IN THE
GAP

*World Christian Series**

Bruchko, by Bruce Olson (Wheaton, IL: Creation House)

Eternity in Their Hearts, by Don Richardson (Ventura, CA: Regal Books)

From Jerusalem to Irian Jaya: A Biographical History of Christian Missions, by Ruth A. Tucker (Grand Rapids, MI: Zondervan Publishing House)

In the Gap: What It Means to Be a World Christian, by David Bryant (Ventura, CA: Regal Books)

Journey to the Nations, edited by Debra Sanders (Pasadena, CA: Caleb Project, USCWM)

On the Crest of the Wave: Becoming a World Christian, by C. Peter Wagner (Ventura, CA: Regal Books)

Perspectives on the World Christian Movement: A Reader, edited by Ralph D. Winter and Steven C. Hawthorne (Pasadena, CA: William Carey Library)

Shadow of the Almighty: The Life and Testament of Jim Elliot, by Elisabeth Elliot (San Francisco: Harper & Row Publishers, Inc.)

William Carey: A Biography, by Mary Drewery (Grand Rapids, MI: Zondervan Publishing House)

---

* Mission Education Movement, Frontier Fellowship, Inc.
  1605 E. Elizabeth Street, Pasadena, CA 91104
  (818) 797-1111

IN THE
GAP

WHAT IT MEANS TO BE
A WORLD CHRISTIAN

DAVID BRYANT

GL
Regal Books
A Division of GL Publications
Ventura, California, U.S.A.

Published by Regal Books
A Division of GL Publications
Ventura, California 93006
Printed in U.S.A.

Library of Congress Cataloging in Publication Data

Bryant, David, 1945-
  In the gap.

  Previously published: Madison, Wis.: Inter-Varsity Missions, c1979.
  Bibliography: p.
  1. Missions.   2. Christian life—1960- .   I. Title.
BV2063.B74   1984   266'.001   84-4880
ISBN 0-8307-0952-5

5 6 7 8 9 10 11 12 13 14 / 91 90 89 88 87

Rights for publishing this book in other languages are contracted by Gospel Literature International (GLINT) foundation. GLINT also provides technical help for the adaptation, translation, and publishing of Bible study resources and books in scores of languages worldwide. For further information, contact GLINT, Post Office Box 488, Rosemead, California, 91770, U.S.A., or the publisher.

To Robyne
My strong companion,
who walks with me
as one . . . in the Gap
(Romans 15:6).

Contents

FOREWORD

I knew a young man who was a "world Christian." Though he did not plan to be a missionary, international studies were a priority for him. He was missions chairman for his Inter-Varsity chapter. A summer in France gave him cross-cultural evangelism exposure. Then when he was barely 21, he died. He was our son, Sandy.

Since then I have told every committed Christian young person I have met, "Sandy has finished his race. Please run yours for Christ—all the way!"

It heartens me to endorse a new edition of David Bryant's IN THE GAP—knowing that it will be used to summon young (and old) to invest their lives in Christ's global cause.

I might summarize David's fine book in three sentences.

We are called to a greater view of God. Our God is no tribal deity. He is the Lord of the nations! In the beginning He created the heavens and the earth. In the end He will bring all things together in Christ. And the Great Creator and Consummator is the Sovereign God Who sends us to proclaim His good news to all peoples.

We are called to a bigger vision of the world. The old "mercator projection" maps of the world are now outmoded. Drawn from a Western viewpoint they showed Scandinavia larger than

India (though India is three times larger) and Alaska as three times larger than Mexico (even though Mexico is larger)! The new Peters Map shows the world in truer proportion. Our "mental maps" of the world may show our neighborhood or nation as bigger, more important than the rest of humankind. Not so for those who know that "God so loved the world . . . " The billions yet unreached must be a bigger priority.

We are called to stand "in the gap" as ambassadors from a holy/loving God to a needy/lost world. With clear biblical teaching, a burning heart and practical advice David Bryant helps us to know how to do that.

I commend IN THE GAP with the prayer that those who read may see more clearly the greatness of God, the bigness of the world and the urgency of their role.

Leighton Ford,
Evangelist
Charlotte, NC

Introductions

FROM ONE EGG TO ANOTHER

This Book Can Help Us Hatch!
It may be hard for an egg to turn into a bird: it would be a jolly sight harder for it to learn to fly while remaining an egg. We are like eggs at present. And you can not go on indefinitely being just an ordinary, decent egg. You must be hatched or go bad.

C.S. Lewis *Mere Christianity* (p. 169)

Lewis is right. Hatch we must! The question is how? One answer is given in this book: get out of our shells and get into the "gap." In a sense, world Christians are hatched eggs. I think Lewis would be satisfied.

To say that *In the Gap* hatches eggs is not subtle hype, because its impact is related not to its "literary genius" but to its focus. *In the Gap* takes basic biblical principles and gives them a contemporary context. Then it helps us lay foundations, both individual and corporate, that insure exciting experiences in Christ's global cause.

Who wouldn't like to end each day, putting our heads on our pillows confidently, saying: "I know this day my life has counted strategically for Christ's global cause, especially for those currently beyond the reach of the gospel." Wouldn't you? That's what's really getting hatched, isn't it? Well, the bottom line impact of the principles in this book have potential for doing just that.

Some examples are in order.

"Don't I know you from somewhere?" interrupted an unfamiliar voice in the United Airline's lounge. I stared back at a willowy-framed, blond-haired youth. "I remember now," he continued. "You're David Bryant, right?" (Believe me, I never get asked that in airport terminals.)

"How do you know me?" I responded in surprise, feeling rather uncomfortable with my newfound popularity.

John introduced me to his parents, standing at each elbow, and then proceeded: "I recognized your picture from the back of *In the Gap*. I read it four years ago, and as a direct result I have driven up from Indiana to Chicago today so that I could catch a plane to Peru. I'm leaving in the next hour to begin my first four years in mission work. And here *you* are! This is no coincidence."

I was sure it wasn't, too. Standing there I felt warm all over. Here was another hatched egg, just like me.

And yet, he was "going" and I was "staying." How could the author of the book that set him toward the plane justify returning to a home in Madison, Wisconsin (not usually considered a mission field, in the technical sense)?

Simple. The issue is hatching eggs, not recruiting missionaries. Hatched eggs aren't measured by whether they "go" or "stay," but whether they live for Christ's Kingdom in such a way that they end each day saying: "I know *this* day my life has counted strategically for Christ's global cause, especially for those currently beyond the reach of the gospel." They are freed to stand in the gap. They are growing as world Christians.

That's what life had been for twenty-six-year-old John over the previous four years. That's what finally got him to the plane.

Recently I sat in a study with the pastor of a large church who had just returned from a trip to Asia.

Before the trip he hadn't thought much about missions. Not because he was against missions, but because the pressures of preaching, counseling and administration left him little time to think about anything else. Or, so he assumed.

But then his missions committee asked him to take a month to visit some of the church's missionaries. He agreed. For one thing it meant a break from all the other pressures, and that wasn't bad! For another, he liked to travel. But most of all, he really did want to understand more about missions.

Before he left someone handed him a copy of *In the Gap*, suggesting he read it on the plane. He did. In the twenty-hour flight he finished it. During his thirty days of visiting mission works he read it again. Flying home he read it a third time. And now he was telling me, "It changed my life. I've returned to my church to work actively at making world evangelization central to all we do together."

"How has it been going?" I asked.

"Let me tell you. First I took a small group through the book. Then each person in the group spawned other groups to study it. Finally we had a weekend retreat of all *In the Gap* 'graduates' to discuss where we should go from here. Many ideas surfaced, from changes in Sunday School curriculum to emphasizing summer missions with our youth. Do you know, this past summer we saw twenty of our congregation go overseas for a short-term ministry. Many were from our working people. We even sent a family. We've never seen anything like that before!"

Of course I was pleased. But I wasn't so much impressed by statistics on summer missionaries. What I saw behind this outward momentum were eggs hatching. A growing percentage of his congregation was developing a life-style as world Christians that allowed them to end each day (and each week in the church calendar) confidently knowing: "This day our lives have counted strategically for Christ's global cause, especially for those currently beyond the reach of the gospel." That, in turn, was opening doors for them to all kinds of exciting dreams for ministry to the world.

As we'll discuss more fully in chapter 6, world Christians are day-to-day disciples for whom Christ's global cause has become the integrating, overriding priority for all that He is for them, in them, and through them. Like disciples should, they have actively investigated all that their Master's Great Commission means, and then built a way of life that prepares them for action in it. Some may go, some may send. But all count strategically for the cause. And in doing so they have entered a freedom and dimension of life they wouldn't trade for anything they experienced before.

It's the life-style Paul speaks of in 1 Corinthians 10:31–11:1: "So whether you eat or drink or whatever you do, do it all for the glory of God. Do not cause anyone to stumble, whether Jews, Greeks or the church of God—even as I try to please everybody in every way. For I am not seeking my own good but the good of many, so that they may be saved. Follow my example, as I follow the example of Christ" *(NIV)*.

What does it mean to live for God's glory? Certainly all of us want to do this. Paul says it means bringing the most practical aspects of our schedule—even eating and drinking—to bear on the advancement of the gospel. We become concerned that Christ's saving work penetrate not only more deeply into the heart of believers (church of God), but in turn our neighbors and families, so very much like us socially and culturally (like the Jews were for Paul).

But we also walk daily in such a way that how we live constantly contributes to the penetration of the gospel among those who are very different from us (as the Greeks were for a Hebrew like Paul), especially where those differences (cultural, linguistic, social, philosophical, etc.), have effectively cut them off from both message and messenger.

To live like this, is to be a world Christian. It is also to imitate the apostolic life-style of Paul (though not necessarily his vocation). And this hatches us into imitators of Christ Himself. That's living strategically for His global cause if anything is!

In the same spirit as Paul, this book can help hatch eggs. Let me give you four good reasons.

Because It's Biblical in Approach

Without the Bible world evangelization is impossible. For without the Bible we have no gospel to take to the nations, no warrant to take it to them, no idea of how to set about the task, and no hope of any success. It is the Bible that gives us the mandate, the message, the model, and the power we need for world evangelization.[1]

Does it strike you, as it does John Stott, that most of Scripture's teachings can be vitally related to Christ's global cause and to the theme of world Christian discipleship? True, some passages aren't as concise on this as, for example, Acts 1:8. But key themes relating to that promise are found just about anywhere you open your Bible. Scores of words like "the nations," "the peoples," "sojourners," or "the ends of the earth" can turn hundreds of passages into valuable commentaries on the world mission of the Church. Highlighting passages that record God's interest in, plans for, and actions toward the nations convinced me that nearly half of my Bible addresses these issues.

For example, did you know the Great Commission is first issued in Genesis 1:26-28? Essentially, God's assignment to Adam and Eve to populate the earth with covenant-keepers is captured by Christ's directive in Matthew 28:18-20. It's repeated in many other places, such as God's promise to bless Abraham so he might be "a blessing to all the families on earth." The New Testament simply explains the original mandate more fully, colors and expands it, detailing it in the light of Christ's finished work. Throughout the whole of Scripture this basic commission is issued to every generation, with binding authority.

Or, take Solomon, who "excelled all the kings of earth in riches and wisdom" so that "the whole earth sought the presence of Solomon" (1 Kings 10:23-24). He became the Old Testament's high water mark. The prophets borrowed from his ideal reign to paint pictures of all God would yet do with Israel. In New Testament times one "greater than Solomon" appeared, more gloriously global in scope. The shadows of Israel's golden age faded before the worldwide reign of the ultimate "Son of David." Have you ever followed *this* thread through the Scriptures? Have you discovered its amazing implications for world missions today, and for your life right now?

The New Testament believers certainly did. They applied all of Scripture to their wider mission in Christ. For them, the ancient biblical records assumed global dynamics. Raised, ascended, and present by His Spirit with power, Christ opened up the whole world to them. He showed them His worldwide *purpose* in a way Abraham or Samuel or Amos never saw it. They awoke to tremendous *possibilities* through Christ for completing the grand design. Their vision stretched beyond their own kind, Israel, to a world full of *people* without Christ. And they thrilled at their world-sized *part* in God's mission because of all Christ would do through them.

W.O. Carver, founder of the oldest continuing seminary department of missions in America, used this "global thread" throughout Scripture to weave a famous series of lectures. They have been preserved in two volumes: *Missions in the Plan of the Ages* and *All the World in All the Word.* The titles say it all! The Bible was written with a world-Christian bent. So, growth as a world Christian unlocks even more meaning from Scripture because, as George Peters reminds us, it contains "a missionary theology—theology in motion." The Bible is basic, therefore, to *In the Gap* (although no attempt has been made to present an in-depth biblical basis for world missions in so few pages).

In the Gap will give you a refreshing perspective on Scripture. It will do so a number of ways. For example, you'll find that chapters 10–13 provide a *framework* with which to interpret much of what Scripture teaches about God's activity among the nations. And, as we tackle personal strategy in chapters 15–17, we'll do so aware that we must first determine through Scripture what direction God is moving us—to insure that our world Christian strategies are synchronized with Him. That's why *Appendix IV* is included to start you as soon as possible in world Christian Bible study.

Becoming a world Christian insures *consistency* with commitments Scripture has already led us to make. Our mission strategies can be justified only as they move us toward a more biblical life-style. But when they do, we become "hatched" people!

After all, two things last forever: the Word of God and people. Our calling is to get God's Word into people. That is precisely what the world mission of the Church is all about: getting God's Word into people of *every* tongue, tribe, nation. Through it God will erect a permanent temple out of living stones—biblical disciples—excavated from thousands of languages and culture groups among Hindus, Muslims, Chinese, Buddhists, Animists and other major blocks of the human race where that Word has not yet penetrated.

Because Christ Is Central as Lord of the Nations
You'll soon discover that *In the Gap* knits Christ's mission among the nations to His saving work in our own lives. He is

presented as Lord in two dimensions: Lord of our lives through His *Word;* also, Lord through His *cause.* Our commitment is, first of all, not to the task but to the Task Master. It's impossible, however, to belong to one and not the other, to love Christ and not obey His commission.

Actually, His mission to the world is the prelude and prototype of our own. The same redemptive drama we find in the Gospels multiplies and intensifies at a world level through the Church, which is His body; and we are members of His Body. So, the more we know of the cause of Christ the more we know of Him. And, conversely, the more we learn of Him the more we'll be led directly into a mission like His for the whole earth.

Simply put, our union with Christ makes us *fit for* the Kingdom of God, and His union with us makes us *fit into* the mission of God. We can't have one without the other. *In the Gap* keeps Christ the center of our lives by His Word *and* His cause.

What do you think: Is Christ Lord of heaven and earth? Is He Lord of history and its sure, redemptive climax? Is He Lord of the nations? Will they come to His feet confessing "Jesus is Lord"? Is He Lord of the challenge before our generation, able to break through any barriers that stand against the impact of His gospel? Is He Lord of the Church at this hour, and Lord *through* her, employing her to fulfill His worldwide purpose? And is He Lord of your life, able to make all that you are and have count significantly for the reaching of unreached peoples to the very ends of the earth? To say yes to these fuller implications of Christ's Lordship is to begin to "hatch" into world Christians! When we embrace all that His Lordship means, the shells around us have to crack!

Because It Takes Missions Seriously

In one sense *In the Gap* is *not* just about world missions. It's about something much larger: Christ's global cause. Missions is only part of that wider movement, although a very critical part.

Chapter 10 ("God's Worldwide *Purpose* in Christ") describes "missions" as one of at least ten issues with which we must be familiar to understand God's plan. There I define "missions" as "the intentional, sacrificial penetration of major human barriers by a global Church through specially sent cross-cultural messengers of the gospel, in order to plant communities of responsible disciples of Jesus Christ among groups of people where none have existed before." In turn, God's worldwide purpose, which includes missions, is one of four major strokes in the overall picture which I call "Christ's global cause" (see chaps. 11,12, and 13 for the other three).

But, *In the Gap* emphasizes the world missions movement over other parts of the larger picture because for one thing, missions is an aspect of the cause most often avoided or misunderstood by the Church at large. And yet missions is so pivotal to the future of the cause. Of course, every world Christian will be concerned with issues like world hunger, economic exploitation, political repressions, nuclear proliferation, and more. That's why I place Christ's global cause, and not *just* the missionary enterprise, as the unifying factor for our life in Christ. But, our missions involvement remains key. Most other needs of the world can be more effectively met once responsible communities of disciples develop within cultural and geographical reach of everyone on the face of the earth.

As you will learn, there are thousands of people-groups (groups with an affinity for one another because of race, language, occupation, class, caste, etc.) where there is not a single church in that tradition that can carry on normal evangelism and social healing. We need millions more indigenous, evangelizing congregations sufficiently equipped to minister within situations, where literally billions wait to hear of Christ for the first time. By recent estimates, we need six million new churches (one for every one thousand people) by the year 2000 if we're going to reach the six billion non-Christians alive at that time. "Missions" targets on this challenge.

But this book is just a thread in God's redemptive weavings in our generation. In an unprecedented fashion, all kinds of Christians are taking world evangelization with intense enthusiasm. I see this worldwide in both churches and student movements. Let me tell you about how some students are "hatching."

At the leading university in Bangkok I talked with students who banded together in Bible study, prayer and evangelism to Thai villages, preparing for the day they believe inevitable when Vietnam invades their nation. They are training to reach unevangelized Vietnamese, even in the face of severe persecution.

In Europe, students from some fifteen nations have formed a movement under the umbrella of The European Missionary Association (TEMA) to challenge local churches in Europe with a new vision for world evangelization, and to go themselves. Every three years they sponsor a student-missions conference in Switzerland. In 1980 it drew seven thousand students and eight thousand in 1983. The Norwegian church has been experiencing tremendous revivals, particularly among its youth. In discussions with leaders of this revival movement I learned that their next great objective is to turn the spiritual ferment outward, to see hundreds moving toward the ends of the earth in obedience to the Great Commission.

In Korea, Campus Crusade for Christ sponsored a conference with a million in daily attendance during the summer of 1980. On the final night, thousands of Korean young people openly testified of their willingness to serve Christ anywhere while thousands of parents stood to offer their sons and daughters to God for mission service, should He call them. Many predict the vision of Korean youth will make it one of the leading missionary sending nations by the end of this century.

I uncovered similar reports at the Consultation on World Evangelization in Thailand in discussions with Asian leaders of the International Fellowship of Evangelical Students, and at the International Student Consultation on Frontier Missions in Edinburgh, Scotland, during the fall of 1980. In Edinburgh, 180 students and student workers from twenty-six nations studied the task of reaching over 2.5 billion who have yet to hear of Christ, and have no one like them, near them, to tell them. Our concern was to challenge students and churches worldwide to join in the task before us. In fact, we adopted as a watchword for the next twenty years, "A Church for Every People by the Year 2000," to indicate how much we believed in the importance of world evangelization.

One spinoff from Edinburgh was Theological Students for Frontier Missions (TSFM), formed in 1981. Seminary students in the U.S. are not only encouraging fellow seminarians to consider cross-cultural ministry for themselves, but also to bring to their pulpits the cause of world Christian discipleship, the urgency of reaching billions without Christ.

"Hatching" students is an essential part of world evangelization. After all, since four million of the twelve million U.S. college students come from evangelical homes, if only one in three are fairly serious about Christ and His mission there are one and one-quarter million ready right now to assume leadership in the Great Commission. By itself, however, this is inadequate. The combined efforts of Inter-Varsity, Campus Crusade, or Navigators will not be sufficient to mobilize them unless local churches become the launching pads behind them for world evangelization. As Gordon MacDonald, pastor of Grace Chapel in Massachusetts, reminds us:

> While I applaud [the student movement] and say it is absolutely super, what worries me is that less and less recruitment is done in the context of the congregation. While I am delighted about the one I wish that there were more of the other. I think it will help when the church congregation sees itself as the seedbed or breeding ground for potential missionaries.[2]

In other words, all of us must hatch new seriousness about missions or the seedbeds may end up burying youthful zeal. *In the Gap* sees this and provides some practical solutions.

You see, God isn't taking a worldwide opinion poll on who wants to become a Christian. He's at work creating communities of sons and daughters within every cultural womb of earth to populate His Kingdom and love Him forever. World missions creates possibilities for God's Kingdom to break through in places where it has not yet come. It is sowing the gospel through new congregations of believers who grow into redemptive forces. In turn, they will overthrow the status quo of the world system and transform the human condition within their own situation.

In the second century, a world Christian named Justin Martyr recorded of the Roman world: "For there is not one single race of men, whether barbarians, or Greeks, or whatever they may be called, nomads, or vagrants, or herdsmen dwelling in tents, among whom prayers and giving of thanks are not offered through the name of the Crucified Jesus" *(Dialogue with Tryphomus)*. Seeing this drama realized on a grander scale throughout all nations in all parts of the earth is a driving dream for world Christians today. And, the more we're "pro-missions" in our dreams, the freer will be our involvement in *all* aspects of Christ's global cause.

Through Larger Dimensions in Practical Discipleship

From another perspective, *In the Gap* is more about *discipleship* than world missions. It develops perspective and strategy for *senders* as much as *penetrators* (such as missionaries). Not only does it ask, "Who will go?" but also, "Who will send?" and, "What kind of goers and senders will they be?"

Every missionary extension needs behind it a missionary *movement* of similar vision, commitment, and sacrifice. The early Church's apostolic bands usually appeared wherever there were missions-minded congregations to launch them. Faithfully engaged in a global cause, local bodies teamed up to do the most strategic thing they could find to do as senders and penetrators. Spiritual growth was linked to serving an expanding mission for their generation. Ultimately theirs was discipleship that put no limits on how far God would go with them or whom He would touch through them.

More than ever we need, in the words of Carl F.H. Henry, "creative disciples who know the world outside and Christ inside and who can bring them together in an authentically Biblical, intellectually compelling and spiritually powerful way." That means discipleship without limits. That means disciple-making *programs* adjusted so that maximum finding of lost people occurs through each disciple.

To this end, *In the Gap* will be practical. Conducting conferences on world Christian discipleship over the past nine years has made me acutely aware of the need for practical follow-through materials on the subject. Students and church lay people alike return from these conferences willing to seriously reevaluate their whole framework for discipleship—God's worldwide purpose takes on new importance. They are willing to let Christ's cause become the unifying focus—the context—for all their other efforts in evangelism and Christian growth. As a result, major shifts begin to emerge in their world views and in how they want to invest their lives. But these changes are short-lived unless resources are available to nurture their world vision. How else can they resist the forces of what I call "pea-sized Christianity," so prevalent in the American church today?

The vision caught needs to become the vision kept and obeyed, a growing vision that outlasts the spiritual high of catching it. Budding world Christians need help to *decipher* the big picture of Christ's cause and to *design* a comprehensive strategy for meaningful personal involvement in that picture. *In the Gap* provides practical handles to get you into both.

The tragedy is that few trained Christians have been discipled with vision and strategy for reaching to the ends of the earth. How many of us are able to come to the end of each day and say: "I know this day my life has counted strategically for Christ's global cause, especially for those currently beyond the reach of the gospel"?

Now, admittedly, the primary thrust I suggest for discipleship entails only three major concerns: learning about, telling others about, and getting involved with those currently beyond the reach of the gospel. This is *not* to suggest that world Christians avoid other issues within the Church or society that affect God's purposes for the whole earth. But for someone, somewhere, discipleship must lead into primary concern for those totally cut off from God's good news. If not you and me, who?

One of the book's primary objectives is to help each of us develop a *personal strategy* that involves us in a *daily discipline* of (initially) only fifteen minutes a day. I often call this the "5-4-3-2-1 Plan." It goes something like this:

> *Build Your World Vision*
> > 5-Spend five minutes some time each day in personal devotions discovering something of what Scripture teaches about Christ's global cause.
> > 4-Spend an additional four minutes reading current world-related literature, such as a magazine article.
> *Reach Out to the World in Love*
> > 3-Every day take three minutes to carry out a mission

to the world through intercessory prayer, using what God gave you in the previous nine minutes of building your vision.

Give Your World Vision to Others

2-Sometime each day in personal conversation with another Christian (such as your family at evening meal, or in a Bible study group, or in a letter) share for two minutes what God has given you in the previous twelve minutes of building your vision and reaching out in prayer.

That averages out to fourteen minutes a day. Finally, before retiring at night give God one more minute of complete quiet when He can speak to you about who you are becoming as a world Christian, based on the other aspects of your daily discipline.

Fifteen minutes a day. Anyone can do it! Is it a significant discipleship approach? Consider this: It means you average ninety *hours* a year! All other things being equal, what kind of increased impact will your life have on Christ's global cause a year from now as a result of those additional ninety hours of world Christian discipleship?

Consider again: Let's say you are part of a congregation with two hundred adult members. If each of you were to experiment with this fifteen-minute daily discipline over the next year, that would average out to eighteen thousand hours (90 x 200) of world Christian discipleship! And, all other things being equal, what increased impact would your church have on Christ's global cause a year from now as a result of those additional eighteen thousand hours?

And yet, at only fifteen minutes a day, it is all so manageable. Who among us cannot find or release an extra quarter hour out of twenty-four hours to get equipped for the sake of Christ's global cause and the billions currently beyond the reach of His gospel?

Clearly, the 1980s demand a new dimension for Jesus' followers. I've met so many evangelicals who are overtrained but underemployed and bored. In light of the tremendous needs, and since world Christians discover exciting adventures in life that won't quit, we must move into discipleship without limits. To return to C.S. Lewis, the world Christian life-style allows us to hatch and fly before we (and the world) go bad. And that's good. That's essential.

Because the Author Is Learning to Hatch

This book surfaces out of almost twenty years of my own pilgrimage as a world Christian. It represents my attempts to understand where God has brought me in this adventure. Both for me and many I've met heading down the same road, it's just the beginning.

It strikes me that my Christian metamorphosis has spiraled through three major cycles. The first six years I concentrated primarily on knowing *Christ* and His Word. Most of it was spent in college and seminary. The second six were my time for understanding the importance and potential of the *Body of Christ,* as I pastored in a church in Ohio. These past years have focused more on the work of Christ in the world. Beginning with studies at Fuller School of World Mission, I've gone on to serve as a missions specialist with Inter-Varsity Christian Fellowship. Notice, if you will, that my three cycles form what some call the Christian's "three priorities." But it was only as I entered the third cycle that I "hatched" enough to soar into a world-sized vision for my life, and for Christ and His Church.

My experience is probably not much different from yours. Every Christian experiences a three-part conversion: (1) a conversion out of the world to Christ; (2) a conversion out of ourselves into the Body of Christ; all tied into (3) a conversion with Christ and others back into the world. Unfortunately, my conversion with Christ back into the world—the third cycle—came long after the other two. If I had known at the beginning what I know now, how much more fruitful my life could have been. (I've detailed this painful but welcomed process in chapter 7.)

The point is, the process is finally coming full circle for me. I'm still neither a missionary nor the son of a missionary. I'm just a day-to-day disciple, like you, called into God's plan for the nations, to establish Christ's preeminence among all peoples. My motivation for this is the same as yours: the Lordship of Christ; the reality of God's yearning grace for a lost humanity;

the right of everyone to know of Christ and have opportunity to come to Him; a biblical vision of Christ's redemptive glory covering the earth as the waters cover the sea and the promise of God to bless me so that I become like Abraham, a blessing to the families of earth.

The questions I've wrestled with in writing this book aren't peculiarly mine. I've met hundreds longing with me to dig for the answers. Maybe you're one of them. For example, have you wondered:

- What is the scope and content of God's purpose for history and the nations?
- How extensive should be the impact of that purpose as it moves forward?
- Why is the fulfillment of His purpose so essential?
- How has it progressed so far? How did progress happen?
- Where are we in His purpose right now?
- What is left to do?
- How will it get done?
- Who will be most affected?
- Where can I fit in most strategically?
- Of all earth's unreached, who are the people God wants me to give my life *for?*
- Of all the Christians, who are the people God wants me to give my life *with* as I reach out?
- What kind of person does God want me to *be* as I give my life for others?

In the Gap shows you how I faced such issues and reoriented my life accordingly. Prayerfully, it will help meet a growing demand of other world Christians across the nation to understand what's happening to them, where to go with it, and how to share it with others.

This book hatches eggs, and here's how it's meant to work. Part One, "Alive in the Gap," defines what a world Christian is and why being one is so important. It gives a biblical, historical, and contemporary analysis of how a movement of world Christians could release the bottled-up resources of North American evangelicalism to the ends of the earth.

The second half, called "A Journey into World Christian Discipleship," changes markedly in pace and style. It helps the reader get into the action with an introductory "curriculum" on what a world Christian sees, chooses, and does. This section is designed for study and reflection on an individual level using the suggested reflection questions throughout, or in small groups using the Small Group Study Guide, Appendix I. Remember, however, this curriculum is introductory. Everything presented here can be expanded through other world Christian resources such as those suggested in Appendixes III and V.

Many have "hatched" with me by using *In the Gap* in various ways. Some have worked through the book privately, studying a chapter a week, referring to some of the questions in Appendix I to help them. Small groups have formed on campuses and in churches to work through the ten-week study guide. Others have passed the book along to friends as one way of giving them a world vision. For Sunday School classes, teachers have digested the ten-week study guide to reteach it in a simpler form. The book has found its way into college and seminary courses. It has been used to train missions coordinators for Christian campus movements, and missions committees in local churches. It has provided missions nuggets to present at weekly large-group meetings and worship services. For those who eventually develop a world Christian strategy, as suggested in Appendix II, *In the Gap* remains a key reference tool as they take action.

And yet, *In the Gap* is only a first brick in rebuilding the framework that puts Christ's global cause at the heart of each day's discipleship and evangelism. It's a springboard into many ways we can make a lasting impact on that cause. My hope is that as a framework and springboard, it will lead to a creative wide-open redirection of many of us toward the uttermost parts of the earth in the 1980s!

A Prayer for Those Ready to Hatch

Let me conclude these introductions "from one egg to another" with a prayer that fits the ideas and opportunities this book offers. It's a prayer of thanksgiving, of praise, and, most of all, of *desire*—desire to become a world Christian, to move with Christ in love and faith, to serve His redemptive purposes in this generation—to the very ends of the earth. It's a prayer for those who want to *hatch*.

For all links in the chain,
O Lord my God,
that brought to me the story of the gospel—
   I thank you, Father, with all my heart.

For Christ himself, author
and finisher
of our faith;
for Christ who is himself the
good news for all mankind—
   I thank you, Father, with all my heart.

For saints and martyrs, teachers
and evangelists; for that
apostolic company; and for Paul,
"unfit to be called an apostle"
whose words I read today—
   I thank you, Father, with all my heart.

And so it goes on; and always at a price.
In toil and labour, in pain and blood,
the good news spreads from place to place,
generation to generation.
For all who shared in the
missionary task—
   I thank you, Father, with all my heart.

And for my chance to be myself a link in this great chain,
a bearer of good news of Christ
to other men,
   I thank you, Father, with all my heart.

And may it be a heart of love,
of joy and praise!
For Jesus' sake, Amen.[3]

Notes

1. John R.W. Stott, "The Bible in World Evangelization," *Christianity Today,* February, 1981.

2. Gordon MacDonald, "Your Church in God's Global Plan," *Christian Herald,* November, 1980, p. 50.

3. Timothy Dudley-Smith, *Someone Who Beckons* (Downers Grove, IL: Inter-Varsity Press, 1978), p. 107.

PART I
ALIVE
IN THE GAP

"I looked for a man among them who would build up the wall and stand before me in the gap on behalf of the land"
—Ezekiel 22:30 *(NIV)*

1

THERE IS A GAP, YOU KNOW

. . . and we're both in the *middle* of it right now! Let me explain.

The Gap Defined

It's the Gap between God and men; between God and all that He is and man and all that he is, in every respect. "For there is one God, and there is one mediator between God and men, the man Christ Jesus" (1 Tim. 2:5). A mediator implies a gap between two parties that cannot or will not accept each other.

It is also the Gap between God's original intention for humankind—to be fruitful, multiply, fill the earth with people in His image and subdue it—and Jesus the Mediator's final restoration wherein a new people will fill and subdue the earth, with Him (see Rev. 5:9-10).

For God, the Gap is a very personal issue. First of all, He is one of the two parties involved. Secondly, He has given the required Mediator to stand in the Gap forever, to close the distance between His own plan for world redemption and the consummation of that plan. He has given His own dear Son. He has "a plan for the fulness of time, to unite all things in [Christ], things in heaven and things on earth" (Eph. 1:10).

But more than that, the Mediator has actually *sacrificed* His own life in the Gap, falling like a seed into soil in order to bring forth fruit (John 12:23-26), to bring many people home from the other side of the Gap.

That is why the Gap is a very personal issue for our heavenly Father; that's why He is personally concerned with the distance that remains between Christ's saving work and the impact of His Kingdom on people from every tongue and nation; between the death and resurrection of our Lord which closes the Gap for all who believe and the imparting of this good news to the billions who have yet to hear it for the first time.

Like Columbus claiming the West Indies for Spain, Christ planted the staff of His Cross in the middle of the Gap and flew the flag of His own broken body to reclaim this world for His Father. He is no "imperialist." He created the world but He also *paid* for the world—all of it. His Kingdom is coming, in the Gap . . . but at great cost.

With that kind of personal investment in such a costly claim, God is deeply concerned for the billions of earth's citizens who have yet to hear that there is a Mediator, let alone believe and walk across the Gap to home. Our God is as personally committed now to reaching these billions as He was the day Christ died for them.

And that's why the Gap is a very personal issue for Christians as well. It lies between what God is doing in your life and mine—as people united forever to the Mediator—and what God still wants to do among all the nations.

Millions of us, for example, have asked the Saviour to quench their thirst with His water of life (John 7:37). But there remains a critical breakthrough in our lives if the living river that flows into the hearts of satisfied disciples like us is to ever lead toward the glorious day when that river flows *out* of us fully to complete Habakkuk's vision: "For the earth will be filled with the knowledge of the glory of the Lord, as the waters cover the sea" (2:14). That's why I say we Christians are right in the middle of the Gap. We have been born again for the sake of the Gap. Someday the waters of life are to cover the whole earth . . . through us. God is committed to reaching earth's unreached people in a very personal way: The Spirit of God extending Christ's Kingdom through *us* who are united with the King (see 1 Cor. 6:9-11,17).

How Wide Is the Gap?

If you measure it by the basic *reason* for the Gap—sin—you could say it's infinitely wide. Sin and rebellion against a just and holy Creator have set us all the same distance from Him. Jesus measured it as somewhere between darkness and light, between the power of Satan and the power of God (Acts 26:14-19). You can't get much farther apart than that!

In this sense, then, the Gap is the same width for everybody. Either you're an old creation in Adam or a new one in Christ; either you're dead or alive; either you're out of the family or you're in it.

On one side of the Gap is a bundle of sins waiting for God's forgiveness; scars waiting for God's healing; needs waiting for God's riches; and potential waiting for God's power. From the other side has come the inexhaustible, yearning grace of God available in Jesus Christ to all nations, with all the forgiveness, healing, riches, and power the human race could ever want or need.

By this measurement the Gap is as wide as sin for everyone but as crossable for all as the Son who forms the bridge is available for all. In one way, the Gap has already been closed for all because Christ has permanently stretched Himself across its chasm. "While we were enemies we were reconciled to God by the death of his Son" (Rom. 5:10). "For Christ also died for sins once for all, the righteous for the unrighteous that he might bring us to God" (1 Pet. 3:18).

Some Are Farther Away Than Others

A second way to measure the Gap, however, unveils some of the tragedy and challenge of the world missionary movement today. This other measurement is the focus of our study.

When you look at the Gap historically, in terms of human *experience* instead of human condition, you find the width varies greatly. Ephesians 2:17-18 notes this variance. Although the Gap is bridged in the same way for all—"through [Christ] we both have access in one Spirit to the Father"—some of us (like the Jews) may be "near" while others (like the Greeks) are "far away." For those who have never clearly heard that the access is available (as most Greeks in Paul's day), the Gap looms wide indeed. This is the disturbing *Gap of opportunity*.

In Acts 1:8 Jesus talked about this other measurement—the Gap of opportunity. When He commissioned His disciples to span the Gap, He promised them that the Spirit's power would transform their lives so that they could contribute directly to peoples' verdict about Him: "You shall be my witnesses." And He drew a map of the Gap that outlined the various widths they would face. He spoke of "Jerusalem, Judea, Samaria and the ends of the earth." In other words, the Gap would vary in at least *three* ways: geographically, culturally, and theologically.

The opportunity to come home would vary *geographically* for those on the other side of the Gap. Although Jerusalem and its surrounding territory, Judea, were important, the disciples would need to physically travel beyond there to Samaria in the north and eventually to the remotest areas of the Roman Empire lest these lands be forever isolated from the people of God and their witness.

Secondly, the opportunity to come home would also vary *culturally* for those on the other side of the Gap. Reaching those in Jerusalem and Judea would demand little in cross-cultural skills. Already Jesus had evangelized them as a Jew to Jews. Samaritans, on the other hand, had enough racial and cultural differences about them that the disciples would need to make special efforts to help them understand the message in a way that fit their own context.

When it came to the "ends of the earth"—the radically unfamiliar Gentile world—the early missionary movement faced major cultural challenges. A message given to Jews in Palestine could be transferred to Cretan, Macedonians, Asians, and Romans only as it came to these groups in relevant terms, using words and concepts that made sense to those the Jew considered "unclean and uncircumcised dogs."

The gospel was universal. The Resurrection remained central to it, as did the Cross. But how Paul, for example, spelled out his message with peasants in Lystra or jailers in Philippi or private clubs in Athens differed noticeably from his preaching to Jewish enclaves in Antioch and Rome. Unless the message "fit" people and their felt needs as family-groups and as cultures their opportunity to genuinely respond to Christ would be very limited indeed.

For some the opportunity to come home would be "near" *theologically* while for others it would be "far away." Jesus taught that "salvation is of the Jews." His message tied directly into the Scriptures and ceremonies that marked the Covenant and its people. All that the Hebrews held so dear, revealed directly by God to His prophets, found its ultimate meaning in Christ Himself who transformed the Covenant and made it new.

The Samaritans, on the other hand, were not quite so "theologically aware." Despite their reverence for the books of Moses and their worship of one God, they held prejudice toward many other covenant doctrines and had incorporated new ones of their own. Still the Gap wasn't that great. At the well of Sychar with Jesus and in Philip's preaching in Acts 8, we see a common ground of moral law and messianic expectations that allowed the good news to find spiritual affinity in the Samaritan soil.

For Gentiles, however, caught in the worship of Roman and Greek deities with little or no exposure to the Old Testament, for whom a covenant-keeping Creator was "unknown" (Acts 17:23), the gap between a biblical witness and the Gentiles' own theological currency presented a major challenge. To give pagans and philosophers alike a just opportunity to cross this gap forced the early Church to face this complex need with clarity and relevance (as John does, for example, in writing his Gospel for a broader Greek audience).

Yes. There is a Gap. Measured by the human condition of sin, it is the same for all of us. Measured by the divine provision of a Mediator, it could be closed for all of us. But measured by the *human experience of opportunity* to know that the sin problem has been bridged, and to respond with faith in the mediator, the Gap differs widely around the globe.

Yet Jesus sent the disciples forth to serve in the Gap, regardless of its geographical, cultural, or theological extremes, that they might reconcile lost sinners to God through faith in the Mediator.

Today the strategy remains the same. Over three billion people stand apart from the Mediator, blocked from an effective, loving witness by geographical or cultural or theological or other

human barriers. It is for them Christ still calls and empowers
Christians to stand in the Gap, especially at its widest end where
there is little or no opportunity to believe and come home.

A Tour of the Gap in Los Angeles

Let me illustrate the different widths of the Gap by taking
you on a tour of Los Angeles. I've taken one similar to this on
many occasions.

In early morning we head for the car. My next-door neighbor, Mrs. Calley, waves a cheerful hello as she cuts roses from
her garden. She's such a kind friend. I wonder how wide the Gap
is for her? I'm not sure that she's ever come to a full faith in
Christ although she has attended church for over thirty years.
With that kind of exposure, if there is a gap for her, it is probably
small. Anyway, since I'm her neighbor I'm actively praying about
how I can narrow the Gap even more for her.

Shall we go?

As our car rounds the corner, notice the rambling house on
our left. The Pritchards hold a home Bible study there every
Thursday evening. Most of the forty-five people who attend
haven't been in church for a long time, or go only on special occasions. But once a week they meet in this house to discuss the
Bible (right now the group is studying John's Gospel) as the Pritchards help them gain a fuller understanding of what salvation is
all about. For these people, the Gap is narrowing quickly. Before
long they'll be able to make intelligent commitments to the Saviour. I think a few already have!

For two people a little farther up the street, however, the
Gap is wider, and not much is happening to change the situation.
Across the street delivering the morning edition is our newspaper boy, George. Last week George told me he has never been
in a church, never had a Christian friend (as far as he knows),
and never read any part of the Bible. (In fact, George hates to
read anything.) Basically, he doesn't know the first thing about
the gospel. Oh, he's picked up a few things about Christianity.
For example, he attended two voluntary assemblies at his high
school this year when someone from Youth for Christ spoke on
drugs and sex. He's also watched some evangelistic type TV
programs on UHF when he got bored with everything else. But

for George, the Gap seems much wider when compared, let's say, to Mrs. Calley, and little is being done to narrow it for him. (That's why I'm trying to win his friendship right now.)

In the neighborhood park off to your right, sleeping on a bench, is a man I've seen there many times. Most people don't know his name. They just call him "the drunk." To my knowledge, he hasn't been completely sober for six years. During this time his family left him, he lost his job, his self-respect and any old friends who ever cared anything for him. What's the Gap like for him?

Years ago, so I'm told by a local pastor, he attended some backyard vacation Bible clubs. He even memorized enough verses to win a trip to a church camp where he learned to recite stories about Jesus. But as he grew older, school chums pulled him away from all that. Some time later he became a corporate executive with all the pressures and distractions this entailed. It left him little time to reflect on the stories of his Bible club days. When his financial world finally collapsed the bottle became his only comfort. For years now he's been cut off from any compassionate help. Few Christians even know he exists; those who do, feel uneasy associating with him. Besides, his mind hasn't been in much shape to make decisions about Christ or anything else. His whole life is disintegrating while the Gap gets wider each day. (I wish I knew where to begin with him.)

Well, here we are on Interstate 10, on our way to the heart of the city. Let's stop briefly at the International Union on a local campus. We've been invited to have coffee with some Middle Eastern students who just arrived in the U.S. this school term. As we sip and chat, you may be surprised at how easy it is to understand one another. Not only do we all speak English, but their Westernized education before coming to the States makes them interested in many of the same topics we are. They're particularly interested in discussing religion and want to tell you about Islam, as well as listen respectfully to what you have to say about Christianity.

We are joined by some Christian students who arranged this meeting. Each student is a personal friend of one of the Internationals. Each hopes to establish meaningful relationships which God can use to reach them for Christ. In fact, the Jordanians, the one from Iraq, and the three from Saudi Arabia attend a dinner and Bible study that a Christian student group on campus sponsors once a month along with a group of Christian laypeople.

What do you think the Gap is like around this table? In light of the geographical, cultural, and theological changes taking place in the Internationals' lives, the Gap which once was very wide continues to narrow. In one sense, each International is now *one person* removed from Jesus Christ: the Christian student who is becoming his or her good friend. That is a great leap from their families and friends back in Middle East towns and cities where the gospel has never been heard, or where its preaching is forbidden.

Our visit is over. Let's head into Little Tokyo. On our way we'll take a swing through a well-known part of Los Angeles, Watts. What's happening with the gospel among the thousands in this black, ghetto community? Who is spanning the Gap, for example, for the teenagers playing baseball down that street, or for those hanging around the corner bar? Who is going into those run-down government projects over there to reach disillusioned tenants with God's love? What opportunity do they *really* have to walk across the Gap to home?

Whites like me can't often do much in such a situation. For one thing, we lack credibility. (What evidence have I ever given before today that I really care about my black neighbors?) Furthermore, in some parts of Watts it might be risky for me even to venture from my car. There is an explainable resentment for what a person like me—white, a middle-class Protestant—represents.

If, for Christ's sake, I did decide to move into this area, as some white Christians have done, the cultural and prejudicial distances between me and those I want to reach would not improve quickly. How long before I could be clearly understood? How much longer before they would even take the time or respect me enough to hear me out?

Of course, they've been exposed to the gospel. They might even give good answers to certain questions about Christian concepts like the Trinity or heaven. And, yes, there are many Christian books, evangelistic shows on cable TV and local storefront churches that could reach them; that is, for those who have been taught to read past a fifth-grade level, or can afford cable TV, or trust the storefront come-on enough to go inside and investigate. But for most of them, and for good reasons, the Gap is wide compared to that of Mrs. Calley or the group at the Pritchards; or, maybe, when compared even to some of the Internationals we met this morning.

Well, here we are at Little Tokyo. There's one sight I especially want you to see—just behind that modern looking Buddhist temple. It's a tall apartment complex built for Japanese senior citizens. About a thousand live there now. Most of them are first generation Japanese; that is, they don't speak much English, they practice most of their cultural traditions, and they are Buddhists.

I wish I could take you in to meet some of them, but the guard at the door won't let us past unless we are relatives or close friends. And many of them are too sick to come out and talk, even if they could speak fluent English.

How wide is the Gap here? What opportunity do they have? Geographically isolated from most believers behind locked doors, culturally and linguistically distinct from most American Christians, and radically unlike any Christian in theology, they sit in their rooms, dying off one by one, just a twenty-minute drive from my front doorstep. The Gap wouldn't be much wider if they lived in Tokyo itself! Who will bridge it for them . . . and how . . . and when?

We have time for one more stop before heading home. I'm leaving on a research assignment to India in a week, so I'd like to pick up my airline tickets at the travel agent's office. As we move down the freeway to the other side of town, my thoughts bounce off the Los Angeles skyline. Here we live in a country of forty million people who claim to be born again, where 70 percent of the population holds church membership and 40 percent attends regularly. Most people in America know what the Bible is, where to get one, and have ten easy-to-understand translations to choose from. Here they can watch Billy Graham preach crusades on prime-time TV or laugh through a comedy show about a priest and a nun in which jokes are based on Christian terminology and concepts. Most Americans with one church for every six to eight hundred people and possibly one evangelical for every three adults (at least by Gallup's findings), have been exposed to the gospel in pretty solid doses, or could be without much additional effort.

But in a week I'll be on an express train from New Delhi to Madras. For thirty-five hours I will pass thousands of villages, and for every one thousand villages I see, there will be over nine hundred fifty that have absolutely no one to give them a clear witness of the Lord Jesus; in most cases they won't even have heard His name. Imagine! A few hours of air travel will place me physically at the widest end of the Gap, a width that can be duplicated for over half of the world's population, most of whom live outside North America.

If we would try to close the widest end of the Gap by herding fifty thousand of its people into a great stadium every day, and if a team of African, Asian, Latin American, and North American evangelists were to preach with cultural and theological sensitivity to a totally different crowd every day, it still would take more than 165 years to let all those billions hear the gospel clearly just one time. In the meantime, billions more would be born. That's a peek at how immense and complex the Gap is at its widest end.

It is in *this* Gap that the Church of Jesus Christ worldwide must stand with Him.

We must not run from it, especially from its widest end. Instead, we must stand in it to close it until all have had a chance to see, hear, believe, and come home. For the whites at the Pritchards, the Internationals on the campus, and the blacks in Watts, we must stand in the Gap. Especially for the 2.5 billion Hindus, Muslims, Chinese, Buddhists and Tribals—those farthest away in every respect from most witnessing Christians—for their sakes, we must span the widest end of the Gap.

Sunrise over the Gap

Fortunately this Gap need not remain the "valley of the shadow of death" that it is. Already shadows are dissipating at the dawn of what some mission strategists call the *sunrise of missions.*

Sunrise of missions does not mean that the world itself is getting better and better or that the sin-problem that created the Gap has ceased to plague us. Rather, it says that the harvesting of people for the Kingdom of God—the opening of opportunity to believe the gospel around the world—is accelerating on a scale never before witnessed in the history of the Church; that the impact of the gospel in the Gap today looks like the sun just breaking over the horizon of God's purpose for all nations.

If this sunrise is complemented by renewal within the Church so that together our life-perspectives, life-decisions, and life-directions reflect a *world* dimension in discipleship and evangelism, we may see the fulfillment of the Great Commission in our lifetime. We may see the closing of the Gap at its widest end!

This sunrise over the Gap shines out in so many ways! The number of Christians in Asia and Africa, for example, are increasing four times faster than the population at large. Over 90 percent of the world's nations are presently accessible to some type of Christian witness coming from the outside. (All of them are if you take into account various forms of media evangelism.) At least 200 million, for example, are accessible to direct missionary outreach in southeast Asia alone.

The sunrise can be seen in the current openings of the People's Republic of China. Internally, there is new freedom for the persecuted church to witness to the light God has shown them in thirty dark years of suffering. Add to this increased travelers from abroad, many of whom will be Christians, and the PRC students sent internationally to campuses often inhabited by faithful Christians ready to love them (ten thousand will be in the U.S. by 1985). God is closing the gap for one third of the world's unevangelized.

Looking at this sunrise, Donald Hoke concludes in his introduction to *The Church in Asia,* that the nations there could be "Biblically evangelized" by the end of this century if the Church rises to claim the possibilities God is giving us.

Many mission strategists agree. Evangelization consultations have been held around the world since the early 1960s. Centers for missionary research and training are expanding to prepare a new force of cross-cultural messengers to share Christ effectively at the Gap's widest end. Even at the local level—in churches and on campuses—God is mobilizing His people for a global impact.

Yes, there is a Gap. But there is also a brilliant sunrise streaming into that Gap. It is shining down on a world where approximately one billion call themselves Christians. Of these possibly 200 million (according to the U.S. Center for World Missions) are committed to Christ enough that they want to share Him with others—they want to stand in the Gap. And what if one million of these "evangelicals" (one for each five thousand to be evangelized in the next twenty years) joined the present world missionary force, to cross over major geographical, cultural and theological barriers to reach those at the Gap's widest end? What if the 199 million other evangelicals supported them by sharing the same intense concern for people with no opportunity to hear of Christ, while maintaining a clear witness to those who live nearby? What if a new movement of world Christians was born? What could God do in our generation?

2

PROBLEMS WITH PEA—SIZED CHRISTIANITY

We Aren't Keeping Pace

Fortunately, what happens with Western Christians doesn't ultimately determine what happens with God's plan for the nations; Christ's Church is worldwide. But *un*fortunately, many Christians in the West are not keeping pace with the Kingdom's worldwide expansion. Many of us are sleeping right through the sunrise of missions.

A 1980 Gallup survey indicated that though winning the world for Christ had priority for 50 percent of U.S. evangelicals (not a totally encouraging statistic itself), the sense of personal, meaningful involvement in world missions for almost all was negligible. Less than 10 percent of evangelical clergy could point to successful missions programs in their churches.

As I've traveled American campuses I've found similar trends among the Christian groups I've surveyed. Again and again the leaders of these groups have confessed to me that they and their members have little world vision and world outreach involvement; view missions as only a career option for a few, or as "threatening" or "foreign" or "something after college"; hear and read little about the global Christian cause; and are in touch with very few if any whom they feel can effectively lead them otherwise. In a typical group, I've discovered, about 15 percent of the membership are enthusiastic about world missions or believe that right now their group can play a vital and direct role in fulfilling the Great Commission.

This sluggish pace is also reflected in the amount North American churches give to missions. Even though North American Protestant giving to missions was $928 million in 1980, only 4 percent of Christians' annual incomes go to all forms of church work and only 15 percent of that is used in world evangelization. Ron Sider calculates that just a tithe from the fifty-two largest U.S. denominations would be $17.5 billion annually. Instead, recent total giving was only $4.4 billion, most of which was spent at home, on ourselves.

We aren't keeping pace in personnel either. Presently four to five thousand full time missionary openings with North American Protestant agencies are begging to be filled. Are such personnel really that hard to come by when we have from twenty to forty million born-again adult American Christians? Research at World Vision International indicates that American evangelical families might have reared and fielded one million young adult short-term missionaries by 1980 had world missions been given the same priority in our homes as the Mormons give it in theirs. How explosive the missionary movement would become if evangelical families would awaken to the "sunrise of missions."

The Greatest of All Gaps

The problem with our pace is not a new issue, however. It has been with us a long time. Why, after two thousand years of countless possibilities for world evangelization by an international Church, are three billion people still unevangelized, most of whom have not even heard Christ's name? One answer is unavoidable. The single greatest gap among the nations is between God's promise to fulfill world evangelization through Christ's disciples and the faith of those disciples to claim that promise and act on it. I call it the *gap-of-unbelief.*

How does the gap-of-unbelief work? For one thing, it puts limits on what Christ can do through us. (Can He really reach the ends of the earth through people like us at a time like this?) For another, our gap-of-unbelief makes us hesitate to take bold risks so that redemption might come to all peoples. (If we lose our lives for Christ's worldwide mission, will we ever see any lasting returns worth our investment?) Our gap-of-unbelief turns us from the many possibilities to fulfill the world missionary movement and concentrates us instead on our own self-preservation. (How can we worry about billions of unreached people when we have so many personal needs that might go unmet in the process?) Our gap-of-unbelief blinds us to the dreams, resources and strategy God would give us to bridge the other Gap, especially at its widest end.

If once aroused by Christ's mighty Spirit, what could hold us back? His presence and His mission would be so compelling that we might tend to *over*extend ourselves and so, periodically, need to seek times to reflect and regroup. If we had any problem, it would be that! Instead, down through history and in the Church today, the constant battle has remained to get Christians to push forward—to stop resting, to wake up, stand together and take hold of the victorious cause Christ has given us for the world. This is the gap-of-unbelief. This explains why the other Gap remains.

Why has unbelief persisted to stifle the momentum of the Christian movement again and again? Underneath disinterest in world outreach, underneath small missions budgets or limited personnel and the scandal of billions yet unreached, hides a culprit I shall call "pea-sized Christianity."

Boxes of Pea-Sized Christianity

When Peter opposed Christ's expressed mission to the cross (see Matt. 16:21-23) he was told: "Get out of my way, Satan. You are a hindrance to me. You're approaching this mission from a human perspective, not God's." Peter was still in his own box of pea-sized Christianity.

Pea-sized Christianity comes in boxes of many shapes and sizes, and at least one box can fit any Christian who allows it. These boxes keep us from a discipleship and an evangelism that's big enough to fill a world-sized Gap. You don't find very many sunrises in a box!

For example, there is a pea-sized box called *convert Christianity*—life in Christ gets no bigger than making it safely inside the Kingdom. Or there's *character Christianity*—life in Christ gets no bigger than pulling one's own spiritual act together. Not far behind this follows *consumption Christianity*—which boxes up life in Christ into meeting one's own personal needs, and that's all.

When life in Christ is no bigger than the warm, secure fellowship I have each week with my good Christian buddies, I'm in the box of *cloister Christianity*. Or, when life in Christ is no bigger for me than getting nicely settled in a good paying job after graduation, then I'm trapped in *career Christianity*. Many of us are groping around the box of *church Christianity*—our life in Christ has grown no bigger than the Sunday School picnic, the choir's Christmas pageant, the monthly finance committee meetings, or scouting out who's absent from midweek prayer service.

A form of pea-sized Christianity that affects all of us to some degree is *culture Christianity*. In this box our life in Christ grows no bigger than a North American, white, middle-class brand of worship and witness. We relish in our tried-and-true traditions, which we erroneously equate with the eternal ways of the Kingdom itself.

In summary, when my Christian experience expands no further than *my* salvation or small group, or church, or future, it's pea-sized. When I compartmentalize my walk with Christ into neat packages of prayer, Bible study, worship, fellowship, evangelism and (somewhere off to the side) missions, it's pea-sized. When my activities and interests don't vitally link me to the reaching of earth's unreached people, I've succumbed to pea-sized Christianity.

Of course, concentrating on missions to the neglect of our personal needs and the needs of the Christians around us, can also be a pea-sized affair. I'm not arguing that we leap from one box into another. Rather, I'm suggesting that we need a new *context* for praying, Bible study, employing spiritual gifts and even for our thinking about missions involvement. That context is the Gap. We need its world dimension for our discipleship.

As many as 2.5 million Americans today suffer from the most common and disabling of all phobias—agoraphobia: the fear of open spaces and unfamiliar situations. Often they've grown up believing the outside world is so dangerous and unmanageable that it's better to stick to familiar routines and only rarely to venture alone outside the house. Similarly, many Christians have grown into spiritual agoraphobiacs—disciples who fear the wide-open spaces of the Gap and would rather stay in the security of a box than venture out with Christ into His global cause. How can anything they do advance God's Kingdom as long as this disorder goes unchecked?

Tragically, there is little place for world missions when our daily mission runs on pea-sized dreams and strategy! Just as tragic, we don't discover the thrill of God using us to close the great Gap between Himself and billions who have never heard of His love. We rarely even think about it. In the end, we contribute little to God's highest priority for this hour of history.

Fortunately, Christ didn't save us to store us in boxes of pea-sized Christianity! He has laid hold of us to stand with Him in the Gap! So, why do we settle for less? Why are we afraid to follow Him?

Reasons for the Boxes

For one thing, *we so easily succumb to the current mood of our own society. Time* magazine studied the American mood in 1976 and concluded:

Narcissism has become a leading topic of research in psychoanalytic circles and one of the most common diagnoses . . . . One difficulty in diagnosing pathological narcissism is that the whole culture has turned in a narcissistic direction. Social critic Tom Wolfe calls the 70's the "Me Decade" . . . Other critics argue that Americans are turning inward because of a sense that individuals cannot have important social or political impact.[1]

Daniel Yankelovich in *New Rules* terms the mood "a search for self-fulfillment in a world turned upside down," though now the trend includes the growing conviction that deeper caring relationships toward others are a way to personal satisfaction.

The world political situation is partly responsible for our narcissistic tendency. More and more we Americans are less in control of world events. We can't seem to manage developments either in the explosive Third-World nations or among our own allies. Vietnam, Watergate, and Iran have disgraced us internationally. We no longer maintain supremacy in energy production and appear weaker to many in military superiority. We feel intimidated by the badgering of the strongly nationalistic emerging nations. And we feel impotent even to deal with many of our own domestic issues. President Carter called it a "crisis of confidence." In a July 12, 1979 column on how we perceive ourselves, *New York Times'* Joseph Sisco writes:

> Skepticism has become a predominant American mood, and we have become a questioning superpower, more uncertain about our role of leadership and seeking to distinguish vital interests from insignificant ones. We are developing a policy of selective engagement in an unpredictable world.

Corresponding to that trend, many U.S. Christians have given up on personally attempting anything significant in the Gap. The mood of our culture—narcissism, and unpredictability coupled with impotence—has spawned fear and unbelief in the Church. Some U.S. church spokesmen and others paralyze us even further by heaping on Americans the major blame for the plight of the so-called Third World and then demanding we pull back altogether. "The theory has it that the advanced nations yanked primitive peoples out of a state of innocent bliss, pressed them into labor and gutted their resources," writes syndicated columnist Jenkin Lloyd Jones. Despite some degree of truth, this charge does not justify the feeling of guilt that British professor P.T. Bauer calls "one of America's few remaining surplus commodities." Jones concludes, "It's time we quit whipping ourselves."

A mood for whipping prevails, however, and too often it is among evangelicals.

As a result of all this, we tend to opt for an undisturbed retreat into our boxes. We rationalize, "There's no use trying to face the complex challenges of world missions today. It's all so far beyond ordinary people like us. Let's concentrate instead on loving each other, or those nearest us who are easiest to love. Maybe that's all we have a right to do."

Think for a moment: How much goes on in local churches, for example, that is just basic self-preservation and a retreat of fear, reflective of the rest of our society?

Herbert Kane, professor of missions at Trinity Evangelical Divinity School, has analyzed some of the barriers to Christian youth's involvement in missionary outreach along these lines: "Young people want a measure of security; never have we had more at home and less abroad. They are uncertain. They have few convictions, few settled opinions, more questions than answers. They are reluctant to make long-term commitments."

Another reason we've settled for pea-sized Christianity is because *the evangelical affluence of U.S. Christians smothers our faith for world missions*. Frankly, most of us suffer from overindulgence in the variety of spiritual food around us. There are scores of organized discipleship programs in and out of the local church on which to feast, along with a wealth of Christian books, magazines, and cassettes on every conceivable issue or personal problem. Famous personalities entertain us at deeper-life concerts and seminars. We can sample an abundance of options for local Christian ministries with all the trimmings needed to pull them off with ease. And for dessert there's a whole menu of charities and organizations ready to help us painlessly discharge any guilt over the distant pleas of the needy.

We become spiritually obese when we saturate ourselves with such a scrumptious input but are devoid of sufficient exercise in a worldwide missionary output! Some have described this as "nominal evangelicalism." We act and look like we're committed to evangelism but we are actually "nominal" when it comes to doing a lot about it.

One expression of our affluence is what I term *smorgasborditis*. So often we're encouraged to pick and choose from the delightful array, to nibble on those things that fit our schedules, our needs, or our interests. In the process, we pass right over God's timetable for the nations who are starving physically and spiritually right now. Smorgasborditis makes us oblivious to needs that are much greater than our own. With so many blessings to choose from at home, we aren't too motivated to choose a sacrificial involvement in the destiny of Chinese in Brazil or Hindus in crowded Calcutta, or a village of Muslim Wolof people in Africa's Senegambia. In fact, we're afraid of all we suspect it will cost us.

In 1978 I returned from India where I observed just the opposite—an indigenous, South Indian missionary movement that actually thrives on the poverty of twenty thousand laypeople. Called the Friends Missionary Prayer Band, these Indians have so few obvious options for significant involvement with Christ that they are willing to give themselves completely to one overriding concern: reaching the thousands of unreached castes, villages, and linguistic groups in northern India. They have far less to work with than we do—financially, educationally, in Bible training, or even in personnel (only 6 percent of south India claims even a remote connection to Christianity). But, from their limited resources they gladly sacrifice in every possible way, and are far richer for it. They are spiritually wealthy but not obese! They've trimmed down their life to the basics: prayer, godliness, love, the Bible, generous giving and a strategy to place 440 of their own members in unevangelized villages by 1985. In place of a smorgasbord they've formed an army to stand in the Gap and close it.

A third reason we have stayed in boxes of pea-sized Christianity is *our own basic ignorance of the facts*. This blindness may be our fundamental problem.

In tests administered to three thousand students in 185 campuses by the Council on Learning, it was discovered that more than one-third indicated they couldn't care less about other nations and world affairs. Their lack of caring was matched by their lack of the facts. The 1981 report concluded: "America's college students are ill-equipped to become national leaders because they are profoundly ignorant of international events, figures and relationships." Council director George Bonham observed that our nation is still poorly equipped in its ability to deal with its innumerable global obligations.

Tragically, many Christians fall under indictment of the same disease, blindness. Only a small percentage are ready to take leadership as God's redemptive agents, to face the global complexities of our generation for Christ's sake.

In a promotional brochure for a conference in Florida on "The Challenge Before Us," Sid McCollum made this honest evaluation:

> Let's face it . . . 99% of us (maybe more) are scared silly of the word *missions*. We really like the idea of someone "forsaking all for Christ and the Gospel" . . . as long as that someone is someone else. "God, you can take my life and use me anywhere you want." we might say. "anywhere except Africa . . . and Asia . . . and South America . . . and Antarctica . . . and Australia. But Hawaii would be OK, God."
>
> What's our problem? In a nutshell, it's this: we see the world differently than God does. We haven't quite caught His plan, His vision, His hope for this world. And until we do, we'll never fully understand what our role can be in the challenge He's set before us."

Honestly now, how many of us even know we're living in the Gap? How often is our vision and courage for the world missionary movement ever stirred by what we've learned concerning its past or future?

Writing in *The Essential Components for World Evangelization: Goals for 1984,* Ralph Winter expresses his personal dismay at this situation:

> Students need a special education just to know the uncensored facts of our world today. The cause of missions is not a simple phenomenon. Common impressions are mainly wrong . . . He may be able to get a course on the history of jazz, but very few state universities or secular colleges (or even Christian liberal arts colleges) offer a course precisely on the history of the Christian mission . . . I am almost more concerned about what the schools do NOT teach rather than what they DO teach. Attacks and criticisms we can grapple with, but the total absence of data is much more subtle and difficult to handle . . . . There is no way that evangelicalism in America has any serious future if 90% of its younger generation is being

undermined on a wholesale basis year after year into the
future.[2]

As I travel to campuses nation wide, I find few students
reading the daily newspaper, let alone catching up on the news
about God's expanding Kingdom around the world today. Their
course work may teach them about world history, international
relations, unusual cultures, and the arts in thirty countries, but
they learn little about how God has been at work in world history, or how international relations open doors for missionary
advance, or how Christ's glory can shine forth through the
redeemed parts of each culture, or (as Winter puts it elsewhere)
how God's grace "transformed those rascally, murderous,
superstitious, head-hunting savages of northern Europe into
builders of Cathedrals."

In his opening address at the Lausanne International Congress on World Evangelization in 1974 Billy Graham noted this
deficiency in our facts:

> Many sincere Christians around the world are concerned
> for evangelism. They are delighted at evangelizing in their
> own communities and even in their own countries. But
> they do not see God's big picture of "world need" and the
> "global responsibility" that He has put upon the Church in
> His world. The Christians in Nigeria are not just to evan-
> gelize Nigeria, nor the Christians in Peru just the people in
> Peru. God's heartbeat is for the world.

Lacking facts on what Graham calls the "big picture" allows
Christians to form all kinds of justifications for not standing in the
widest end of the Gap. We could call these justifications our
myths about missions.

For example, some think the Gap is pretty well closed
already (a sad lack of facts, to say the least). Others think the
Gap is too wide to ever be closed, and so give up (equally sad).
Some opt for the Second Coming as God's way to close it (they
only have part of the biblical facts). Others are concerned that
too much attention on the Gap will disrupt good, solid spiritual
growth right where we live (they need to know some historical

facts). One myth says that when God is ready to close the Gap He will do it without much help from any of us. Another claims that some Christians stand in the Gap, while the rest of us "work for a living." Of course, there's always the myth that only super-spiritual people would even dare to stand there, and that these are few and far between.

Let me give you a folksy proverb I've coined: "God cannot lead us out of boxes of pea-sized Christianity on the basis of facts we do not know and refuse to learn." Daily we should build our own discipleship on the facts of God's worldwide purpose, of all the possibilities and the many unreached people before us right now, and of what it means for believers to get strategically involved where they are.

Narcissism, smorgasborditis, blindness—all these have kept the gap-of-unbelief alive for too many of us too long. As a result we have remained in our boxes of pea-sized Christianity. God doesn't intend that we persist in this useless condition!

The "Lausanne Covenant," embraced by delegates from over ninety nations at the International Congress of World Evangelization in 1974, and again in 1980 during the Consultation on World Evangelization in Thailand, affirms God's desire for all of us:

> We affirm that Christ sends his redeemed people into the world as the Father sent him, and that this calls for a similar deep and costly penetration of the world. We need to break out of our ecclesiastical ghettos and permeate non-Christian society.

He who gave His own Son to close the sin-gap yearns for a people who will effectively keep pace with the critical hour in which He has placed us. He's looking right now for a global church with the courage to embrace the sunrise of missions and to stand by faith with Christ in its light until the Gap of opportunity is closed throughout the earth.

Notes

1. "Narcissus Redivivus," *Time* Magazine, September 20, 1976, p. 63.
2. Ralph Winter, *The Essential Components for World Evangelization:* Goals for 1984 (William Carey Library, 1980), pp. 12-14.

3

SO, WHO WILL STAND IN THE GAP?

The history of God's worldwide purpose has been marked from the beginning by people who repented of their boxes and *stood* in the Gap. You and I can join their ranks. And look at the company we'll keep!

Some Biblical Case Studies

For example, God wanted someone to stand in the gap between a great society turned sour and the new beginning He intended for the human race. So God called Noah to preach righteousness to his generation and build a craft that would take a remnant into the post-Flood world. Later, God wanted someone to stand in the gap between His gracious resources for all nations and their fullest distribution everywhere. So He called Abraham and Sarah to leave their home, to go into a land of promise, to believe that God could give them children in their old age to receive the inheritance that would one day bless as many as the stars of heaven. When God wanted someone to stand in the gap between a nation of slaves and their deliverance, He called Moses to leave Egypt's comforts. Moses, Aaron and others led Israel into God's plan to make them a nation of priests, and as a result, directly changed the course of history for all peoples everywhere.

In one sense the entire Old Testament might be viewed as a series of case studies on different forms the Gap took through the centuries, and of those who responded to the call to stand in it, and what that stand meant for them.

But it wasn't just others called to stand in the Gap. The mystery and majesty of our God is that ultimately He Himself stood there! Jesus forever became God's way home across the Gap. He fulfilled all the efforts of those who stood there before Him. He became the foundation for all the new efforts of those whom He drew forth to stand in the Gap with Him, to finish the reaching of the unreached in a way no Old Testament saint ever could or ever dreamed possible!

Here's a major theme of the four Gospels: Jesus was progressively breaking His disciples out of the boxes that prevented them from believing they could effectively help close the Gap with Him.

In the last forty days following His resurrection, the parallel passages of Luke 24:36-53 and Acts 1:1-8 tell us that Jesus concentrated on three areas of the disciples' faith: their faith in His *person* ("everything written about me"; "many proofs"); their faith in His *purpose* ("that . . . forgiveness of sins should be preached in his name to all nations"; "be my witnesses to the end of the earth"); and their faith in His *promise* ("you shall be my witnesses"; "you are clothed with power"; "you shall receive power when the Holy Spirit has come upon you"). Jesus knew that if their faith focused on these three truths, they would be free to stand in the Gap with Him and to close it. In fact, that's precisely what happened. Through them the gospel penetrated much of the first century world.

Some Christians have the mistaken notion that when we're redeemed we cross *over* the Gap between us and God and out of it to live safely ever after on the other side. But that isn't altogether accurate. Jesus, in bringing us back to the Father, calls us to lose our lives with Him in this world, stating that "if anyone serves me, he must follow me; and where I am, there shall my servant be also" (John 12:26). Where is Jesus right now? In one sense, He is at the right hand of the Father's throne. But He is also active in the Gap! The living Mediator *remains* the mediator! If He wants His people to be where He continues to work then we must serve Him *in* the Gap.

The attitude that was in God's Son when He entered the Gap for our salvation is the same He wants for all His disciples (see Phil. 2:5-10). We're to stand with Him as He stood and stands there. According to 1 John 1:1 that means Christ's approach, and ours like Him, is to be "heard" (speaking good news so that others understand it clearly), "seen" (available to people because we come to where they are), "looked upon" (visible to those we want to reach, being a living model by which they can discover God's love for them), and "touched" (directly and personally involved in bridging the distance between God and specific unreached sinners somewhere in the world). That all adds up to standing in the Gap.

Paul understood this. He claims to be personally "appointed" to stand in the Gap (1 Tim. 2:7). According to his own testimony, that appointment came the very day He met Christ on the Damascus road. In that hour Jesus called him to "rise and stand" for a "purpose": to "serve and bear witness" not only among his own people but "the Gentiles—to whom I send you" (Acts 26:12-23).

But then, Paul turns around and instructs all of us Christians to "be imitators of me, as I am of Christ . . . as I try to please all men in everything I do, not seeking my own advantage, but that of many, that they may be saved" (1 Cor. 11:1,10:32). Of course, we're not all called to be apostles. But like Paul, we should testify about the focus of our conversion: "But when he who had set me apart before I was born, and had called me through his grace, was pleased to reveal his Son to me, [He did so] in order that I might preach him among the Gentiles" (Gal. 1:15-16). God desires the whole Church to imitate Paul's sense of priority and purpose, each of us saying of our lifelong journey in the Gap: "I was not disobedient to the heavenly vision" (Acts 26:19).

Two Important Questions

Will I *stand* in the Gap? That is, will I fully assume the privilege Christ has given me to serve His global cause? A second question is of equal concern: In *what part* of the Gap will I stand? That is, what will be the width of the Gap where I serve Christ's global cause? At what geographical, cultural, and theological distance from a clear witness to Christ are the ones I will reach with God's love? Who will have an opportunity to hear of Christ for the first time because I care?

God is looking for people to stand in the Gap. He's looking for people who believe the Gap exists, that Christ can close it and that they must be in it with Him. He's looking for people to walk in it with Christ, making a strategic impact for His saving mission among all nations, especially among those at the widest end of the Gap.

God is looking for people to stand in the Gap not only because they love Christ but because with Christ they love those on the other side. Only the toughest love will take the kind of action that brings lost sinners home.

God isn't looking first of all for missionaries. No! He's looking for Christians who are willing to be changed, wherever that may lead. He wants disciples who will stand in the Gap humbly, knowing that what is wrong with the world is also what is wrong with them, who are willing to be broken and remolded until they fit strategically in some needy part of the Gap, as God chooses.

God is looking for the change I saw illustrated in India as I watched seven workmen rebuilding part of a collapsed stone wall, about fifty feet down the road. The wall had a hole in it that ran from top to bottom and about six feet wide. Their supply of stone to fill the hole came from some nearby boulders. First, they dynamited the boulders to break them down into chunks. Then they chiseled each chunk to form a stone that would fit perfectly in the next layer of the hole. Slowly the break was closed as one stone after another was fashioned and laid in its exact place.

Like a foundation stone Christ has been set in the Gap. No one else could ever be that rock. But God is looking now for "living stones" to be built on top of Him. He is preparing stones that He has broken and remolded to close the Gap like a "royal priesthood" that "declares the wonderful deeds of him who called you out of darkness into his marvelous light" (1 Pet. 2:9). God has a place for disciples like us who will allow our plans, gifts and abilities, schooling and training, our most intimate relationships, and even our hopes for future Christian service to be broken and remolded so that our lives can count most strategically for the reaching of earth's unreached billions.

To stand in the Gap means to place no limits on how fully God may use you, or for whose sake. It means that, as God directs you, you're willing to take on any role, any time, any place, by any means, with anyone, and at any cost that will help close the Gap, even at its widest end. After all, that's precisely what it meant for Jesus to stand in the Gap.

So, who will *stand* in the Gap? And, *where* will they stand?

There's nothing ho-hum in all of this! It truly is an adventure. To stand in the Gap means to discover all that we are meant to be in this moment of history—to discover the cause for which God has placed us at this hour in His world.

4

THE UNIFYING CAUSE

Put on the Spot

"I've been a Christian for twenty years," he said, "but I must admit that there's something missing in my life. Can you tell me what it is? Can you tell me if there's something more?" There I sat in his living room, only two months into my first pastorate, with a great chance to do the things I had been prepared for . . . and I really bombed!

"Have you tried a private devotion time, Bill—you know, fifteen minutes a day for Bible study and prayer?" Yes, he did that regularly. "Is there sin in your life? For instance, are you a kind husband and father? Maybe you harbor bitterness toward someone." He was clean on all counts. "Well, have you discovered the Spirit-filled life? What role does the Holy Spirit play in your walk with Christ?" His two-minute response told me he had the facts down straight and was truly seeking all God had for him in this area. As his pastor, I knew he attended church faithfully and tithed so I couldn't offer that solution. He did admit he wasn't the witness to his neighbors he ought to be, but he wanted to change this and was praying for them regularly.

So I read some Scripture with him, offered a brief prayer,

promised I'd give it some more thought, and walked away . . . into many similar sessions with other frustrated Christians until I finally learned what my friend was searching for.

Quite simply, despite all the good points, *Bill lacked a cause.* He needed something bigger than the issues we discussed that day, to pull together everything else in his daily life and send it out to bless the ends of the earth. He needed to get beyond pea-sized Christianity, to put his Bible study, or prayer, or family life, or evangelism into a world dimension. He needed a global cause.

What Would I Say Next Time?

I wish I had looked my friend straight in the eye and said, "Bill, I'll tell you what's missing. You need a cause to live for! Something bigger than personal spiritual maintenance or church activities. And you can have it! Focus your life in Christ on the whole world, nothing less, and you'll have a cause on your hands! Discover that you don't have to be a spectator in God's global drama but can become a teammate with those who are reaching out to earth's unreached billions, and you'll have a cause on your hands. Let your discipleship overflow with a world-sized challenge and compassion, and you'll have a cause on your hands, and your life will touch the ends of the earth.

"Beyond the people around you, Bill, that you can touch, see, and care about, is the cry of a larger world: human beings with no knowledge of Christ, that God touches, sees, and deeply cares about. And, Bill, as you make that discovery you'll find a cause that's really the 'something more' you're looking for. It will turn everything else you are and do as a Christian into an adventure without parallel!

"It strikes me that this was Jesus' point with the rich ruler who questioned him on eternal life. Let me paraphrase our Lord: 'After all your good and moral activities, you still lack one thing. You need my cause. Start by selling all you have so you're free to really reach out to those most neglected and most often unaware of God's love. Then, continue with my cause by following me only. I'm on the move. You don't know it yet, but I'm headed into a world full of physically and spiritually poor people. I'm headed toward the ends of the earth!'

"Bill, the frustrations of pea-sized Christianity can be overcome by what I like to call 'Christ's global cause.' Beyond the multitude of crusades and issues that compete for your involvement and mine is this unifying cause that either justifies or eliminates all the rest. I recall how Elton Trueblood once put it: 'This missionary program of the Church of Christ is not simply one aspect of the Christian cause. It is, instead, the concept which is capable of bringing order and meaning into the entire Christian enterprise.'"

Don't get me wrong. I wouldn't tell Bill that the way out of pea-sized Christianity is simply through giving larger percentages of his time and energy to world missions, or worse still, that his only hope is to become a missionary. Rather, I'd tell him that through a bold new faith that turns the sweep of world missions into the integrating factor for all his other efforts at discipleship and evangelism, he'd find a cause so compelling that he'd have his "something more"—and more.

This concept of world missions at the heart of the Christian life is what I mean by "Christ's global cause." Let me explain further.

Christ's Global Cause Defined

First, world missions springs from a cause: the reality of the Gap. To use the dictionary terms for a cause we could say the Gap is the "basis for motivation and action" in the Christian life. At this moment of history it is the "aim and purpose" for all we do as disciples. Until the unreached billions are reached it must have "highest priority" for the whole Church. World missions, then, is the activity of being so concerned with this cause that we actually stand in the Gap; that we persistently *seek* God's Kingdom, and His righteousness, wherever it has yet to break through.

Secondly, the cause belongs to Christ. Our mission in the Gap is because of Him, through Him, and about Him. Our efforts depend on His concern and His provisions for each unreached person and for their societies. He is the One the Church proclaims to the nations, the One we invite them to trust and worship, and the One who will be eternally glorified by all who cross the Gap through Him.

Thirdly, since the Gap exists worldwide, the cause is global in scope. Many today pursue global activities that unify all their other concerns: communists, Muslims, oil cartels, IBM, the United Nations, and Coca-Cola. How much more should we think globally about Christ's cause. After all, the scope of His mission encompasses all tongues, all cultures, all people-groups, all nations, and all places where humans dwell. It includes people like us, true. But it also includes people very different from us. God's focus goes far beyond the minority who can make an intelligent verdict for or against Christ. He is targeted on earth's majority who have too little information to reach any verdict. We should be so targeted as well.

Christ's global cause. How can something of this magnitude not be the integrating factor for everything a Christian does. We must decompartmentalize our discipleship by taking missions out of the closet where we've stored the bits and pieces picked up along the way, things which never seemed to relate to anything else we were in Christ. We must give the cause of missions' grand sweep center stage in the Church's life and in our lives in this generation.

I should have asked Bill the crucial question for all of us in the Gap: "Bill, what is your cause? To *what end* are you dreaming what you dream, wanting what you want, and doing what you do? For example, to what end do you have Quiet Time, Bill? To learn more about Christ and His global cause and how to get better involved? Or is it merely for a temporary spiritual "fix" to help get you through today's eight-hour grind at the office?

To what end does your small group from church meet? Do you discover more about Christ's global cause and equip one another to get more effectively involved in it? To what end are you going to the Christian businessmen's retreat this fall? Will it strengthen your commitment to Christ's global cause, and to nothing less? To what end do you care for your family's needs day by day? To build, encourage, and help them move out with God's love, ultimately for the ends of the earth?

"Bill, that's what's missing! You need this kind of unifying cause or your life will continue to seem splintered and unfulfilled."

Of course, some may hesitate to put world missions at the heart of the Christian life. Even Bill might object.

"It's Not Our First Priority"

Bill might come back: "It seems to me that before we can do anything for the world, our number one priority should be to know Christ Himself."

"Yes, Bill, I agree. But you can't separate knowing Christ from His global cause. It's true, when we get the gift of salvation we also receive the Giver of salvation, and we should desire to learn all we can about Him. But He remains a giver. So, He won't allow us to keep Him to ourselves, nor can we ever fully know Him as long as we try. True, since Jesus is the food for our hungry souls we should feast on Him continually. But He doesn't intend for us to keep eating at a banquet table with so many empty chairs. His food strengthens us to go out and invite others to the same feast. Otherwise, we will soon lose our taste for His presence.

"I'm with you, Bill. I want Christ to reveal Himself to me fully. But we can never see the Redeemer of mankind the way He should be seen unless we care about helping others behold Him and worship Him as we do, especially those who have never heard His name. You see, beyond all our personal encounters with Christ in salvation, in daily Bible study or in the Christian community, looms a larger encounter with Him: learning to know Him as we stand with Him in the Gap, especially at its widest end. This encounter brings us a world-sized revelation of His glory and love that we can find no other way."

"All God Asks Is Obedience"

"Be careful," Bill might caution next. "What counts first in the Christian life is faithful obedience to Christ. And there are other commandments in Scripture that take precedence over the Great Commission, such as God's original command to mankind in Genesis or the two Great Commandments on love by which Jesus summarized all the others."

I understand Bill's hesitation here. Of course, a cause that lacks faithfulness to God's Word can turn into an egotistical, fanatical binge. But, although obedience is essential, Christ doesn't ask us to obey Him just to prove to Him we can be obedient. (That's the circular reasoning by which Islam often looks at God.) Instead, He asks our obedience to specific actions in order to free us and equip us to love with a love that has no limits—a love that reaches out to the ends of the earth!

"As far as these others commandments of Scripture, Bill, isn't the cause of the Great Commission the key at this moment of history to restoring God's original intent for creation, as well as to igniting love for God and one's neighbors in the breasts of us selfish sinners? In this moment of history can anything but the gospel proclaimed, believed, and lived among the nations ever bring individuals or societies or creation itself back to obedience to God's perfect will? Of all things to be faithful to, should we not be faithful to the Great Commission?"

"Shouldn't Our Own Society Come First?"

"After all," Bill argues, "aren't there enough needs around us to worry about? What about all the unreached people on our campuses and in our urban sprawls, for example? Why should we expand our efforts to other nations when the tone of our own culture seems so decadent. Can't a cause like missions undermine our sense of responsibility for a country in crisis?"

Good questions. The answers aren't easy. Certainly we recognize that outreach isn't merely overseas. It is into wider parts of the Gap—cultural and social and theological, as well as geographical—wherever we find them. Furthermore, the expansion we do seek is of God's Kingdom through the growing witness of its ambassadors, not of America's economic or political influence abroad.

As to the fear that we'll concentrate on world missions to the neglect of our own national problems, I would offer Bill two observations: "Over the years I've noticed that publications and groups committed to prodding the social conscience of U.S. evangelicals (like *The Other Side* and *Sojourners)* have increasingly done so by raising our sights to the same problems on a worldwide scale. The implication of this may be that people with a heart for Christ's global cause will respond with new concern for the social, moral and political issues in the Gap around them. Calling evangelicals to embrace world missions more firmly may be a solid way to produce Christians more sensitized to our own country's perils.

The second observation comes from an interview with Ruth

Bell Graham, daughter of a distinguished missionary to China and wife of a world-roving evangelist. I remember reading . . .

> She believes it is vitally important to reach the greatest number of people possible because "If God does not judge America, He will have to send a letter of apology to Sodom and Gomorrah." She is serious. She is firmly convinced that judgment of the United States has been delayed as long as it has only because Americans have sent so many missionaries around the world.[1]

"Could it be that an expanded missionary outreach from the U.S. will develop such significant new spiritual growth here, that the mysterious preserving influence of Kingdom-salt against our own national decay will actually be increased?

"I guess it boils down to this, Bill. In our modern global village all nations and societies are interlinked and interdependent in so many ways. So, it isn't an either/or question. The involvement of American Christians in a global cause on a global scale will strongly determine their impact on their own society."

"Local Outreach Is Hard Enough"

Bill's frustration in evangelizing his neighbors around him prompts the next objection. He knows how much they need the Lord Jesus and how long it takes before they listen to him: "If I'm not successful in reaching them, won't my sense of frustration just increase if I take on concerns for people thousands of miles away?"

I've felt the same tension. He's right. Increased frustration might result. Here's how I would resolve the tension for Bill:

"Most of the people around me have heard the basics of the gospel and have everything from mass media to friends like me to sharpen their understanding. The day came when I faced this and realized that if it's appropriate for me to offer those at the narrowest end a way across the Gap, then surely it's even more appropriate—and crucial—that I pour much of my effort into bridging the Gap for those at its widest end.

"Furthermore, trying to give my love to those who have needs but refuse to admit it can be far more frustrating than giving it to those who have deep needs, know it, and admit it even if they are of another culture or language. Often those nearest me are pampered by overindulgence in prosperity and hardened by overexposure to the gospel. But when I get involved in outreach at the global level, I find many people crushed by deep needs they cannot hide, and openly seeking for answers that are found in Christ alone. What's more, most of them have never once heard the gospel, and desperately need someone to give them the facts in love.

"For example, what greater thrill can I have than loving a few of the millions of tribal peoples who are undergoing tremendous upheaval and crises due to the advance of modern technology? I could do this by praying faithfully for missionaries I know working on community development in a remote village in Irian Jaya, or by actually joining them for two months in the summer. Another example happened just last week. After months of frustration in neighborhood evangelism, a friend of mine was deeply fulfilled as he shared with a Lebanese on campus whose family was threatened by fighting near Beirut. This foreign student had no idea of what Christ could mean to him or his family in such a crisis.

"But there's more. With experiences like these I find myself newly motivated to be more persistent in my love for those nearby who are often so indifferent to me and to Christ! Once you can find some places to let your love flow, even with people very different from you, the thrill keeps you loving even those who couldn't care less!

"And here's another curious thing. My growing concern for those at the widest end of the Gap has actually intensified my outreach to those most like me because I realize that the harvest is so great and the laborers so few. Those around me that I can win and disciple to Christ can someday play a strategic part in harvesting the unreached somewhere else. So, I evangelize them not only to bring them happily into the Kingdom (my first concern) but also to multiply laborers for the greatest cause a person could ever serve.

Acts 1:8 Says It All!

As past generations of disciples, we too have been given a

global cause for our moment in history. I can see Bill sitting back, reflecting on his new understanding. Quietly I would study his face, enjoying his moment of discovery with him. Then, to help him nail it down with Scripture, I would pick up my Bible.

"Bill, from the day you and I entered the Kingdom we've had Christ's cause as our high calling. In fact, from the day the Church was born it has been her grand inheritance. Listen to Jesus' summary of the cause in Acts 1:8 (and I read to him): 'You shall receive power when the Holy Spirit has come upon you; and you shall be my witnesses in Jerusalem and in all Judea and Samaria, and to the end of the earth.'

"Let me tell you what this passage means to me." I proceed to show Bill that the "you" and "upon you" are plural: the cause is given to the whole Body of Christ and is fulfilled through them together. I point out that the "Holy Spirit" refers to the living God indwelling His people in order to unite us to Christ and to one another, to transform us, and lead us forth as Christ's ambassadors to all nations. Only the Spirit can take us beyond the security and comfort of our little groups into the overwhelming challenge of the Gap that He continues to close through those who stand there with Christ.

"Power" designates the Spirit's primary ministry in fulfilling the cause through us. He gives us ability, authority and effectiveness—all this is wrapped up in the word *power.* Even more, His power means love-without-limits, both in how far it reaches and how fully it meets others' needs. Not just any love, either. Christ's love!

"'My witnesses,'" I would explain to Bill, "describes the ultimate impact of the Church's worldwide mission. We bring other people to such a clear understanding of who Jesus is that they can render an intelligent verdict for (or against) Him. What a courtroom witness does for a judge and jury we do for those who have never heard of Christ. Bill, what more strategic impact could any of us ever make for Christ's cause?"

Finally, I would show him how "the ends of the earth" defines the cause as nothing less than global. The disciples weren't to stop with those near to them geographically, culturally, or theologically, nor with those relatively close at hand, like the Samaritans. There was "something more" for them! Christ wanted them (and us) to embrace a cause that would sweep to the ends of the earth before it finished. He wanted them to serve Him in the world dimension.

I can see Bill's growing excitement. He sits up on the edge of his chair: "If this is so, then no cause the world has ever known should be more consuming or more satisfying!" Right, friend. And knowing this, Christ put rock-bottom stability into His challenge with a two-fold promise: "You shall receive power" and "you shall be my witnesses." In the swirl of such an overwhelming task, His Word secures us.

Frankly, it would be foolhardy for Bill, or me, or anyone else to unite all we are and have around a cause of this magnitude unless its triumph was sure. The One who paid the ultimate price for its fulfillment and reigns over the nations to lead it forward guarantees the victory in this two-fold promise. His promise gives us the right, in the words of William Carey's famous directive, not only to "expect great things from God" but also to "attempt great things for God."

"Bill, this discovery of the cause can end your search. If your life seems incomplete because it is sectioned up like a *Time* magazine—if our church seems sluggish because it is fragmented into twelve equal but unrelated programs—then Acts 1:8 provides the new 'cover' to bind up all those themes into the adventure for which we were made. Christ only asks you to 'staple' the whole thing together with your faith—faith working through love."

Actually, the apostle Paul sums it up in much simpler, more beautiful words: "Above all these things put on love, which binds everything together in perfect harmony" (Col. 3:14). Love—love for those on the other side of the Gap. Faith working through that love. Faith and love that result in worldwide missionary activity. That is the unifying cause.

The love we need is not only for those nearest to us and like us, but also for those at the widest end of the Gap. It's love for those very much *un*like us. Love for those who have never heard of Christ and have no one to tell them. Love for those far away from us and far from the good news we could give them about our Saviour. Love for those who will never know of us or listen to us unless you and I and other believers together love them enough to make those radical efforts that put us and the gospel into their part of the Gap. Love that acts especially on behalf of these. That is the unifying cause that gives wholeness and harmony to all the rest of life.

"It's like this, Bill. God's will for us can be put into a single word: *people*—the people *for* whom He wants us to give our lives and the people *with* whom He wants us to give our lives. By making the act of love called world missions our unifying cause we're saying that the people-issue is world-sized. I need to know, therefore, who the people are at the widest end of the Gap God wants me to give my life for. And in order to effectively face that challenge, I must also seriously consider who the Christians are God wants me to give my life with in order to reach them."

What if—what if that day in Bill's living room I had already made this discovery myself so I could have shared all these thoughts with him? What if I had already wrapped my own life in Christ around His global cause?

Or, what if Bill had sat that day with another who sees Christ with a clear eye, theologian Elton Trueblood. What if Bill could hear him say:

The full commitment of millions of Germans, prior to and during the Great War, was to Adolf Hitler and his cause. Other millions are today committed to Marxism, Christians have no monopoly on commitment; they simply have a different object. A Christian is a person who confesses that, amidst the manifold and confusing voices heard in the world, there is *one Voice which supremely wins his full assent, uniting all his powers, intellectual and emotional, into a single pattern of self-giving*. That voice is Jesus Christ . . . he believes in Him with all his heart and strength and mind. Christ appears to the Christian as the one stable point or fulcrum in all the relativities of history. Once the Christian has made this primary commitment he still has perplexities, but *he begins to know the joy of being used for a mighty purpose by which his little life is dignified.*[2] (Italics added.)

Notes

1. Julie Nixon Eisenhower, *Special People* (New York: Simon and Schuster, Inc., 1977), p. 65.
2. Elton Trueblood, *Company of the Committed* (New York: Harper and Row Publishers, Inc., 1961), p. 23.

5

IS THE CAUSE HEALTHY FOR US?

Nothing Could Be Healthier

Living in a world dimension . . . it all seems too big and hard and complex to manage. Couldn't we collapse trying? Is this cause truly healthy, you may wonder, for practical day-to-day growth as Christ's disciples? From my conversations with Bill you won't be surprised if I tell you I believe nothing could be healthier for us!

Of course, it would be *un*healthy for anyone to try to assimilate every fact on the world situation, or to respond to every impulse to be compassionate toward the world community, or to assume personal responsibility for all the world's woes. Even contemplating a witness to all three billion unreached people could easily drive any of us insane unless there is a balanced strategy.

But despite such global-sized eruptions into our lives we can remain healthy if we have *simplified* the issues. For example, our great cause doesn't depend on us going at it alone. We are part of a movement of disciples from many nations who have shouldered the cause together. We can relax. We can work on our own important roles in the complex picture knowing that God sees it all and will effectively coordinate the efforts of His international team.

Furthermore, we can keep our sanity if we concentrate on *one* major cause at a time: closing the Gap of opportunity, fulfilling God's worldwide purpose. This is no pollyanna cop-out on the world's myriad needs.

Research confirms beyond a doubt that the world is full of "unreached peoples." There are at least 2.5 billion who have never been exposed to the gospel and have no one like them, near them, to tell them. Most have never seen a Christian, let alone a church. Among most culture-groups there is not one missionary currently trying to reach them. Consequently, the *fruits* of the gospel are having little direct impact on their lives. They know nothing of the reign of Christ in their midst.

But, we know that as unreached peoples hear, believe, and follow Christ as responsible members of His Church, the rest will follow; the Kingdom will expand its influence, a new basis for solving other world problems will be laid, and a reservoir of compassion and justice will be uncovered among these millions, among culture-groups in every city and every village.

Conscientious Christians, faced with the modern evangelical smorgasbord, are crying out for a style of discipleship that thrives on such clarity and simplicity—and significance. The single-minded focus of standing in the Gap may be the healthiest answer of all.

One who stood for many years in the Gap in India, Donald McGavran, cautions against seeking any other answer:

> As soon as we separate quality from the deepest passion of our Lord to seek and save the lost, it ceases to be Christian quality . . . Even if we produce Christians who live as full brothers with men of other races but do not burn with desire that those others may have eternal life, their "quality" is certainly in doubt.[1]

Missions is not just an emphasis or phrase of the Christian life. Growth in the Christian life, and realistic understanding of evangelism, involves an increasing realization that the field is the world.

What exactly is healthy discipleship anyway? It involves the gradual discipline of our characters until we become like the Saviour. It also involves the growing development of our potential to glorify God. For those standing in the Gap full discipline and full development occur the more we get fully involved in the basic cause for which Christ came.

Didn't Jesus encourage this single-minded discipline and development when He summoned the Twelve to follow Him and learn to fish for others as He took them with Him into His own mission? Wasn't their quality of growth as disciples permanently affected as He helped them integrate and simplify their lives around the one cause of love in the Gap? So, eleven became healthy apostles ("sent ones"), sent out in His power to fish to the ends of the earth.

Practically speaking, healthy, quality discipleship involves learning to give away what we already have. We grow from point *A* to point *B* only as we first give away what we've received at *A*. And, the larger the giveaway the greater the growth. Discipleship is training someone to give better and farther. A mature Christian isn't one who practices the rules more. He's one whose disciplined living helps him love others better and farther. Is this the kind of discipleship you are experiencing?

This is why world evangelism is central to our health as disciples. The best we can give to others is God's love through the gospel. And, while we should love everyone we meet this way, giving the gospel to non-Christians at the wider end of the Gap provides us opportunities to discipline our characters and develop our potential to glorify God farther and farther. Paul Little observed that:

Obedience in evangelism is one of the keys to spiritual health.... When we evangelize, we pray specifically, laying hold on God for victory in the spiritual struggles within the soul of an individual we care about.... With anticipation we watch God answer prayer.... Meanwhile, the Bible becomes increasingly alive and relevant as we see others responding to its truth. Passages that once seemed dry and extraneous appear practical and pertinent. And, remarkably, when we're concentrating on evangelism we don't have time to pick at other Christians and their faults.[2]

What Paul Little claims for local evangelism is doubly true for those involved in world evangelism. "Christianity does not remain healthy among those who are not actively trying to give it away to people at a cultural distance," wrote Ralph Winter.

For example, a person in a wheelchair enjoys some degree of physical health. But the person who walks his dog a mile a day is probably more healthy. And the person who jogs five miles cross-country every day is the healthiest of all. Even so, Christians who stretch their spiritual lives to bridge wider parts of the Gap will discover a healthier faith, hope, joy, and love than they have ever known before.

The more opportunities we take to get out of our cultural and our Christian ghettos, to love those radically different from us, the more we will grow as disciples. We'll grow in our understanding of ourselves—of our real strengths and of our total dependence on the Spirit. We'll grow in our appreciation of the gospel—of how it is God's power for the salvation of all kinds of people. Salvation itself will mean more to us as we watch how God transforms other cultures and world views into something that glorifies His Son. We'll be more committed to the Church— to that global Body whose diversity becomes Christ's rich resource for fulfilling His world mission. And, most of all, we'll grow in our understanding of God's love as we ourselves experience His kind of sacrificial caring and giving to reach those for whom the Gap is widest.

If that's not evidence enough, let's look at other healthy changes the cause brings to those who stand in the Gap.

A Healthier Prayer Life

The cause provides a healthier perspective on what we pray about and the results we expect. This healthier dimension of prayer is illustrated by Psalm 67. Here we learn that our personal requests—bless my family; strengthen the love in my small group; heal me of this disease; help me make the right decisions about a job; give me shelter from the cold winter; bring my best friend to Christ—should contain one overriding provision "that thy way may be known upon earth, thy saving power among all nations" (v. 2).

When we articulate personal requests in keeping with our

growing concern for revealing God's name, Kingdom, and will among all earth's people (the opening concerns of the Lord's Prayer), we are praying about the things God wants to do most. As a result He will show us great answers! When His answers to our prayers make an impact on the reaching of unreached peoples, then our praying will be truly effective. We will have asked for and received the right things. And we will be motivated to pray even more.

As we learn to pray beyond our own little worlds, for people and nations where darkness reigns and the evangelistic task remains so critical, we'll discover new vistas of faith for praying about our own needs as well. When we pray for things at the widest end of the Gap, the challenges at the narrowest end won't seem so impossible anymore.

Here are just five examples of this healthier prayer life. When George reads the daily paper, he prays over the front page headlines. They remind him to pray for persecuted Christians in Asia, or for a Middle East summit meeting that might influence the future of missionary work, or for a missionary in Africa who may be the next victim of guerrilla raids, or for Indian Christians to have new opportunities to show Christ's love in the midst of the century's worst monsoon.

Every evening Tina and her husband Carl spend a half-hour after dinner in prayers that cover everything from their children, to their church, to those who wrote them letters recently, to missionaries and international events. But in keeping with their world vision, they always begin their prayer time praising God for His greatness and glory and His worldwide purpose in Christ. From there they intercede for the needs at wider parts of the Gap and gradually work their way back to their own personal needs. This approach puts their more immediate problems into perspective when compared with far greater tragedies in the Gap, and expands the scope of their concerns. It also provides them with a new faith about how God will answer their own needs, as they learn to trust Him for bigger answers in the Gap.

A Christian group at a large university has planned six evangelistic Bible studies in the dorms. But their prayer is not only that students would come or that some would receive Christ,

but also that through their efforts God would raise up new laborers to go into the harvest, even to unreached people in other
places of the world.

A church in the East gathers every Saturday evening for
prayer. They pray about personal and congregational needs, of
course. But they also discipline themselves to give equal
amounts of time to pray for the Church in other nations and for
missionary outreach. In fact, they actually divide their ninety
minutes of prayer into two major segments. First, prayer for
revival in the Church, locally and worldwide. Then forty-five
minutes is given to issues touching the Great Commission,
locally and worldwide. As a result, many believe these prayer
meetings are some of the most stimulating and life-changing
they've ever been a part of. No wonder they keep coming back!

Jim had such lower-back problems that he was put in traction
for a week. It's still very stiff. But he's asking God to heal him.
And he does so with this provision: that as a healed person he
might be physically freed to go anywhere and do anything Christ
asks of him for His cause.

Healthier Bible Study

The cause changes what we look for and what we find in our
Bibles. Among other things, healthy Bible study will uncover
perspectives and principles that not only lead to Christ but also
out to the world with Him.

Clearly, Bible study that turns into a spiritual sedative isn't
healthy. Instead, the Bible should stir up our faith in Christ's
global cause, build our vision for His world, anchor our decisions
to get actively involved, and equip us to stand wherever the Gap
needs us.

For example, as Jack has his devotions in Joshua, he looks
for principles that God gave Israel for possessing the land, then
he applies these to his desire to help "possess" India for Christ
through his ministry to Indian students on his campus. Mary is
memorizing some of the great promises of Isaiah. As she medi-
tates on each one, she tries to picture how they could be fulfilled
not only in her own life but generally among the nations who are
often the direct focus for the blessings described.

John's small group is studying Christ's Sermon on the Mount

this quarter, but not only as a devotional commentary. Rather, each verse helps to form their thinking about a strategy for a mission they face next summer. As a group they want to reach out to Nigeria by sending two of their members there. In the Sermon they're discovering much of the why, the how, and the what for their mission.

On Sunday evenings First Church is enjoying a series that scans Paul's Epistles. Pastor White intends to help them see that these are also missionary letters written to churches Paul considered partners with him to reach the ends of the earth. Each week he illustrates this fact by suggesting ways the members can apply what they're learning to their own involvement with the church's missionaries.

One day I bought an inexpensive Bible and a pink highlighter pen. For a solid month I studied the Scripture from cover to cover, underlining all the passages that recorded God's interest in, plans for, and actions toward the nations. To my surprise almost half of my Bible turned pink! Again I was impressed that Scripture is full of world-sized themes to think on and live by. If we let it, the Bible will stretch us in new directions beyond ourselves and out to the whole world! Nothing could be healthier for us!

Healthier Motives for Godliness

When we discover that each of us is personally vital to a global cause for world redemption, our motives for staying morally clean begin to change. We find ourselve wanting to flee sin and pursue righteousness for more compelling reasons than just to remain trophies of moral spotlessness. Bitterness, greed, lust, or pride can't be tolerated any longer by those who want God to make their lives count significantly for reaching the unreached. Love does fulfill the Law—particularly love for those at the widest end of the Gap.

The more we accept the fact that we are part of the hope for three billion unreached people, the more we crush our desire to sin. The more we understand that godliness gives support to the credibility and power of the gospel's worldwide advance, the more we will flee the traps of sin. As we accept our solemn privilege to help tell all peoples that Christ can cleanse the world's sin, we will *want* to be righteous like the Lamb of God who takes that sin away.

I observed these healthier motives with Paul and Sally. They thought they loved each other. But their Friday night dates, one of the few times they saw each other, had turned into a steady, exclusive relationship that sometimes left them with nothing better than to drive around in Paul's car, trying to find something fun to do they hadn't done before. In time their physical attraction to one another began to overshadow every other option. They both felt empty about it but they couldn't find the strength to stop until Paul made friends with Kim, a student from Korea. When Paul realized that Kim and many unreached people in Korea stood in the balance, he and Sally found something more compelling to fill their time than their romantic turmoils. They put their relationship into the Gap and it changed everything, including Friday night dates. They actually spent a few minutes each date praying for Kim's salvation and learning about Korea. Some Fridays they would take Kim on an outing and eventually they were able to share Christ with him.

Peter found that the more concerned he became for world missions through his weekly missions study group at church, the more he really wanted to invest some of his earnings in a specific missions project. He chose to work among recent migrants from poverty-stricken rural villages in Mexico, forced into equally discouraging housing in a shanty town outside Mexico City. Peter also found that the more he sacrificially committed personal funds to this ministry, the less willing he was to pad reimbursements from his expense account at work. Somehow that kind of "taking" couldn't coexist with his new-found "giving" in the Gap.

Allen and his wife wrestled with a different problem. They often argued, and their arguments made them misfits with everybody. It's hard to love others when there's a wall of bitterness in the home. Then Allen's pastor asked him to start writing to one of the church's missionaries who was going through some real spiritual lows in his outreach to a mountain tribe in Taiwan. Writing a weekly letter to heal the wounds and build the faith of a key person at the cutting edge of world missions doesn't come easy. Allen knew it wouldn't come at all unless he and his wife kept their relationship full of forgiveness. Christ's cause was too important to fool around with petty bickering. Many arguments didn't seem so necessary after all.

A Healthier Life Together—In Smaller Groups

Warren Webster, a missionary leader who has seen the cause's healthy impact, observes: "The spiritual vitality of any fellowship of Christians should be measured not simply by the number of believers it attracts but by the number of disciples it sends out empowered for witness and service."

Such vitality can be found in many kinds of smaller groups. *Marriage*, for example, should result in the sending forth of two disciples newly equipped to close the Gap as "one flesh." A couple I know willingly put their engagement before the Lord, asking that He bring them together only if it would enrich their involvement in the Gap. In this way they risked all their dreams for the sake of those who've never heard the gospel, as they gave time to search out God's answer. Another couple I know are presently self-supporting missionaries in an Arab country. One of the primary reasons they married was their conviction that their combined strengths, shared in love for one another, would increase their effectiveness in reaching Muslim peoples.

Another kind of small group is *the family*. Family life should also result in disciples empowered to stand in the Gap. I know a father who has given ten years of his life bridging the Gap as an artist-evangelist in the Hindu world. Every night he and his wife present their three young sons before the Lord in prayer, asking that God would someday call them to be missionaries to reach more Hindus. (How many Christian parents could be comfortable praying this way?) Other families pray faithfully each night at dinner on a rotating basis for different missionaries they know personally. One family gradually cut its life-style back to the standard of living of the missionary family in Kenya it helps support. Although the father makes $20,000 a year, they're living on $14,000 so that they can free up the remaining $6,000 a year for those standing in the Gap for the unreached Masai people in Kenya.

The cause can also make for healthier small support groups formed by campus fellowship.

Jesus' support group demonstrated the correct approach. In

contrast, any support group that nurtures self-indulgence, vague commitments and isolation from a needy world isn't healthy at all. In fact, it's terminal. How many support groups are no more than "retirement centers," where the members enjoy a weekly game of "Christian shuffleboard" as they shove a few Bible verses around and talk about their latest spiritual aches and pains. How few support groups are like "caravans"—companies of disciples on the move, traveling together for protection and encouragement as they journey from where they are to touch other parts of the Gap, to serve together wherever and however God asks.

With a global life-or-death cause before it, a support group won't settle for being just a collection of individuals. It will be a team-on-a-mission that has integrated its caring and fellowship into the worldwide mission of Christ Himself. Fellowship will be more the by-product of such a team than its purpose! Howard Snyder writes:

> Groups exist for service. But the mere existence of small groups is not enough. Their function must be clearly understood. Their purpose is objective, not merely subjective. If the focus is only on personal spiritual growth the groups turn inward and become self-defeating—like regularly pulling up a plant by the roots to see if it is growing. Rather, the purpose of such groups must be defined in objective terms that involve work to be done and goals to be achieved. They exist for service; they are "enabling groups" for Christian obedience in the world.[3]

Let me illustrate this with the support group to which Tom and Dick belong. Since they want to keep the cause at the center of their life, they call it a "World Action Team." All the benefits of small groups are theirs, plus they attempt to place everything in the world dimension.

For example, they pray together, and not just for the personal needs within the group. They also pray for the world. Dick has a copy of a handbook on prayer needs for all the countries. Each week a member of the group is responsible to prepare a three-minute report on one country, showing its location on a map, and then leading the group in the handbook's prayer suggestions.

Their small group frequently studies the Bible's great passages about God and the nations. Tom prepares the inductive Bible study each time. They intend to cover key Scriptures in both Old and New Testaments before the year is over.

During their two-hour meetings the group spends time sharing personal burdens and needs. They encourage or counsel each one as they share. But they also try to build up one another's faith in what God wants to do through them individually and as a team to reach the ends of the earth. They try to put all their needs into that perspective.

Finally, each session finds the group at work to develop their strategy for a mission to the world. They study basic materials on world missions. They lay plans for direct involvement in world missions. (Last year they sponsored an orphan in India. This year they're also staging monthly dinners for international students.) And they prepare ten-minute spots on world missions (called a "World Christian Focus") to be given weekly to their Sunday School class.

In order to evaluate their effectiveness as a World Action Team, they keep four questions before the group:

1. Is each facet of our life together (Bible study, prayer, support, and other activities) relevant to the cause we're a part of?
2. Does each facet of our life together strengthen our vision of and involvement in the cause?
3. Does each facet of our life together move us together toward Christ and toward the world He loves and wants to reach?
4. Does each facet of our life together help free us and equip us to more effectively reach the unreached—to the ends of the earth?

Let me tell you about one other support group that never stopped. It was made up of Fred, Joan, and Len (plus one or two others) who met together while they were at a university. Fred and Joan married and three years later took on a mission to an Eastern European country. The vision for that mission, however, came to the whole support group back on the campus. So a year later it was no surprise when Len joined them overseas.

Two years later he also married. Now a small group lives in that country, reaching people at a much wider end of the Gap. The group is identical in many respects to what they were together in college. They're still a healthy support group because at the very beginning they made the cause their overriding concern, and that commitment has never changed. God just took them in their love for Christ, for one another, and for the world and transplanted them six thousand miles away from where they started.

A Healthier Life Together—In Churches
Larger gatherings of Christians—in churches, weekend retreats, or conferences—will be even more healthy when we conduct them for the sake of the cause. Of course, some things like joint Bible studies or bearing one another's burdens usually have their deepest value at a smaller group level. But a meeting of the whole congregation is the logical time for healthy instruction among support groups and families involved in the Gap. During these larger group meetings, Christians in the Gap cross paths to share one another's missions and reinforce one another's commitments to go on with them.

Fortunately for us, our Father led Robyne and me into a church in Madison actively pursuing this. In all honesty we all still have much to learn. But six years ago we rewrote our church objectives to incorporate three major thrusts: worship, build (discipleship), send (world ministry). Then we formed committees (we called them "components") to guide us in each thrust.

When we looked at "sending" we meant this: we were certain that if we developed a congregation of people hungry to send some of our own number into the widest end of the Gap, God would have no trouble raising up those who were hungry to be sent.

We developed a statement of purpose on our sending thrust that reads, in part:

> Our church is to be a mission training and sending center as we grow together into a church of world Christians. And, in sending we will give highest priority to those peo-

ples, both locally and worldwide, currently beyond the reach of the gospel.

Experience has taught us, however, that even the very best purpose statement will get us little action unless we seek to *integrate* a world vision into all we do in worship and in discipleship.

So integrate we have! And the result has been measurable vitality for our regular weekly "housegroups" (where 25 percent of our meeting time is committed to sending concerns), and our newly formed "Institute for Christian Studies" (where we offer prevocational training for potential missionaries, as well as lay leadership courses that have a strong emphasis on the Gap).

We've seen the greatest fruits of integration, however, in our corporate worship each Sunday. For example, behind our pastor and musicians is a large map of the world (the biggest we could find) that indicates—in brilliant orange dots—where we have sent out our own (so far, 10 percent of our Body). It looms over us weekly as we seek God's face in hymns, liturgy, and sermons. That way we can't forget the world as we look at Christ!

Then, a twenty-minute portion of each worship service is actually given to *sending* topics: we see and touch the Gap in creative, challenging and practical ways each Sunday.

But even more, we study the whole Sunday morning experience to insure that *sending* circulates through all we do in our ninety minutes of worship.

We seek to stress *sending* throughout by keeping the following four questions informally before us:

- *Celebration:* What has God recently accomplished through the world mission involvements of our people for which the congregation should praise God together this morning?
- *Motivation:* What will encourage our people in this worship time to move on with their world mission involvements (through Bible messages, world event updates, singing about the cause, testimonials of how personal growth is taking place through a specific mission, etc.)?
- *Training:* How can our people help each other improve their effectiveness to carry out their missions-to-the-world (through up-front teaching, literature tables, reports on how others have done it, etc.)?

• *Intercession:* What are the specific needs and opportunities for our church and our missions-to-the-world that call for immediate prayer?

Results? One example. Recently some members insisted that once a month we set aside forty-five minutes after the worship service for any who could remain behind to join in additional intercession for expanded mission thrusts resulting from church renewal. In light of the increasing numbers of young and old alike volunteering for ministry among the unreached (locally and overseas) they sensed a desperate need for united prayer as part of our Sunday experience.

Anytime a local church's corporate life produces that kind of response, wouldn't you consider Christ's global cause a very healthy focus?

Enlarged Scope of Outreach

No more obvious evidence of spiritual health occurs than when someone's witness for Christ reaches to more and more people. Wherever you find people who make the Gap their life concern, you will find their outreach expanding, where they are and beyond.

It will expand at the local level for a number of reasons. First, the challenge of billions of unreached people demands that outreach in general be given highest priority in our lives. If we live with a sense of urgency about worldwide evangelization it will naturally overflow toward those around us. Second, most of those yet to be reached are vastly different from us, culturally and in many other ways. Concern with reaching them will require of us an increased sensitivity to these differences. In turn, this will stretch us to be more sensitive to those around us who are like us. In the same vein, missionaries depend on cross-cultural communication skills. So, the more we learn from them about what it takes to clearly communicate the gospel across major human barriers, the more skillful we will be in relating to those where the barriers are minor. Finally, concern for the cause puts evangelism and the sovereignty of God into perspective. A global challenge demands that we learn to trust God's grace and power in new ways. All of this can't help but increase our confidence and boldness in evangelism right where we live.

Outreach will also expand beyond those around us to those at the widest end of the Gap. Look at some of the many examples of how the cause is so healthy in this way. David Wilkerson, a one-time rural preacher from Pennsylvania, began standing in the Gap for teenage gangs in New York City, and many teenagers since, even outside our nation, have been changed as a result. John Perkins not only stands in the Gap for poor blacks and whites in Mississippi through his Voice of Calvary ministry but has established an International Study Center to help reproduce his approach to evangelism in other parts of the world. Mother Teresa, an Albanian, went to India to serve Christ in a convent and made the Gap between the gospel and the "poorest of the poor" (as she calls them) her life cause. She and her Missionaries of Charity have spent over twenty-five years revealing the love of Christ among the disinherited on the crowded, dirty streets of Calcutta, and in major cities throughout India and around the globe, including New York City, Detroit, and Los Angeles.

My friend Bob, while completing his Ph.D. in physics, studied Russian to prepare himself for a teaching assignment that would put him in the Gap in Moscow. God did not disappoint him. Joy Ridderhof couldn't go overseas as a missionary due to medical problems. But the cause remained her highest priority. God gave her a vision for reaching remote tribes whose language had never been written down. The tools were portable recordings of gospel messages translated into the native tongue. For decades Gospel Recordings, Inc. has bridged the Gap for unreached people worldwide in seemingly impossible situations.

Tom Brewster was paralyzed from the neck down in a swimming accident when he was eighteen, yet he refused to abandon the Gap. In time God gave him a skill in linguistics, and a wife with similar training and concerns. Tom became a language trainer for hundreds of missionaries. Sometimes Tom travels to over sixty countries a year to equip people serving at the widest end of the Gap. Keeping this cause central has been healthy for Tom. It has enlarged the scope of his outreach. What could be "healthier" than something that frees a paralytic's abilities and his spirit to help glorify Christ around the world?

Notes
1. Donald McGavran, *Understanding Church Growth* (Grand Rapids: Wm. B. Eerdmans Publishing Co., n.d.), p. 52.
2. Paul Little, *How to Give Away Your Faith* (Downers Grove, IL: Inter-Varsity Press, 1966), p. 25.
3. Howard Snyder, *The Problem of Wineskins* (Inter-Varsity Press, 1976), p. 145.

6

WHAT IT MEANS TO BE A
WORLD CHRISTIAN

What, then, shall we call this discovery that can change us so radically and yet make us so healthy? And, what shall we call those who have experienced it?

By now it should be obvious that *all* Christians are born again *into* the Gap between God's worldwide purpose and the fulfillment of it. But there's more than one kind of response to that Gap.

Some are asleep, some are on retreat, and some are determined to stand in the Gap, particularly at its widest end where billions await the opportunity to hear of Christ for the first time. Some are heading into the "sunrise of missions" while others huddle in the shadows. Many move along at a sluggish pace, changing little in the Gap because of their own internal gap-of-unbelief. Others run the race before them, setting no limits on how, where, or among whom God will use them.

Some are trapped in boxes of pea-sized Christianity, full of myths about missions that rob them of incentive to care about the unreached. Others have broken through into cause-Christianity, ready to reach out with God's love to the ends of the earth. They are determined to make Christ's global cause the unifying focus—the context—for all they are and do in the Gap. Yielded to the Mediator, they are willing to be broken and remolded to fit in the Gap wherever they can make the most strategic impact. In turn, they're growing to know Christ, obey Him, and glorify Him as the Mediator.

So, what shall we call the discovery that redirects Christians toward the needs of the Gap? And how shall we distinguish those who have made it?

Some Christians in the Gap are stunted by selfishness and petty preoccupations or by a cautious obedience and love reserved for those closest and easiest to care about. How shall we distinguish the others in the Gap whose growth in discipleship is unmistakable, with a vitality that comes only to those who help bring home lost sinners from many nations?

What shall we call this distinct group of Christians who have taken a stand that says:

> We want to accept personal responsibility for reaching some of earth's unreached, especially from among the billions at the widest end of the Gap who can only be reached through major new efforts by God's people. Among every culture-group where there is no vital, evangelizing Christian community there should be one, there must be one, there shall be one. Together we want to help make this happen.

For a moment, let's call them *World Christians.* Of course, any new term might be misunderstood. For example, some might think I said "worldly" Christians, not "World Christians." By now we know, however, if you are one, you can't be the other. If you are one you don't *want* to be the other!

No, the term is not in your Bible concordance. Don't worry. It isn't another cliche like the words of the bumper sticker that read "Honk-if-the-Rapture-starts." Nor is it an attempt to label some new spiritual elite who have a corner on a super-secret blessing. Rather, the term describes what all of us are meant to be and what some of us have started to become.

The term "World Christian" may have been coined first by Daniel Fleming in a 1920 YMCA book entitled *Marks of a World Christian.* More recently the term has appeared in publications of such groups as Worldteam, Conservative Baptist Foreign

Missionary Society, United Presbyterian Center for Mission Studies, Overseas Missionary Fellowship, National Prayer Committee, and United States Center for World Mission, as well as Campus Crusade for Christ and Inter-Varsity Christian Fellowship. Of course, we mustn't forget a recently launched periodical, considered by many to be the *National Geographic* of missions magazines—*World Christian* magazine.

A World Christian isn't better than other Christians. But by God's grace, he has made a discovery so important that life can never be the same again. He has discovered the truth about the Gap, the fact that he is already in it, and the call of Christ to believe, think, plan, and act accordingly. By faith, he has chosen to *stand* in the Gap as a result.

Some World Christians are missionaries who stand in the Gap by physically crossing major human barriers (cultural, political, etc.) to bring the gospel to those who can hear no other way. But every Christian is meant to be a World Christian, whether you physically "go," or "stay at home" to provide the sacrificial love, prayers, training, money, and quality of corporate life that backs the witness of those who "go."

World Christians are day-to-day disciples for whom Christ's global cause has become the integrating, overriding priority for all that He is for them. Like disciples should, they actively investigate all that their Master's Great Commission means. Then they act on what they learn.

World Christians are Christians whose life directions have been solidly transformed by a world vision. This is not a term for frustrated Christians who feel trapped into the world missionary movement and sporadically push a few buttons to say they've done their part. Having caught a vision, World Christians want to keep that vision and obey it unhesitatingly.

World Christians are (in Corrie Ten Boom's phrase) tramps for the Lord who have left their hiding places to roam the Gap with the Saviour. They are heaven's expatriates, camping where the Kingdom is best served. They are earth's dispossessed, who've journeyed forth to give a dying world not only the gospel but their own souls as well. They are members of God's global dispersion down through history and out through the nations, reaching the unreached and blessing the families of earth.

By taking three steps we become World Christians. First, World Christians *catch* a world vision. They see the cause the way God sees it. They see the full scope of the Gap. Next, World Christians *keep* that world vision. They put the cause at the heart of their life in Christ. They put their life at the heart of the Gap. Then World Christians *obey* their world vision. Together they develop a strategy that makes a lasting impact on the cause, particularly at the widest end of the Gap.

Many years ago a World Christian named John R. Mott, leader of the Student Volunteer Movement that sent out twenty thousand new missionaries, outlined similar steps:

> An enterprise which aims at the evangelization of the whole world in a generation, and contemplates the ultimate establishment of the Kingdom of Christ, requires that its leaders be Christian statesmen—men with farseeing views, with comprehensive plans, with power of initiative, and with victorious faith.

Catch! Keep! Obey!—these are the three steps to becoming a World Christian. Let's examine them a little more closely in outline form:

Step one: Catch a world vision
- See God's worldwide *purpose* in Christ
- See a world full of *possibilities* through Christ
- See a world full of *people* without Christ
- See my world-sized *part* with Christ

Step two: Keep a world vision
- *Be* a World Christian
- *Join* with other World Christians
- *Plan* to obey the vision

Step three: Obey a world vision
- Obey as you regularly *build* your vision
- Obey as you *reach out* directly in love
- Obey as you *give* your vision to other Christians

How can someone know if they've taken these three basic steps toward becoming a World Christian? Here are some important clues:

Have I caught a world vision? (step one)
- PURPOSE: Do I see the big picture of Christ's global cause from God's point of view?
- POSSIBILITIES: Do I see the Church's potential in our generation for closing the Gap between God's worldwide purpose and its fulfillment?
- PEOPLE: Do I see the great scope of earth's unreached peoples, especially the billions at the widest end of the Gap who have yet to clearly hear the gospel?
- PART: Do I believe that I along with other Christians can have a strategic impact on Christ's global cause right now?

Have I kept a world vision? (step two)
- *Be:* Am I willing to stand in the Gap with Christ, to unite my whole relationship with Him around His global cause?
- *Join:* Am I willing to team up with other World Christians to stand in the Gap together?
- *Plan:* Am I willing to design specific ways to obey my world vision and help close the Gap?

Do I obey a world vision? (step three)
- *Build:* Do I take time to study the case? Am I letting my world vision grow?
- *Reach-out:* Do I get personally involved in the cause? Am I helping to reach unreached peoples, especially at the widest end of the Gap?
- *Give:* Do I transfer my vision to other Christians? Am I seeking more World Christians to stand in the Gap and serve the cause?

Ultimately, however, becoming a World Christian goes beyond "steps" that we take. It is the gracious work of Christ Himself! Our faith must always be in Him, not in any simple three-step process. It is Christ who opens us up to catch His world vision. He alone anchors us to that vision and then empowers us to effectively obey it. With the hymn writer, all

World Christians appeal to Christ: "Be Thou my Vision, O Lord of my heart."

Do you know any World Christians? Are *you* one? Would you like to be? Would you like to wrap your life in Christ around His global cause and nothing less? Every night when you place your head on the pillow would you like to say, "I know *this* day my life has counted *strategically* for the global cause of Christ, *especially* for those currently beyond the reach of the gospel"?

7

AN IDEA WHOSE TIME HAS COME—AGES AGO!

The Christian movement is the story of thousands of World Christians burning with a world vision, disciples who have lived and died standing in the Gap.

Examples from the Past

World Christians have been around since the apostles preached on Pentecost to multitudes from most known nations under heaven; since Philip, a Jew, planted churches in Samaritan villages and then shared the gospel with an international visitor from Ethiopia; since Peter crossed the threshold between Jews and Gentiles to bring Christ to a Roman centurion and his family. The New Testament is full of World Christians: the members of the Jerusalem church, scattered abroad by persecution, preaching the message to Jews and Greeks as well; Paul and Barnabas, sent out by the church at Antioch to establish other churches throughout Galatia; Aquila and Priscilla who formed the nucleus of a mission-minded church that evangelized all of Asia Minor in less than three years; the Thessalonian church, whose life together established a witness that reached far beyond them into Macedonia and Achaia; John, banished to an island dungeon because he proclaimed Christ in the face of great political and theological barriers, but given there a prophet's overview of the global climax of the Christian movement.

Thousands of other World Christians have preceded us in the Gap. A fourth-century World Christian, John Chrysostom, stood in the Gap for the Barbarian Goths of the Balkans, training and sending missionaries to reach them. He defined his world vision this way: "We have a whole Christ for our salvation; a whole Bible for our staff; a whole Church for our fellowship; and a whole world for our parish."

Patrick stood in the Gap for the Celtic people in Ireland to plant the church there in the fifth century. In the sixth century, Columba, building on this foundation, founded a missions community of the Irish coast on the island of Iona where Celtic World Christians were trained and sent into the Gap between the gospel and the unreached tribes of Northern Europe.

In the thirteenth century, a youthful World Christian named Francis left his family's wealth in Assisi, Italy, to stand in the Gap. Initially he and his wandering band worked in a narrower part of the Gap in Europe, but gradually the Franciscan Order became a World Christian movement that reached around the globe!

Another World Christian movement, the Dominicans, produced compassionate Bartolome De Las Casas. In the 1500s he stood in the Gap for Indians oppressed by the Spanish in the New World. He worked for their conversion and struggled with the Spanish government to institute laws that secured their humane treatment. Later, a Puritan, John Eliot, gave his life in the Gap on behalf of abused Indians and Negro slaves in our own country.

An amazing movement of World Christians were the Moravians, a society made up of families from Bohemia who sought political refuge in Germany. Throughout the eighteenth century, they sent out teams of missionary communities to stand in the Gap for peoples in North America, South America, Africa and China, as well as other parts of Europe. Those Moravians who did the "sending" were as fully World Christians as those who went. For example, their German sending base sponsored a twenty-four hour prayer chain that lasted almost one hundred years! The chain backed their commitment to send forth 10 percent of their number.

The "father of modern missions" was an ordinary cobbler who met monthly in the late 1700s with a small group to pray for "the revival of religion and the expansion of Christ's Kingdom around the world." William Carey caught a world vision. His own research on the Gap, entitled "An Enquiry into the Obligations of Christians to Use Means for the Conversion of the Heathen" is an explosive volume that describes his findings on millions of unreached peoples who stood at its widest end. His book turned English Christians around and broke the logjam in Protestant missionary efforts that had blighted the cause since the Reformation. Eventually, Carey relocated to another part of the Gap to obey his world vision on behalf of India. He translated Scriptures into over thirty languages and planted churches around Calcutta.

Less than a century ago the Gap was flooded with thousands of World Christians issuing from the Student Volunteer Movement of the late 1800s and early 1900s. Twenty thousand college graduates sailed to most countries of the world to preach the gospel. Thousands more remained behind as the sending base, spreading the challenge of Christ's global cause throughout the churches, leading many laypeople and church leaders into the experience of World Christian discipleship.

Examples from Today

The Gap continues to close as many today have made the same discovery. Over seventy thousand Protestant missionaries from North America and Europe, standing in the Gap worldwide, are joined by over fifteen thousand additional missionaries from Third-World nations sent out by over four hundred Third-World missionary societies.

For some in this vanguard, being a World Christian has required tremendous courage. In 1976, for example, a friend of mine visited missionaries working in the resistant parts of the Muslim world. As he traveled from country to country and missionary to missionary, he found that the spiritual battle was so great that only where missionaries labored long hours each day bridging the Muslim gap through intercessory prayer was there any noticeable fruit.

We noted earlier one courageous Third-World movement of

World Christians—the Friends of Missionary Prayer Band—
that is twenty thousand strong, meeting in five hundred prayer
bands with a goal of sending four hundred-fifty south Indian missionaries by 1985. Sacrificially they have reached out to countrymen who are separated from the gospel by great chasms of
castes, cultures, languages, and Hindu traditions. Furthermore,
their world vision has brought revival to churches in south India
because the FMPB has inspired fellow Christians to make the
same World Christian discovery and form their own prayer
bands as a result.

In America we have many examples of World Christians on
the move. A church in Arizona pledged as much to world missions as they would spend on themselves when they entered a
five-million-dollar building program! A Southern California
church puts world vision and challenge into all their teaching programs, from Sunday School to morning worship to Bible clubs.
As a result God has raised up scores of missionaries within their
own congregation and hundreds more to send them. Two hundred members of a church in the San Fernando Valley sold second cars, while others mortgaged their homes, in order to give
full support to a team of five couples who became missionaries
to the Tonga tribe in Zambia. That was ten years ago. Today that
church of World Christians is responsible for bringing thousands
of Tongans to Christ!

A large church in the Northwest conducts numerous prayer
meetings throughout their city every day of the week. Each
meeting concentrates on a different part of the world. Members
are encouraged to attend the one for which they have the greatest burden. Another metropolitan church has organized what
they call "Circle of Twenty" groups. Each group is composed of
nineteen church members and one missionary. But all become
World Christians as the nineteen get as fully involved with their
missionary as any sending base could be. A church in the Midwest put the word "missionary" in their name, indicating where
they intended to give priority. Over the past fifteen years, they
have grown in world vision and involvement, while many of their
members have actually become missionaries.

Take the case of another Midwestern church that has set a
goal of sending ten thousand missionaries (either professional or

self-supporting) by the year 2000! That will not happen unless all eleven hundred members become devoted World Christians.

A new movement called the Episcopal Church Missionary Community is comprised of laypeople who want to help fellow Episcopalians "catch the vision." They are seeking hundreds of missions prayer cells which may eventually send out their own missionaries. Across the country, World Christian pastors and missions committee members from churches in over fifty denominations have banded together to form, for the first time, an Association of Church Missions Committees in order to help maximize the impact of local churches in the Gap.

World Christian dynamics have also surfaced in major campus movements in North America. The Navigators, with field offices for every continent, are presently reproducing disciple-makers in over thirty-four countries while increasing their ministry to international students in the U.S. Campus Crusade for Christ has almost five hundred staff working in over one hundred countries outside North America. Along with its Agape program (vocational witness overseas), its International Summer Projects and its intensified training for witness to Internationals here, CCC is also committed to spend one billion dollars to reach one billion people by 1985 through its Here's Life World! campaign (especially through the Jesus film).

Operation Mobilization and Youth with a Mission (YWAM) have trained thousands of young adults to serve overseas on short-term mission assignments. Many are working in some of the most difficult parts of the Gap. And most return to the States with renewed vision for the world that fires up their local churches. Right now YWAM is at work to mobilize trans-denominational "Concerts of Prayer" for spiritual awakening and world evangelization in every one of our state capitals. At the same time, they hope to thrust out twenty thousand short-term (two-year) missionaries during the next three years.

In addition to inviting furloughing missionaries to meet with students in its over eight hundred-fifty groups, Inter-Varsity Christian Fellowship (the world's oldest and largest interdenominational campus ministry) is developing a reservoir of staff specialists for various kinds of cross-cultural ministries. Within the mainstream of its discipling ministry there has emerged Overseas Training Camps in Latin America, Asia, Africa, and Europe, along with credit-bearing extension courses in missions right on campus. Its Student Training in Missions program continues to gear toward six hundred or more abroad by 1985. And since 1976 the challenge of Christ's global cause has received increased visibility through its World Christian Conferences conducted nationwide.

Further, IVCF currently has data on computers on the missions commitments and experiences of over twenty thousand students. The personal printouts on each suggests that IV's goal of mobilizing five thousand new career missionaries and fifteen thousand committed "senders" by 1986 is quite within reach.

It needs to be said again—and all these examples bear it out—that most World Christians today are not missionaries. They are like any Christian, with the same struggles, fears, and potentials for Jesus. What marks them is their discovery of a *world vision* around which they've reordered their lives. They've discovered the truth of John Stott's words to the seventeen thousand students at Inter-Varsity's triennial Urbana student mission's convention: "We must be global Christians with a global vision because our God is a global God."

In the early seventies, Bruce Graham was studying at Massachusetts Institute of Technology to become a career astronaut. As a small boy he had sat on his back porch and gazed at the moon, determined someday to walk on it. Now his dream was about to come true. But at MIT he became a Christian and was discipled by another Christian student from India. That was when Bruce began to catch his world vision.

During his graduate studies in aerospace engineering Bruce and his wife Christy attended a six-week program cosponsored by Inter-Varsity that explored the dimensions of a world vision. Challenged to become a World Christian at the Summer Institute of International Studies, Bruce took the next step: he made his world vision a life cause.

In the months that followed, Bruce laid a strategy to obey that vision. God changed Bruce's passion from a mission to the moon to a mission in the Gap, particularly at the wider Muslim end. Today in California, Bruce trains other young adults to stand effectively in the Gap. He and his wife, along with a community of World Christians who lived in their house until recently, prepare themselves for the day some of them may physically go to reach people in the Muslim or Hindu worlds. The "Haggai Community" continues on with their dream.

Here's how Bruce describes his own "conversion" to World Christian discipleship:

There came a time, though, after I had realized that He was Lord that I became aware that He wanted to use my life to reach others. I was, in fact, useful to Him. This had tremendous ramifications in the choices of future occupations in my life. Even beyond this there came a point in my growth as a Christian when I realized that Jesus wasn't just for me or for those here in the U.S., but that He was for all the people of the world. Jesus Christ was desiring that I help make Him known to the ends of the earth. There are people around the world very different from me who are looking for a relationship with Christ just as I was. No longer could I keep Him for myself or be content with making Him known to friends and those like me, but He was desiring to use me to help make Him known to people different from myself. The scope of His concerns and now, therefore, my concerns was the world.

Here's How It Happened to Me

I was leading a three-day conference on World Christian discipleship. During Sunday lunch a student shared with me how she had been depressed the entire weekend. Finally she'd figured out why. As she caught a world vision that weekend, she realized she had spent the past two years as a new Christian without Christ's cause as her highest priority, and she deeply regretted the lost time. But, I told her, nothing was lost. All of her growth as Jesus' disciple would be valuable as she now took her stand with Him in the Gap. "Be grateful it was only *two* years," I said. "Many have labored ten to twenty years at Christian discipleship without making this great discovery."

I was one of those. When I became a Christian my freshman year in college, I thrived on Bible study, sang my heart out with newly found hymns, drank in the fresh warmth of Christian fellowship for the first time, but ran scared from the missions study group on campus. That's where my pilgrimage toward being a World Christian began.

And I kept on running! Right through undergraduate studies in religion and graduate studies in theology, successfully avoiding every missions course that was offered along the way. There was something about the whole topic that seemed dull, peculiar, and above all, threatening in my own plans for Christian service. I was stuck in pea-sized Christianity, boxed-off from the thrill of Christ's global cause by my gap of unbelief.

But the Lord Jesus wanted for me exactly what He wanted for His first disciples: that I catch a world vision and move out on it. My discovery of this began when, during my years of graduate study, He put me into an inner-city Bible club ministry in the black neighborhoods of south Chicago. At first I was unaware of what was happening to me. But there Christ gave me a vision for people where the Gap was much wider than I had experienced before.

Next, He led me into the pastorate, and cracked open my pea-sized boxes. For six years He helped me discover the potential of a local congregation to make a worldwide impact on His cause.

Like many pastors I struggled to give meaningful leadership to our church's involvement with three or four missionaries. I had never met any of them. How difficult it was to teach my church how to pray for them when I knew little about the big picture of missions myself and had little desire to find out and few clues where to begin. But God had a surprise for me!

It happened that our church was located near Ohio's Kent State University. Many students from Christian campus organizations attended our services. To hook up these students with our church families we began what we called our "adoption program." As the years passed God sent many of our "adopted" students into other parts of the U.S. and into the world. We woke up to this fact the year we placed a map on the wall of our educational wing and marked with flags the places our student friends came from and the places they were going. To multiply those flags over the previous five years of ministry and to see how we were literally touching the ends of the earth was simply overwhelming. (Incidentally, I would recommend that any student fellowship or local church take a map and try the same experiment. You'll gain a new perspective on how to fit into God's plan for the nations.)

Truly God had placed our church right in the middle of a mission-training, mission-sending ministry. The possibilities were unlimited. And, the vital link between the church as a base and the students in its worldwide extension were the families who adopted them. As students and young couples from our midst went forth in many capacities, our whole church could make a lasting contribution to the cause. The training we gave them, the quality of community life we showed them, and the deep support of individual family units would go with them. We could become a church of World Christians.

Standing on the Commons as National Guard bullets struck down four Kent State students in May of 1970 I saw these possibilities even more clearly. Individuals involved in something in one small part of the world rocked a whole generation and affected the consciousness of nations toward a war. For some time after the shootings people traveled from everywhere to declare their solidarity with those who died, with a life-and-death cause of international proportions. I thought: Could not a local group of World Christians—students and church laypeople bound together for the sake of the Gap—have a similarly far-reaching impact on Christ's global cause?

All this created in me a longing to expand my own world vision in order to lead in our church's mission. My hunger grew as I met with concerned laymen to pray eight hours each week for six weeks about our church's future. We prayed through the book of Ephesians (a theology of the cause), using one chapter each week as the basis of what we praised God for and asked Him for. One evidence of what God taught us those days was the motto He gave us for our church: "Applying the gospel of Christ to the world of Kent—and the world beyond."

My hunger increased in 1970 when my wife Robyne and I attended Inter-Varsity's Urbana Student Missions Convention. There we met with many mission agencies, heard great sermons on the world mission of the Church, and discovered through a computer printout where we could serve Christ in other parts of the world. In 1973 my hunger took a more personal turn through a loving relationship God gave me with a Buddhist Japanese student doing graduate work in the Kent State physics department. (That relationship continues through mail and over the years has offered tremendous opportunities to share Christ with him.)

Finally it happened. Becoming a World Christian took me out of the pastorate. The situation had created in me such a craving to know more about Christ's global cause that I knew I wouldn't be satisfied until I found out.

Leaving behind financial security, a fulfilling ministry, and the comfort of family and friends, Robyne and I ventured to Southern California to spend a year at Fuller Seminary's School of World Mission. Not only did God provide for every physical need (that's a story in itself!), but He built in us the world vision we longed for. For nine months of classes I sat at the feet of leading mission strategists, furloughed missionaries (with a combined fifteen hundred years of missionary experience), and church leaders from the Third World.

Like the student I mentioned before, I too experienced a time of depression during these months as I realized how much my previous twelve years as a Christian had lacked. I was hit hard by statistical studies and multimedia presentations describing the one billion people who were starving physically and the two billion who had never heard the name of Christ. Why should this be? And, why wasn't I told before? Then the harder questions: Was I willing to open up to these people? Was I willing to love them? What changes would this make in my life? What would it mean for *me* to stand in the Gap? And for Robyne and our marriage? What impact could the two of us have on those with such compelling needs? How would we get started?

Fortunately, during this time God put us with other Christians who had caught the same vision and were working through the same questions. We labored together to build our vision, learn how to put it into practice in very practical ways, and how to pass it along to others. Many kinds of world-sized ministries sprang from that fellowship of World Christians, not the least being the U.S. Center for World Mission with its many new frontline ministries.

Since then the global cause of the living Christ has continued to transform my life; not only in terms of occupation and ministry but even in marriage Robyne and I have seen the effects of this grand discovery. The broad sweep of world missions has become the unifying cause—the context—for our relationship.

For example, our prayer life continues to grow in its focus on missionaries, unreached people-groups, and current international events. Our new priorities have changed everything from what magazines we take, to the kinds of social events we attend. We want to save our time and money for those things that will help us obey our world vision. We delayed investing in a house, for example, until we thought God had moved us where He wanted us to settle for a time of maximum involvement in the Gap. Then we purchased in a neighborhood where the Gap is culturally wider than in other parts of town.

Being World Christians has influenced our hospitality ministry. Often we invite in fellow World Christians to work at building our vision together, or potential World Christians so that we can help them catch the vision. Our guests include missionaries from the front lines so that we can refresh them and learn from them, to non-Christian international students so we can love a few at the Gap's widest end, who just "happen" to live nearby. Recently two other "guests" joined us permanently: an abandoned child from Kerala, South India named Adam and beautiful two-year-old Bethany from an orphanage near Bombay. Robyne and I adopted both because God set them before us and called us to love them as our own. (We were delighted to comply!)

Some people don't understand all this, or us. But stretching back two thousand years stands a great company of disciples who do. And that's enough for now.

8

NEEDED: A GREAT AWAKENING IN THE GAP

Walk with me along a very special beach, one with over four billion grains of sand. It's the same beach Habbakuk described when he wrote "For the earth will be filled with the knowledge of the glory of the Lord, as the waters cover the sea" (2:14).

For two thousand years the knowledge of God's glory in the face of Jesus Christ (2 Cor. 2:14) has spread like ocean waves over the sands of peoples, languages and cultures. Some day the gospel will cover all of it. Throughout the past centuries the gospel's advance along this beach has fluctuated. But, now God's Spirit has stirred up new waves of global outreach to thunder farther up the shore than ever before. Church historians call these waves of renewed missionary activity the "Great Awakenings." During the past two hundred years, concurrent with the greatest missionary advance in two millennia, there have been three such mighty spiritual surges. Many mission strategists today believe we're on the crest of another Great Awakening, called by some the "sunrise of missions." (C. Peter Wagner's *On the Crest of the Wave* puts hard facts behind this claim.)

What Does a Great Awakening Look Like?

One of the foremost authorities on these waves of awakening, J. Edwin Orr, describes them in three distinct phases:

1. A spontaneous outpouring of the Holy Spirit revives Chris-

tians to the point that they band together in fervent prayer.

2. Out of united prayer meetings spring cooperative evangelism, increased lay leadership in the churches and a new zeal for present missions activity, both at home and abroad.

3. Rising from the first two phases the church mobilizes the talents and energies of its best trained men and women to carry forward the missionary advance with unparalleled results.

(Dr. Orr substantiates this in three detailed volumes: *The Eager Feet, The Fervent Prayer,* and *The Flaming Tongue.*)

Can it be that awakenings similar to those in the days of William Carey and the Student Volunteer Movement are upon us again? Since World War II, a new crest of spiritual ferment has erupted worldwide. Much of this is seen in the formation of 250 new North American Protestant missionary societies since 1945 and of 400 more in the Third World. Consultations on world evangelization at the national and international levels, including Lausanne's 1980 worldwide consultation in Thailand, Amsterdam '83 for itinerant evangelists, and the Korea '84 International Prayer Assembly, are also evidence of the crest.

As in past awakenings, people of many denominations are coming together in the Gap to seek all God wants to do through them, to throw off the shackles of unbelief, and to fully commit themselves to serve the cause. In the past thirty-five years many in the church have moved through phases one and two as described by Dr. Orr. What remains is the explosion of this spiritual ferment into an awakening of all God's people in the Gap, so that we mobilize every resource to fill the widest end of the Gap in this generation.

Missionary and seminary professor J. Christy Wilson remarked to me one morning on our way to breakfast: "I believe we've entered the fourth Great Awakening—it has already started—and it may be the last one. Because in this awakening God can complete His plan for the nations." I believe this too.

What will another awakening mean for Christians like you and me? Primarily, we'll experience a world-sized answer to Paul's prayer in Ephesians 1:18-23:

[I pray that you may have] the eyes of your hearts enlightened, that you may know what is the hope to which he has called you, what are the riches of his glorious inheritance in the saints, and what is the immeasurable greatness of his power in us who believe according to the working of his great might which we accomplish in Christ when he raised him from the dead and made him sit at his right hand in the heavenly places, far above all rule and authority and power and dominion, and above every name that is named, not only in this age but also in that which is to come; . . . and has made him head over all things.

What is the world-sized awakening Paul expects God to do for every believer?

Prior to this, in verses 1-17 we learn who Paul prays for: the Church. He describes it as "destined and appointed to live for the praise of [God's] glory . . . according to the counsel of his will" (vv. 12,11). The counsel of His will is "a plan for the fulness of time, to unite all things in [Christ] things in heaven and things on earth" (v. 10). To put it another way, Paul is praying for those destined and appointed to stand in the Gap.

When the hearts of such people are able to really see, they will make an extraordinary discovery in three important areas, and the awakening will happen! Paul asks God to awaken us to (1) the *hope* of our calling in Christ (v. 18)—the contemporary as well as the eternal victories awaiting those "destined" to stand in the Gap; (2) God's *resources* in the saints (v. 18)—Christ's global Body, adequately equipped to bring praise to God's grace among all the nations; (3) God's *power* at work in us (vv. 19-23)—the very power that is right now summing up all things under Christ as Lord and doing so through the Church around the world.

Paul carefully notes in his prayer that only the Holy Spirit can bring this awakening to pass. He alone can give us new eyes for the world. As Paul prays further in Ephesians 3, the Spirit strengthens God's people in their inner being with the mighty love of Christ, which, in turn, can fill the height, depth, width, and length of the whole Gap through them (vv. 14-19).

Could we desire any more than that God would give His people such an experience? What if this prayer were answered in your Bible study group or your church—and in groups like yours around the whole world?

I observed one way God can create this awakening following a church missions conference on the theme "Becoming a Church of World Christians." During the weekend we gave a questionnaire to the one hundred fifty members. Twenty-eight responded that they felt God was leading them into some form of cross-cultural ministry within the next three years. Six of these were between the ages of eighteen and twenty-four (maybe the most mobile and ready to go) and three were fifty and above (which meant they wanted to be mobile; they weren't ready to stop!). But forty-one others indicated a willingness to seriously *explore* the possibility that God would have such a ministry for them, and most of these were over twenty-five years old (again, these had a mobility and maturity that made them prime candidates for new mission efforts). Because the facts of their church's potential were coupled with the strategy of the Ephesian model in Acts 19, and because they were given practical tools for tapping that potential, the congregation exploded.

As a result of these findings the church's missions committee reevaluated the definition, policies, and strategy of their entire missions program. Above all, they asked themselves how to release into the heart of Christ's global cause the tremendous people-resources God had given them. How should they mobilize the sixty-nine with a cross-cultural concern, together as a church? One of their answers was to set new goals: (1) their missions thrust would focus primarily on unreached people-groups; (2) they would ask God to raise up people from their church family to reach them; (3) they would provide learning situations to help the whole church family research and prepare themselves for the outreach they assumed.

I've watched similar awakenings stir a number of churches since. God's Spirit has placed new eyes in other hearts to see a world vision. If that's the potential in just one small group, think of what could happen within the evangelical church at large if a Great Awakening came with full force in our generation! I believe it will.

Watch It Surface in the Student World

If such an awakening is imminent, look for it to surface dramatically among those usually more open and more mobile—the student world. In 1975 Billy Graham observed: "I believe there has never been as many committed young people worldwide as there are today. They are waiting to be challenged and lead in the greatest revolution in history: the evangelization of the world."

From the campus can come a movement that renews the Church and provides the thrust for fulfilling the Great Commission. As so often in the past, today's Christian students are key to helping the whole American church break through the logjam of pea-sized Christianity. They could set a new pace for all of us in aggressive concern for the world's unreached.

Again Dr. Orr gives historical perspective to these possibilities:

> The college revivals of the early nineteenth century provided volunteers for the missionary societies that they themselves provoked into action, and continuing revivals supplied a steady stream of missionaries to India, South Africa and the Islands of the Pacific. The awakenings of 1858—59 provided volunteers for the existing missions and the new, interdenominational "faith" missions that carried the Good News and good works into East Asia and other parts of Africa and Latin America—as well as the earlier-opened fields. Subsequent awakenings on campus and in quadrangle supplied a veritable torrent of thousands of missionaries for overseas service.[1]

In his book *Student Power in World Missions,* David Howard reviews a number of student movements for missions, including the one begun at the rainy afternoon "haystack meeting" in Massachusetts in 1806 when Williams College students prayed about the world and their place in reaching it. Those students helped found the first American Protestant foreign missionary society. Similar campus awakenings lead Howard to this observation:

> God's concern is world-wide. How the Church has responded to that mandate is also clear in the light of history. All too frequently the Church has fallen into lethargy in relation to its world-wide obligations. But God does not

leave Himself without a witness. Whether it be a Nicolas Von Zinzendorf, a Samuel J. Mills, a C.T. Studd, a Robert Wilder, a John R. Mott, a Jim Elliot or a hundred others who could be named, God singles out a man to prophecy to His Church. And with remarkable frequency that man has been a student.[2]

The Student Volunteer Movement

The coming awakening could well follow the pattern of the Student Volunteer Movement. It began when one hundred students volunteered for missionary service in 1886 at a Bible conference led by evangelist Dwight Moody, himself a product of the Great Awakening of 1858. The movement grew for the next forty years. It placed twenty thousand new missionaries overseas and tens of thousands more missions-minded laymen in the Church around the world. By 1920 about 70 percent of the total North American missionary force came from the SVM.

Although they called themselves "Volunteers," not World Christians, they gladly took the same kind of stand in the Gap. By signing a pledge that read, "It is my purpose, if God permit, to become a foreign missionary," a student became a Volunteer. Even those who never traveled overseas maintained a strong commitment to their world vision by supporting those who went. Many full-time Christian workers at home, both on campuses and with ministries in the church and society, first found their calling as Volunteers and continued to obey that vision where they were.

The SVM had dramatic repercussions on the Church at large. It mobilized the vision of laypeople through extensive study programs on world missions and directly through the Laymen's Missions Movement. It disseminated literature on missions and influenced Christian periodicals to feature missions in a fresh and vital way. It convinced many Christians that such a stupendous enterprise as world evangelization was feasible through the resources available to them. Local churches found a new faith for missions through their personal interactions with enthused Volunteers. Whole denominations were inspired to increase the efforts of their own missions boards. Giving to missions increased sharply.

Nominal Christians were renewed and unbelievers won to Christ as society became aware that Christianity was a present-day, vital, worldwide, world-changing movement, sufficient for the needs of people everywhere. Christians were moved to aggressive evangelism at home by their growing commitment to it abroad.

Christians from different denominations found a rare sense of unity when world missions became a higher priority than the lesser things that often divide. A large portion of the Church's outstanding leaders in the twentieth century missionary movement came from the SVM. The groundswell of the SVM contributed significantly to the dramatic 1910 Edinburgh meeting of world mission leaders, the first in history. Two major associations of evangelical missionary societies today have roots in the SVM: the Interdenominational Foreign Missions Association and the Evangelical Foreign Missions Association. And the SVM was a model for other student movements for missions such as the Student Foreign Missions Fellowship of Inter-Varsity, the large Urbana Student Missions Conventions, the International Fellowship of Evangelical Students, and the Agape Movement of Campus Crusade for Christ.

Is the Time Ripe?

Can it happen again? Are Christian students today looking for a cause this big, this compelling, this life-changing? Or has the campus mood changed significantly enough from the SVM days to make such a movement unlikely?

Despite small-scale demonstrations against U.S. involvement in El Salvador or Lebanon or marches for nuclear freeze, students today do appear more traditional, more cautious, less rebellious and more pragmatic than their counterparts a decade ago. They look at college as a stepping stone to monetary and personal satisfaction in career. Some surveys indicate they are more religious, but less likely to care what affect this has on those around them.

Yet, Pat Yeghissian, an advisor to student groups at the University of Michigan, thinks this student generation's silence and apathy may stem partly from the fact they haven't been compelled, as a group, by challenges as forceful as the Vietnam war and the draft. "They are very specialized, very goal-oriented, very specific," she observes. And yet, out of this silence has emerged a long, diverse list of activists such as feminists, gays, black and Jewish groups, environmentalists, right-to-life, anti-nuclear groups, and even former anti-war groups protesting U.S. irresponsibility regarding Cambodian and Vietnamese refugees. Does a legacy from the anti-war and civil rights years lie dormant in the subconscious of today's students? Are these various activist groups tremors of potential student movements just ahead?

Noted campus watcher and UCLA psychologist, Alexander Astin, says today's students have given up on campus demonstrations and protests, but they are still firmly anti-establishment and anti-regulation. They want to move and act freely. He claims that "activism" could be easily revived if the right cause came along. Students might get involved in things that change the world, but only in a people-to-people context; and they want something that works.

In its Christmas 1978 essay, *Time* magazine commented on "The 70's: A Time of Pause." There Frank Trippett interprets U.S. society as a whole in a very encouraging light, suggesting that what we call apathy is merely a momentary pause in the spirit of activism that marks the American psyche. His words apply equally to the campus scene:

> The waning decade has remained elusive, unfocused, a patchwork of dramatics awaiting a drama . . . [When] Jimmy Carter tried to whip up a moral crusade for energy conservation, much of the country seemed to have perfected the knack of shrugging off the alarms of crisis. It was easy to read that mood as indifference, but it is more reasonable to suppose the country just needed a rest . . . Some have called it the "apathetic age," but to accept this is to be blind to countless activity by innumerable social and political groups . . . A thousand times as many Americans are to be found at any time—around hospitals, churches, offices, schools, neighborhoods—all as lost as ever in the volunteerism that has been a striking phenomenon of the national character since Tocqueville came meandering about.[3]

The predictions were on target. Despite the look-out-for-number-1 narcissistic mood today, a renewed mood of volunteerism is surfacing in our land. "Probably in no other country in the world," writes sociologist Daniel Bell, "is there such a high degree of voluntary communal activity." More and more Americans are discovering that self-sacrifice can actually fulfill a person rather than hurt him. But it goes further. "Today the demand for participation is real," suggests George Pickering at the University of Detroit. "It is not a demand for therapy. It is a demand for access to the world." Could another student volunteer movement be the natural result of this trend?

In *New Rules,* social analyst Daniel Yankelovich forcefully argues that the search for self-fulfillment in the 1970s will not disappear but will, instead, reach a new and more intense expression in what he calls "an ethic of commitment." He believes Americans are entering into a cultural revolution where we "shift the axis away from self (either self-denial or self-fulfillment) toward connectedness with the world"[4] as each stops "treating himself as his own work of art and instead refocuses his creative energies on the world."[5] The upshot of this revolution, says Yankelovich, will be accelerated volunteerism. Should we look for less than this on our campuses?

Best-seller *Megatrends* by futurologist John Naisbitt, describes one fascinating trend for American society over the next two decades: the revolutionary change of outlook from thinking nationally and acting selfishly to thinking globally while acting on it locally. In other words, having a world vision will lead to corporate and very interpersonal action within local communities. Certainly such widespread volunteerism can, therefore, be anticipated not only among churches, and especially in society at large, but even more in local campus fellowships. In fact, it may be the young, as emerging leadership for the twenty-first century, who set the pace for all of us. This has happened repeatedly in former generations.

I believe today's Christians on campus are (in Trippett's words) "a patchwork of dramatics awaiting a drama?" That drama could be Christ's global cause. The 1981 *Mission Handbook,* a directory of North American protestant ministries overseas, reports that by 1979, 35,861 career personnel were joined by 17,633 short-termers, up over the 5,764 in 1976. "The growth in numbers of short-termers has been nothing short of spectacular," writes Sam Wilson, handbook editor. This trend was matched on campuses where thousands of Christian students attended missions-related events, formed missions study groups and explored missions opportunities. Nothing like this was seen in the fifteen years preceding 1976.

One strong indication that the Spirit of God may be challenging today's student with a new vision for Christ's global cause is the tremendous response to world missions at the Inter-Varsity Urbana Student Missions Conventions, held every three years during the Christmas holidays at the University of Illinois. Students who indicated in writing their willingness to seriously explore how they might volunteer to stand in the Gap rose from 8 percent of twelve thousand delegates in 1970, to 28 percent of fifteen thousand in 1973, to 55 percent of seventeen thousand at Urbana 79. *Time* magazine correctly predicted Urbana's statistics: "The U.S. Protestant missionary movement has depended on collegiate enthusiasm, and that enthusiasm is increasing at a remarkable rate . . . The Evangelical movement clearly treats overseas missions as a growth industry."[6]

My own travels nationwide since Urbana 76, speaking to students in various campus movements, have uncovered similar evidence that they are waiting for a global drama. Repeatedly, when they are challenged to make Christ's cause the unifying focus for their lives and to stand in the Gap with Him, the response is overwhelmingly positive. It seems they have already been searching for deeper meaning for all they do as growing disciples. But world missions never appeared to be the logical place to find it. As they wrestle with the reality of the Gap, however, and the drama of the cause finally breaks through, they don't hesitate to move together in new ways toward the ends of the earth.

If an awakening in the Gap is possible among today's students, then campus ministries could play a major role, under God's Spirit, to precipitate such a move. That Inter-Varsity, for example, is opened to this role seems evident in their statement of purpose:

Inter-Varsity is an evangelizing fellowship which reaches beyond itself to introduce the campus to Jesus Christ, and which helps Christian students bring life and learning into focus and challenges them to involvement in God's Plan for world evangelization.

Across the country Inter-Varsity (as well as the other solid Christian campus movements) is there to challenge and lead students to face the wider implications for all they are and have in Christ. It is there to teach them that world missions doesn't start after college for a select few with a special occupational calling. Rather, students learn that world missions is for *all* thirty-five thousand I-Vers, right now, gathered in over 850 chapters nationwide. College can be a training ground for a lifetime of standing in the Gap.

God's great desire is to awaken our students to the world-sized vision of Acts 1:8 and its fulfillment in this generation through them, and through the churches who obey that vision with them.

None of this emphasis on students is intended to lessen the significance of the local church in missions. As someone has said, "It's the local church that changes the world." Illustrations of local churches mobilized for mission action abound today as never before.

But the fact remains, the commitment and godly zeal of young people *is* the future of the local church. And further, history proves that when God has mobilized the youth as World Christians, local churches themselves find renewed determination to be the discipling, sending base of operations for the new mission surge at their doorstep. We might call a revived student mission movement the "firstfruits" of the mighty mission revival God is preparing for the whole Church.

Clearly, today God is reviving a new movement of student involvement in world missions. This new movement will not exactly duplicate previous ones. The issues are broader and the possibilities far greater than before. But the *fact* and the *spirit* of this movement will be consistent with God's ways through students in the past.

Look with me as the "sunrise of missions" hits our campuses:
• As the past ten years witnesses the largest student missions conventions of their kind in the history of the Church, followed

by scores of local missions training weekends involving as many as five thousand at key locations around the nation.

- In a small action group of six men in the Midwest that justifies its existence by their regular ministry to international students on their campus.

- In the determination of the chapter leadership at a north central university to put world missions at the center of their year-round plans.

- As Inter-Varsity, Campus Crusade, Navigators, and International Students Incorporated jointly sponsor "Operation Prayer" to mobilize all their students in a common effort of prayer, to intercede together each day for the same country of the world, using a "prayer diary." And, as a result, in 1984 they call for regular united prayer on campuses nationwide.

- As a New England black student is commissioned by his white friends to begin an evangelistic Bible study in the black fraternity among students who are cut off from the witness of most white Christians by cultural and prejudicial barriers.

- As a team of Mississippi students prepares to go out together on a short-term missions project—something none of them would have dreamed of doing before.

- In the efforts of a southern university group to sponsor bimonthly friendship dinners for non-Christian Internationals on campus.

- As Christian student groups come together for two-day workshops on cross-cultural careers, to meet with missionaries and plan and pray.

- In the weekly *World Christian Newssheet* published by an aroused World Action chairman in an eastern college.

- As over 250 students, after four weekends of intensive cross-cultural training, go to serve with missionaries in sixty foreign countries through Student Training in Missions (STIM) program, and return to share expanded world visions with their own groups.

- As a small group in the midwest decides after three years that God is calling them to a lifetime missionary outreach as a team, some going and some sending; and as they prepare together to make this dream come to pass.

- As a group of seminary students link up to travel to churches around the U.S. to share their world vision and challenge laypeople to become World Christians with them.

- In a group of undergraduates and recent graduates who share a house together as a World Christian community in order to help one another keep Christ's global cause as their highest priority, especially as it relates to their reaching some of the world's Muslims, Hindus, or Chinese.

- As thirty students in Pennsylvania, from five campus movements, develop a dream called the "Caleb Project." They ask God to use them as a sending-going team to penetrate a major closed door in missions today, to accomplish an "impossible" task in that country for the gospel. Then they fan out to other campuses to challenge Christians to trust God for similar miracles—to tell how God answered *all* their prayers!

- As two Christian leaders who, burdened to train students to serve in the American ghetto, move into ghettos themselves to strengthen their own witness among those who usually have only a fuzzy understanding of the real gospel.

- In the desire of seventy students in one campus-oriented church to link up with missions-minded families and explore whether God would have them involved together in the Gap, particularly as the students assume a cross-cultural ministry.

- In an intensive week-long investigation into World Christian discipleship sponsored by a west coast group two hundred strong.

- As a group at a southern California school organizes its own conferences on world evangelization and accommodates hundreds of other students who share the weekend with them.

- As 185 students and student workers, representing various campus Christian movements in twenty-six nations, meet in Scotland for consultation on mobilizing students and churches in their various countries to reach the two and one-half billion people at the widest end of the Gap.

- In thoughtful discussions with delightful men and women across the country who know the certainty of their missionary call and only ask how to best use their college years to prepare for it.

- As a seasoned collegiate staffer, after one summer of short-term missions work in Africa and another of hard study in world missions strategy, returns to campuses near his church declaring: "With heartfelt commitment I dedicate myself to the Lord to do everything I can to contribute toward the Body of Christ in my city becoming a Body of World Christians, strategically involved in reaching the nations for Christ."

• As hundreds in seminaries and colleges, in the U.S. and around the world, embrace a common declaration of intent and vision, for now and the rest of the century, that reads: "By the grace of God, and for His glory, I commit my entire life to obeying the commission of Matthew 28:18-20, wherever and however God leads me, giving priority to those peoples currently beyond the reach of the Gospel (Rom. 15:20-21). I will also endeavor to share this vision with others."

In 1978 I saw the sunrise of missions in the face of a graduate student in the South who had just "awakened." She woke up to the possibility that the many friendships God had given her with Chinese students might be God's signal that He desired to use her in a lifetime ministry to Chinese people. Her testimony captures the new direction in which God's Spirit can lead *anyone* who rises to stand in the Gap:

> I just had to write to say how much my life has changed since this past weekend of exploring what it means to be a World Christian. It seems that everything about my Christian life has taken on a new perspective, because I was waiting for God to speak to me the way He did this weekend.
>
> What really hit home to me the most was the fact that God wants us to live beyond the getting of things in life. Even as a Christian, I could see myself becoming an average college graduate, concerned only about getting through, getting out, and getting a job. I was feeling boxed in by my career in special education because preparing for it was taking too much of my time and energy.
>
> But as God spoke to me about being part of the great adventure of life by being a World Christian I started to see my career through God's eyes. I can see now that a career in special education is significant only as it relates to God's total plan for my life as a World Christian.
>
> And I see my relationships differently, too, especially my relationships with the Chinese students at the univer-

sity. God has a plan for me and them in our relationships, and it includes more than just good friendships.

And I feel free, freer than I've ever felt. I can dream and not be afraid of my dreams. I can dream that someday maybe I will be in mainland China with my Chinese friend, working for God and showing His love to the Chinese.

I'm praying daily for the Chinese, and I'm going to start praying for the salvation of those Chinese students I know. I'm going to budget my money more carefully and give more to world missions.

On the way home from the conference, we talked in the car about having a small group that will focus on becoming World Christians. If it comes together, I'm going to be a part of it. I'll never be the same, praise God!

That's the stuff Great Awakenings are made of! It can be dramatically multiplied in the near future, by God's grace, if we will seek it, ask for it, and receive it; then let it flow through us, through the campus, through the church, and out to the ends of the earth. That's precisely what the Christian movement needs at this critical hour! As Ralph Winter envisions:

No one is promising the emergence of a new Student Volunteer Movement. God alone is able to bring this to pass. But what an awesome effect on world evangelization the appearance of a new SVM would have. Nothing could be more significant in this hour of history than a vast, new, responsible student initiative. We need a great new initiative in order to reach the three major blocks of humanity as yet unwon to Jesus Christ who number ten times the U.S. population, and are virtually out of contact with any effective mission outreach from any church anywhere.[7]

Notice please: Winter wrote that in 1974. In 1981 missiologist Arthur Glasser, surveying the intervening seven years, boldly suggested the challenge before us is no longer to create a new student missions movement, as it is to prepare for the one that's forming:

Actually, 1980 was the busiest year in the history of the

Church in terms of training and sending youth to share the gospel with those who have yet to hear it. Although all their activities are highly diffused and decentralized, the sheer numbers involved quite overshadow the Student Volunteer Movement, even in its best years . . . So then, let us brace ourselves! Our society (of missiologists) will have far more tasks to perform and far more problems to explore in the days ahead than it has had in the past. And why? Largely because of the resurgence of missionary concern among Christian youth all over the world.[8]

Considering that presently the single largest block of missionaries are young adults worldwide serving with Operation Mobilization and Youth with a Mission, it would seem Winter and Glasser have accurately analyzed the emerging awakening in the Gap.

Notes

1. J. Edwin Orr, *Campus Aflame* (Regal Books, 1972), p. 120.
2. David M. Howard, ed., *Student Power in World Missions,* 2nd ed. (Downers Grove, IL: Inter-Varsity Press, 1979), pp. 109-110.
3. Frank Trippett, "The 70's: A Time of Pause," *Time* Magazine, December 25, 1978, p. 84.
4. Daniel Yankelovich, *New Rules* (New York: Random House, 1981), p. 250.
5. Ibid., p. 257.
6. *Time* Magazine, January 10, 1977, p. 56.
7. Ralph Winter, "Is a Big New Student Mission Movement in the Offing," *Christianity Today,* May 10, 1974.
8. Arthur Glasser, "1980—Where Were the Students?" *Missiology,* January, 1981, p. 13.

9

A DECISION, A PARABLE, A MAP

A Decision

Like Frodo and friends in Tolkien's *Lord of the Rings,* the experience of being a World Christian is a high adventure, calling for eventful movement from here to there, in a word: a *journey.* Not just any journey but one between life and death—a journey in the Gap! Now the time has come to either close this book and set it aside for good, or else rise and go hence.

This is a significant moment for you the reader. Up until now we've surveyed together what it means to be a World Christian and why we each need to become one. We've also discovered that the journey into this marvelous adventure moves forward in three major steps: catch a world vision, keep a world vision, obey a world vision. Now you, the reader, must decide whether or not to take this journey.

The remainder of *In the Gap* borrows these three steps to draw a map of what a World Christian sees, chooses, and does. Like a map it will give you a sense of what to look for as you travel in the Gap and help you get where God wants you to be. Only those interested in such a journey would need what follows.

To help you decide about the journey I want to give you a parable. If a picture is worth a thousand words, a parable is worth at least five hundred. It will summarize why this journey is so important and what it will mean if you decide to take it.

A Parable

Imagine . . .

   for a moment . . .

      that . . .

As long as you can remember you've been seated in a darkened theater. Alone.

Well, not completely alone. You've noted other shadows brooding in the dimness. Some have even mumbled their names to you. But the chill, the mystery, the emptiness of perpetual night—that's been the extent of your life. Until now, that is.

Imagine that one day a spotlight bursts its brilliance across the distant stage. Light. At first it startles you. Then, it intrigues you. You sit and stare.

Gradually your eyes focus. Now you're aware that a Man has stepped into the spotlight. How unusual He is. He's laughing, dancing—and singing! In time you notice that others are up there too, dancing with the Man in the Light, happy and free as He is.

It's hard to resist their enthusiasm. You want to hum along. Your tapping foot betrays you.

Suddenly, without warning, the Man halts, turns, looks straight at you and beckons. What's this? An invitation to leave the dark and dance with Him in the Light? Now?

Your heart jumps. You hesitate, but not for long. Surely that stage promises you a joy, a freedom, and a love like you've never known before. You must have it! You bound forward, leaping to the stage to join the chorus, circling with them hand-in-hand. Your new Friend holds tightly to you. Round and round. How can anything ever be the same?

Time passes.

You sense that His laughing eyes are looking directly at you again. But as yours meet His you're immediately struck by how His have changed. They whisper a strong sorrow that you never noticed before. Why?

He points away from Himself to the theater seats. The Light reflecting from His face outlines the silent shadows below. The audience! You'd forgotten. You understand His sorrow now. You also care. His joy in you makes you care.

As He motions, the chorus—spontaneously it seems— sweeps off the stage and down through the aisles, singing hope and love. Gladly you run with them. Reaching out. Encouraging the shadows to "take my hand! Come join my Friend! Come dance with me onto His stage, into His Light!"

Some don't. Some do. Gradually a new throng encircles your Friend. Freed dancers, laughing with Him in the Light.

Time passes.

You sense something new is about to happen again because your Friend has left the stage. There He stands by the back double doors. Evidently He plans to leave your theater. But He's waiting—for you.

His gentle quietness reassures you. And yet, inside, you feel as you did that moment He called you up from your lonely seat into the Light. You're afraid, unsure, insecure. Still, you're too intrigued, too full of dreams of possibilities, to turn away. Besides, you love your Friend.

Step by step you join many of the others moving off the platform and toward the exit sign glowing in the back. Wondering, you crowd against your Friend and watch. He turns. His strong arms push evenly against the steel doors until they swing wide open.

Oh-h-h-h-h-h! What unspeakable brilliance splashes its warmth over you. For a moment you're stunned. Another stage spot? No, it's the sun! You had no idea. How blue the sky! How green the leaves!

Breathlessly you scan the expanse around you. Now it makes sense. There's an adventure before you unlike any you knew back on your little stage. You've followed your Friend right out of one very small theater and right into His "universal studios!"

Look where you're standing. You're surrounded by thousands of other theaters, encasing countless shadows like you once were. Each theater waits for someone like you to flood their auditorium with the Light; to strike up joy and laughter on their stage; to sing and dance before them in a way that they can understand and join in if they will; to introduce them to your

Friend, the Great Producer, who has a place for them as He did for you, in His Grand Eternal Finale.

Once you leaped alone into a single floodlight. Once you danced up very narrow aisles. Now you chase the sun with a great Chorus-Set-Free. Now you dance and sing throughout all the streets—all the doors.

You've emerged into the full light of Christ's global cause. You've come face to face with the Gap—the gap between the spotlight on your stage and the thousands of theaters that have no light. You've danced with your Friend into God's heart and God's plan for all the nations. Your life in Christ has become "World Christian!"

You've burst upon the adventure for which you were made. Now you can become all you were meant to be!

Welcome! Shall we run together?

Good. I'm glad you've decided to come along.

A Map

In a moment, you'll notice how the pace of *In the Gap* changes. It becomes a map for your journey, as it gives you:

- An overview of what a disciple with a world dimension sees, chooses, and does
- A framework for thinking broadly and correctly about Christ's global cause, with "hooks" on which to hang further discoveries as you explore world missions on your own
- Guidelines to measure your own progress as a World Christian, particularly as it relates to the three main steps.
- A curriculum for individual and small group reflection and action, to help you learn to study about world missions and to get meaningfully involved.

Don't feel overwhelmed by the large sweep of this journey. Instead, let it be a time of exploration. Come back later to the parts that seemed hard to grasp or that interested you the most and make them a starting place for your life as a World Christian. You might use a color pen to mark those thoughts you do find new, challenging, or even confusing as you travel along.

If you're traveling alone, take time to think through the "Reflection" questions. If you're traveling with a small group you may want to set up a series of discussions using the "Small Group Study Guide" found in Appendix I.

Remember, plenty of back-up literature is available through publications, resources, and organizations listed under Appendix III. One key resource is the six-hundred-page compilation of sixty-six authors called *Perspectives on the World Christian Movement* (available through the William Carey Library).

Our journey begins with the first step: "Catch a World Vision!" (chaps. 10–13). Here you'll learn about four words that summarize the four-fold vision every World Christian should have.

"Keep a World Vision!" (chap. 14) is the next step. Here you'll learn about the kind of personal response you should make once you've caught a world vision. This step forms the hinge that opens the door between catching the vision and obeying it. From here on your journey will head into wide-open spaces, with no limits but the ends of the earth!

The third step is "Obey a World Vision!" (chaps. 15–17). It outlines a three-fold plan for continuing your journey the rest of your life. It introduces a few of the options available to those who let Christ fulfill His global cause through them.

All of this will finally converge in a way that can help you (individually or corporately) to end each day confidently saying, "I know that this day my (our) life has counted strategically for Christ's global cause, especially for those currently beyond the reach of the gospel."

Ready to go? Enjoy your journey into World Christian discipleship!

> We face a *humanity* that is too precious to neglect.
> We know a *remedy* for the ills of the world too wonderful to withhold.
> We have a *Christ* who is too glorious to hide.
> We have an *adventure* that is too thrilling to miss.
>
> —words of Theodore Williams,
> a South Indian World Christian
> who has led many Indian mission teams
> into the Gap.

PART II
A JOURNEY INTO WORLD CHRISTIAN DISCIPLESHIP

"And the Lord said to me: 'Rise and stand . . . I am sending you to the nations to open their eyes, that they may turn from darkness to light and from the power of Satan to God, that they might be forgiven and stand with those who have bridged the Gap through me.' Wherefore, I have not been disobedient to that heavenly vision" (Acts 26:16,18-19, Author's paraphrase).

Step One—Catch a World Vision!

The Vision Every World Christian Should See
"I was not disobedient to that heavenly vision . . . "

10. See God's Worldwide *Purpose* in Christ

11. See a World Full of *Possibilities* Through Christ

12. See a World Full of *People* Without Christ

13. See My Own World-Sized *Part* with Christ

10

CATCH THE VISION! SEE GOD'S WORLDWIDE *PURPOSE* IN CHRIST!

KEY QUESTION: Do I see the big picture of Christ's global cause from God's point of view? (The following studies will help you answer the question.)

FACT: There IS a Worldwide Purpose

God's worldwide purpose is working its way out through history and among the nations. From Adam to Abraham to Israel to the exiles who returned to rebuild the Temple, that purpose was active but often channeled through one family, one clan, or one tribe. But from Christ to the Twelve to the early Church to Paul's missionary band and through the two-thousand year impact of the Christian movement, it has flowed widely in a global direction that might be outlined as follows:

- *Penetrate* all human cultures with the reconciling gospel and power of Jesus Christ so as to
- *Persuade* all kinds of peoples to become obedient disciples of Christ and responsible members of His Church where they live, so as to
- *Project* into every society the redemptive alternatives of God's Kingdom against the destructive forces of evil, so as to
- *Press* the course of history toward the climactic return of the

Lord Jesus to reign visibly over His victorious Kingdom, so as to

- *Permeate* the whole earth with the knowledge of the glory of God as the waters cover the seas.

It is a purpose marked by love. In one sense world missions is the extension of the love shared eternally among the three Persons of the Godhead. That same love reaches out toward His lost children at the widest end of the Gap. As we face a world of over three billion who have never clearly heard the good news of God's purpose, we must never forget that ultimately the fulfill-ment of all that is in God's heart does not depend on the limita-tions of their faith or ours, but on the boundlessness of His eter-nal love and justice.

> *Turn to me and be saved, all the ends of the earth! For I am God, and there is no other. By myself I have sworn, from my mouth has gone forth in righteousness a word that shall not return: "To me every knee shall bow, every tongue shall swear." Only in the Lord, it shall be said of me, are righ-teousness and strength; to him shall come and be ashamed, all who were incensed against him. In the Lord all the off-spring of Israel shall triumph and glory* (Isa. 45:22-25).

REFLECTION: How would *you* describe God's worldwide pur-pose in one sentence? In practical ways, how should this vision affect your life's purpose the next year? Your life's purpose for the next twenty-five years?
You Might Explore: A Biblical Theology of Missions by George W. Peters. Also *Eternity in Their Hearts* by Don Richardson.

CHRIST: The CENTER of the Purpose

Christ's coming isn't one in a series of equally significant events in God's worldwide purpose. Rather it is the fulfillment event. He came in the fullness of times, giving ultimate meaning and direction to everything else God is doing among the nations. As Abraham's nobler heir, Christ receives God's purpose to bless all earth's families and is Himself its guarantee. Through Him who takes away the sin of the whole world, God's purpose extends once and for all beyond one nation to the ends of the earth; beyond any one cultural form of the Kingdom (Israel) to break through to all kinds of people everywhere. His blood can and will ransom sinners from every tongue, tribe, and nation.

And, since Jesus rose and lives, He continues to lead God's worldwide purpose to its ultimate triumph: when all things are finally summed up in Him, all His enemies destroyed, and all glory given to His Father. The kingdoms of the world will become the Kingdom of our God and of His Messiah. Then, He will shine like the sun for that cosmopolitan city the Bible calls His Bride and Wife. From beginning to end—from before the foundation of the world until the New Heaven and Earth—Christ remains the center of God's worldwide purpose.

Therefore, He is also central to our own involvement in God's worldwide purpose. Since *He* gave the Great Commission, its priority has not been diminished by two thousand years of the Church's historical ebb and flow. The fundamental basis of the Christian world missionary movement is Christ's universal authority. As John Stott observes, His authority on earth allows us to dare to go to all the nations. His authority in heaven gives us our only hope of success. And, His presence with us ("Look! I am with you always to the climax of this age!") leaves us no other choice.

> *In everything He might be pre-eminent. For in him all the fulness of God was pleased to dwell, and through him to reconcile to himself all things, whether on earth or in heaven, making peace by the blood of his cross* (Col. 1:18-20).

REFLECTION: How would *you* describe in one sentence Christ's place in God's worldwide purpose? In practical ways, how should this vision affect your daily relationship to Christ? *You Might Explore: The Unshakable Kingdom and the Unchanging Person* by E. Stanley Jones.

THE NATIONS: The TARGET of the Purpose

Christ's Body has become the most international society in the history of mankind. This should not surprise us. Almost every book of the Bible records something of God's intentions for and actions toward the nations. Whether we look at the table of nations in Genesis 10 or the citizenship of the New Jerusalem in Revelation 21, we find that God's purpose has maintained one great target throughout: the world of the nations.

Even early on, when God summoned Abraham to come out from his kindred and be a part of His purpose, it wasn't for Abraham's sake alone. All the nations were summoned with him. "I will bless you so that you can bless the families of the earth." All along God has intended to include people from every family and race in the inheritance of His dear Son.

In some cases the phrase itself—"the nations"—refers to those outside the people of God: that is, mankind in general, separated by sin from their Creator-Redeemer and His Covenant. But in a majority of cases, and often in the New Testament's use of *ta ethne* (Greek for "the nations" or "the peoples") the meaning becomes more specific. It refers to the thousands of cultural groupings around the world that make up the grand, creative, diverse community of humankind.

Today we know of at least 19,000 such culture groups, speaking at least 5,700 distinct languages and dialects. For example, the U.S. Center for World Mission estimates that the world's 750 million Muslims speak 580 languages and are divided into many distinct sub-cultures. There may be actually as many as 4,000 significantly different Muslim culture-groups or "nations." Or, among the Chinese there can be found at least 50 distinct spoken languages with an estimated 2,000 sufficiently different varieties of Chinese people that each one must be dealt with separately. Thus, each is a "nation" within its own right. One more example: God's target isn't just the political state of India. The fact is that of its 3,000 castes and tribes only 21 have really responded to the gospel; in 50 others are found small, struggling congregations. But God's purpose is focused as well on the other 2,929 "nations" within India's borders where there is no witness for Jesus Christ.

God desires to declare His glory in the face of Jesus Christ within every one of these societies. He desires to reach them in ways expressive of who they are and in keeping with their own unique ways of experiencing His salvation.

When the Spirit came at Pentecost He hurled the Church toward God's global target, across the national, cultural, and racial boundaries, all the way to the ends of the earth. Today, as a result, Christianity is the only world religion without a cultural home base or headquarters, a constant reminder that God is on target. The world missionary movement is both international and inter-cultural, from, to, and within all six continents. No doubt about it: a day will come when people from every tongue and tribe will be gathered before the throne in praise, to reflect like a grand mosaic the Father's glory through Christ Jesus, their Saviour. And every piece of that human mosaic once it has been penetrated and purified by the fire of the gospel, will make essential contributions in creating that spectacular display.

> *When you read this you can perceive my insight into the mystery of Christ, . . . that is, how the Gentiles are fellow heirs, members of the same body, and partakers of the promise in Christ Jesus through the gospel . . . . [to me] this grace was given, to preach to the Gentiles the unsearchable riches of Christ, and to make all men see what is the plan of the mystery hidden for ages in God who created all things; that through the church the manifold wisdom of God might now be made known to the principalities and powers in the heavenly places. This was according to the eternal purpose which he has realized in Christ Jesus our Lord* (Eph. 3:4-11).

REFLECTION: How would *you* describe in one sentence who the nations are in God's worldwide purpose? In practical ways, how should this vision affect the target of your daily Christian living?
You Might Explore: All Nations in God's Purposes by H. Cornell Goener.

THE GOSPEL: The POWER of the Purpose

In this moment of history, God's Kingdom demonstrates its presence and power through the impact of His Good News in Jesus Christ, proclaimed by word and deed. God's great redemptive purpose expands throughout the earth—His Kingdom breaks through into individual lives and into whole societies—as the gospel is properly understood, believed, and obeyed. Do you want to see evidence that God's Kingdom is near? Look at the spread of the gospel for almost two thousand years across numerous human barriers around the globe to create a truly worldwide community of faith. This is more than human ingenuity or historical accident. The best explanation for all of this is the power of the message in the hands of faithful witness.

Of course, the gospel never works in a spiritual vacuum. Wherever missionary feet have trod God has prepared the way. Creation has set the stage for the message by testifying God's presence and glory and goodness (see Rom. 1). Conscience has set the mood for this message by testifying to man's sin and guilt, and his coming judgment (see Rom. 2). Both creation and conscience press mankind toward all that the gospel offers.

Furthermore, the gospel's power is inseparable from the convicting and convincing power of the Holy Spirit (see John 16). The Spirit works with the messengers, driving their witness deep into the hearers' hearts. After all of our cross-cultural skills have been plied, the Spirit translates it at the heart level, so that anyone, anywhere can believe and be saved.

But there is more. The gospel's power lies not only in its call to trust Christ for salvation, but also in its summons to believers to fulfill their destiny in Christ—it is good news about their direct involvement in His global cause. It is good news not only about what Jesus is for us and in us, but what He will be *through* us. The gospel invites us to both faith in Christ and a new life of concern for other unreached peoples for whom Christ died. Submission to His Commission is a response totally consistent with submission to His Lordship. He saves us not only for Himself but for His saving mission. Properly understood, the gospel should ignite a radical obedience that thrusts us out together to follow our Saviour to the ends of the earth. The gospel is God's power to save *and* send (see Luke 24: 45-48).

I am under obligation both to Greeks and to barbarians, both to the wise and the foolish; so I am eager to preach the gospel to you also who are in Rome. For I am not ashamed of the gospel: it is the power of God for salvation to every one who has faith, to the Jew first and also to the Greek. For in it the righteousness of God is revealed through faith for faith;

as it is written, "He who through faith is righteous shall live"
(Rom. 1:14-17).

REFLECTION: How would *you* describe in one sentence
where the gospel fits into God's worldwide purpose? In practical
ways, how should this vision release the power of the gospel in
your life even more?
You Might Explore: Christian Mission in the Modern World by
John R.W. Stott.

THE CHURCH: The AGENT of the Purpose

World missions cannot happen without a vital, growing,
global community of disciples who burn with the fire of a world
vision. Christians aren't meant to be a collection of spectators
whom God asks to watch as He puts on a global extravaganza.
We're not to sit by passively waiting for the Kingdom to suddenly materialize before our eyes. The Church is the agent of
God's worldwide purpose. We're to be more like a caravan of
ambassadors, going forth to bless the families of the earth, than
a royal entourage basking in the sunlight of God's love for us.

It is just as proper, maybe even more so, to say Christ's
global cause has a Church as to say Christ's Church has a global
cause. Because the Church exists more for the benefit of the
unreached world outside her own community than for those who
are already safely inside. Citizens of Christ's unshakeable Kingdom are empowered by Him with exclusive authority to be co-
workers with Him in fulfilling His global cause.

We could characterize this community as both a family and an
army. Married to Christ the Church has an implanted desire
from God's Spirit to lovingly reproduce new children for Him
within every cultural womb on earth. She wants to be the
"household of God." And yet, wherever this household is found
it is always a colony of settlers from another land, planted among
earth's families as God's agent of Kingdom-life in their midst.

But as an army—a "bulwark"—she is equipped with grace
and truth to march through the Gap, overthrowing the rule of sin
in human hearts, as she carries out her role as the great change-
agent for the Kingdom in this world. "When we say with Paul, 'O
Death, where is thy sting? O Grave, where is thy victory?' we

are shouting out our battle cry as God's liberation front in the world, moving through the world freeing the captives" (John Perkins).

Know how one ought to behave in the household of God, which is the church of the living God, the pillar and bulwark of the truth. Great indeed, we confess is the mystery of our religion [our right to be God's agent for the purpose: Christ] was manifested in the flesh, vindicated in the Spirit, seen by angels, preached among the nations, believed on in the world, taken up in glory (1 Tim. 3:15-16).

REFLECTION: How would *you* describe in one sentence the Church's place in God's worldwide purpose? In practical ways, how should this vision affect your relationship with other Christians locally? And, around the world?
You Might Explore: Community of the King by Howard Snyder.

MISSIONS: The PROCESS of the Purpose

The world missionary movement is the longest sustained human enterprise in history, and today it is touching the world with unparalleled impact. What exactly is missions? Certainly it is more than the Protestant missionary machinery developed over the last two hundred years. Missions could be defined as "the intentional, sacrificial penetration of major human barriers by a global church through specially sent cross-cultural messengers of the gospel, in order to plant communities of responsible disciples of Jesus Christ among groups of people where none have existed before." Missions focuses on the billions of unreached peoples without *culturally-near* neighbors to whom they can turn for spiritual reality. The process of missions in our generation must move toward planting churches among the 16,700 culture-groups and in the hundreds of thousands of geographical locations where no church presently exists.

Of course, the process of missions requires more than just preaching the gospel at people. The missionary enterprise confronts all levels of human need. But top priority must be given to the undiminished tragedy of billions of people unreconciled to the Father and also unaware of how this could happen. Today five out of six non-Christians in our world have no hope unless missionaries come to them and plant the church among them. Every day eighty thousand of these die without having any contact with a church of their kind that could make the gospel intelligible in their language and within their culture. That's why missionary strategy must concentrate on cross-cultural evangelism and church-planting. All other Christian ministries and good deeds should be balanced with this great effort, so that maximum finding of lost sinners takes place.

And who are "missionaries"? They are the specialists who fulfill the task of missions by actually working with people at wider parts of the Gap. Not every Christian is a missionary in this sense, but only those who move out across the major human barriers (usually cultural) that keep a people-group from receiving the gospel. "Missionary" is less an adjective (like "missionary doctor") and more a noun to indicate one who penetrates major frontiers in order to plant the church where none previously existed.

But these specialists can never stand alone. Every missions *extension* (through societies and teams) must have a mission *movement* behind it, through local churches and Christians who pray and sacrifice. Although this process can happen by the spontaneous response of God's people to opportunities God lays directly before us, it often rises from the planned efforts of experienced, mobile missionary groups sent out by the Body of Christ in response to His clear command, and to the pressing challenge of specific people isolated from the gospel.

Now those who were scattered because of the persecution that arose over Stephen traveled as far as Phoenicia and Cyprus and Antioch, speaking the word to none except Jews. But there were some of them, men of Cyprus and Cyrene, who on coming to Antioch spoke to the Greeks also, preaching the Lord Jesus. And the hand of the Lord was with them, and a great number that believed turned to the Lord . . . . Now in the church at Antioch there were prophets and teachers . . . the Holy Spirit said, "Set apart for me Barnabas and Saul for the work to which I have called them." Then after fasting and praying they laid their hands on them and sent them off

(Acts 11:19-21; 13:1-3).

REFLECTION: How would *you* define the word *missions* in one sentence? In practical ways, how should this vision affect your own involvement in today's world missions scene?
You Might Explore: I Believe in the Great Commission, by Max Waren.

MULTIPLIED CONGREGATIONS:
The STRATEGY of the Purpose

God's worldwide purpose has a more specific strategy than just the vague objective of "reaching the unreached." His strategy is to multiply congregations—living models of the Kingdom of God—among all the cultural, linguistic, and ethnic groupings of the world, which in turn will carry out the reaching of their own people around them. In fact, in most places of the world, each congregation must not only be culturally like those they desire to reach around them, but must also be geographically accessible, within walking distance. Ultimately the world won't be evangelized by multiplying the number of times evangelistic invitations are given or evangelistic activities and programs conducted, nor even by multiplying individual disciples. Ultimately the purpose will be fulfilled by multiplying obedient, evangelizing congregations of disciples, who can invite those around them to Christ and to a taste of His Kingdom in their midst.

India illustrates the need for this strategy today. Out of three thousand castes and tribes less than a hundred have culturally or socially similar Christian communities. But in India, caste position usually determines those you eat with or marry or mourn for or follow after. Most won't be open to any important message (the gospel or otherwise) if it comes from those of another caste. Certainly they won't be easily evangelized into fellowship with a church of another caste. These are the stark realities of how human societies work.

But God is willing to *begin* with people at this point. (After all, the gospel isn't "accept Christ, plus change your mind about your social structures, and you will be saved.") In India (and everywhere) our initial strategy must be to plant churches within every village and within every major stratum in each village. Then, from these local bases of operation God can bring about a moral revolution that eventually overcomes prejudice.

This is because every congregation is potentially like a time-bomb within its own culture-group, ready to explode with Kingdom-style changes as new Christians grow and reach out to their friends and neighbors. No matter how poor or talentless a local church may appear it is still God's base of operation within its locality. In that congregation dwells the living Christ in all His fullness. And out of His fullness they can penetrate their society with His grace and truth until the ultimate transformations emerge.

But our strategy goes one step further. God desires to multiply not only sensitive, evangelizing, transforming congregations, but also *missions-minded* ones. They are to become the new sending bases who commission their own people to cross other cultural frontiers into wider parts of the Gap. For God's strategy to have its fullest expression, missions must spring from the concern of thousands of new churches worldwide, committed to fulfilling Christ's global cause.

I heard behind me a loud voice like a trumpet saying: "Write what you see in a book and send it to the seven churches [in Asia Minor], to Ephesus and to Smyrna and to Pergamum and to Thyatira and to Sardis and to Philadelphia and to Laodicea." Then I turned to see the voice that was speaking to me, and on turning I saw seven golden lampstands, and in the midst of the lampstands one like a son of man . . . in his right hand he held seven stars, from his mouth issued a sharp two-edged sword, and his face was like the sun shining in full strength . . . the seven stars are the [messengers] of the seven churches and the seven lampstands are the seven churches (Rev. 1:10-13,16,20).

REFLECTION: In one sentence, how would *you* describe the strategy of multiplied congregations in God's worldwide purpose? In practical ways, how should this vision affect what you pray for and look for in your own missions involvement?
You Might Explore: Understanding Church Growth by Donald McGavran.

NUMERICAL GROWTH: A MEASURE of the Purpose

To Abraham God gave the promise of descendants as numerous as the stars in heaven. As the Bible ends we are confronted with an international throng that can't be numbered, gathered from every people-group of earth to praise the Lamb forever. And between the beginning and the end of time the Scriptures continue to emphasize that numerical growth—the winning of many peoples to Christ—is one key evidence that God's worldwide purpose is being fulfilled.

Growth in quality must be matched by growth in quantity. Without numerical growth there will be no one around through whom the purpose can be fulfilled any qualitative way. Christ works among the nations through *countable* people saved to obey and serve Him. Note that numbers are not an end in themselves. This emphasis on quantity is not an encouragement to pad our personal tally of converts. The numbers are *people,* redeemed people who in turn can love other people. If the billions unreached today are to hear of Christ there must be a visible swelling of responsible disciples and congregations of disciples throughout the world.

True, growth in quantity doesn't lessen the need for growth in quality. But quality itself can often be determined by quantitative measurements. For example, in medicine, physical fitness is measured by body temperature or height and weight or heart beats. In farming, good soil can be determined by the abundance of crops it produces. A successful hunger relief program isn't concerned only with the vitamin content of the food distributed, but also with how many are getting fed.

So it is with God's worldwide purpose. Numerical growth determines much about its fitness, about the heart-soil where the gospel is shared, and about our success in relieving spiritual hunger. Even in Jesus' parable about the sower and God's purpose, this comes through. There He not only frees us from discouragement over those who don't respond (the story shows us many won't) but He also teaches that faithfulness in sowing insures a measurable and often abundant response. He teaches us to expect it!

This measurement gives us a whole new set of questions to ask about God's purpose. In Nigeria, for example, our question isn't just, "Is the Nigerian church healthy?" We must also ask: How many churches are in Nigeria? How many people in each church? Are Nigerians coming to Christ within a few tribal groups or within each of the almost five hundred tribes? And, what percentage of the total population are the Christians within each tribal group? A large enough percentage (at least 20 percent according to research) to make their witness truly visible and available to all?

God is not willing to settle for a "token presence" in each of over two hundred countries, satisfied with a few sheaves of gathered wheat, while ignoring the massive harvest still standing in the fields. If large numerical growth is possible anywhere it should be aimed for everywhere. Wherever culture-groups are accessible and ready to hear and respond, missionaries must be immediately deployed. One measure of the Kingdom's advance and of the faithfulness of us its citizens is the growth of the Church by *conversions,* conserved within vital, evangelizing congregations.

After this I looked, and behold, a great multitude which no man could number, from every nation, from all tribes and peoples and tongues, standing before the throne and before the Lamb, clothed in white robes, with palm branches in their hands, and crying out with a loud voice, "Salvation belongs to our God who sits upon the throne, and to the Lamb!" (Rev. 7:9-10).

REFLECTION: How would *you* describe in one sentence the importance of God's purpose of emphasizing the numbers of people converted? In practical ways, how should this vision affect what you pray for and look for in your own missions involvement?
You Might Explore: Measuring the Church Growth Movement by J. Robertson McQuilkin.

COMPASSION: The PULSE of the Purpose

Compassion is caring deeply enough about people's needs to meet those needs. The world missionary movement has been driven with compassion—caring not only about other peoples' discontents (which can often be unholy), but about their deepest longings and their real need for Christ and His Kingdom (whether they realize it or not). Compassion sees people as whole people, and cares about everything that truly concerns them. Compassion acts! God's compassion moves the Church to proclaim the gospel, and plant congregations where none presently exist, so that a base of operations can be established within specific groups from which all other needs can be met.

Considering the plight of billions of unreached people today, most of whom are in the Third World, compassion morally obligates us to speak out and live out what we know to be the source of life and liberation for all peoples. It must lead us into acts of love and justice that help ease the unreached out from under the heavy loads (whether physical, psychological, social, economic, political, or demonic) that strangle the joyful reality of the message we bring them. Acts of compassion become major steps in establishing trust, so that the people we desire to reach will trust us enough to investigate who we are, what we stand for, and what we offer in Christ. Not that our compassion is conditional, depending on how favorably they respond. But as we touch people who are hurting, we will naturally build bridges over which the supreme act of compassion can reach them: reconciliation to the Father by faith in Christ Jesus.

Contrary to popular myths, missionaries have usually been highly motivated by this pulse. Their acts were not confined only to a "passion for souls." Their contributions to raise up the needy have exceeded any of their mistakes. Most often they have taken up the plight of those they reached as if it were their own. They have been found helping the oppressed and, by so doing, creating situations around the world for major advances in God's saving purpose.

Compassion is the pulse of missions. It urges us to cross all human barriers, at whatever sacrifice, to identify with the unreached, to share the Good News, and meet their needs through local congregations that glorify Christ as Lord on a permanent, ongoing basis.

> *The Spirit of the Lord God is upon me, because the Lord has anointed me to bring good tidings to the afflicted; he has sent*

me to bind up the brokenhearted, to proclaim liberty to the captives, and the opening of the prison to those who are bound . . . They shall build up the ancient ruins, they shall raise up the former devastations; they shall repair the ruined cities, the devastations of many generations . . . . For as the earth brings forth its shoots, and as a garden causes what is sown in it to spring up, so the Lord God will cause righteousness and praise to spring forth before all the nations (Isa. 61:1, 4, 11).

REFLECTION: In one sentence, can *you* define compassion as you see it in God's worldwide purpose? In practical ways, how should this vision affect the pulse of your daily Christian living? *You Might Explore: Bring Forth Justice* by Waldron Scott.

CULTURAL TRANSFORMATION:
The IMPACT of the Purpose

God's worldwide purpose will create an impact on both individuals and the community to which they belong. This will spring from the influence of faithful disciples whose living faith leads them to active, daily obedience where they are. Through the gospel, God incorporates new believers into local congregations where they learn obedience, experience personal liberation, and engage in creative evangelism that liberates others. World missions and a biblical transformation of earth's approximately twenty-five thousand cultural groups go together.

Cultures never remain the same, anyway. Cultural change is a natural, historical phenomenon. The question is: What and who will guide the direction of that change? Today many forces are at work for cultural changes: communism, technology, multinational corporations, Islam. But only the missionary movement holds potential for the significant, lasting changes that all people need.

A missionary isn't sent to direct a social revolution. But his work will lay a foundation for one. By bringing God's message of reconciliation and new life, he creates the opportunity for the Kingdom to break through in concrete ways, and for lives and societies to be transformed. As he teaches the implications of the Kingdom and invites new Christians to live out their allegiance to Christ, he creates the conditions for righteousness, justice, and love to eventually permeate the whole society. Since sin touches all aspects of who people are and of their cultures, God's redeeming work in Christ should not be expected to do less on either level. A new allegiance to Christ as Lord through the gospel becomes the standard by which the believers can interpret everything else in the culture and then accept or reject or transform what they find.

One example of this impact can be seen in Nigeria. Through 140 years of missionary outreach the Bible's transforming work has brought forth over thirty million Christians with a government that is asking right now for thousands of expatriates to come to their country as "Bible knowledge teachers" in government schools. There religious instruction is a compulsory subject at the secondary and teacher training levels. Not only has past cultural transformation opened the door, but this biblical molding of Nigeria's future leaders holds promise of even greater changes ahead. A ripe opportunity awaits evangelicals, even from the U.S., to share in the impact of God's purpose there, if we act now.

Every culture is full of treasures unique to it that have often been abused and misused for evil purposes, but that wait to shine with the glory of God. When Christ reaches and redeems people in a culture there is much He finds there—unique to that people as a culture-group—which He desires to transform and place in His Father's house forever. What a day it will be when He will "shake the heavens and the earth" and "shake all nations, so that the treasures of all the nations [including treasures out of the 16,700 culture groups not yet reached] shall come in [to fill this house]" (Hag. 2:6-7).

We pray for you, because we have heard of your faith in Christ Jesus and of the love which you have for all the saints, because of the hope laid up for you in heaven. Of this you have heard before in the word of the truth, the gospel which has come to you, as indeed in the whole world it is bearing fruit and growing—so among yourselves, from the day you heard and understood the grace of God in truth, as you learned it from Epaphras our beloved fellow servant (Col. 1:3-7).

REFLECTION: In one sentence, how would *you* describe the impact of God's purpose on cultures and societies? In practical ways, how should the vision affect what you pray for and look for in your own missions involvement?

You Might Explore: The Mustard Seed Conspiracy by Tom Sine.

SATAN: The ENEMY of the Purpose

God has not abandoned our age to the powers of Evil. But the Old Age is still hostile to any world missions activity, and its citizens won't allow us unalloyed success. We are engaged in constant spiritual warfare with Satan's hosts, who oppose and attempt to frustrate the world missionary advance. Those willing to follow Christ into the widest part of the Gap can't avoid the conflict of this age-long battle.

There is no neutral territory. Among the nations God is at work calling citizens in the kingdom of darkness to a verdict about His dear Son through the gospel. Every advance in missions, especially where the Church has never been planted before, will be marked by a "fight" with the Enemy of our souls. When a person or a people-group gives allegiance to Christ as Lord, enemy held territory (see Luke 4:5-6) is "captured." Accordingly, Satan's only alternative is to set himself against those most deeply involved in the sending/going process of missions. The temptations, oppressions, and persecutions that these Christians experience often come from aggressively operating in the whirlpool created by the convergence of two diametrically opposed spiritual powers, one of which knows his time is very short and one of which is assured of ultimate victory.

Sometimes Scripture describes this battlefield as the "world." Used in this way the term does not refer primarily to the physical world of nations but to a *system* of organized evil, put together by Satan himself to oppose the Kingdom's advance. This system might be organized as a form of nationalism or traditionalism or technocracy or military expansionism. Or, it may be expressed in the more obvious forms of idolatry, superstition, and demonism. But in every instance, our real enemy remains the Evil One. Ultimately our battle isn't against communism or racism or "human nature." It is against the principalities and powers behind all these things, who exploit them in order to oppose God's worldwide purpose.

Of course we need to be careful not to label every resistance to the gospel as satanic. Whenever the missionary movement is rejected or opposed we must first ask: Are they really opposed to Christ Himself? Or, do they misunderstand my communication about Him? Is my nationality or my culture suspect? Are they reacting to my insensitivity or lack of evident love? In other words, is the problem with the hearer or the speaker? Should I assume part of the responsibility for the problem rather than blame the devil?

But when we're faced with Satan's most threatening activities we can always have hope. Actually, growth of the opposition forces remains a clear indication of the even stronger growth of God's kingdom, not of its retreat. Scripture teaches that evil is to grow concurrently with good as God's purpose reaches its climax. Many believe the book of Revelation details this final global clash between both Kingdoms over a global missionary movement. As Satan is threatened with an accelerated worldwide harvesting he will have no choice but to deploy his forces in one last onslaught against the Church that has brought it to pass.

> *And the great dragon was thrown down, that ancient serpent, who is called the Devil and Satan, the deceiver of the whole world—he was thrown down to the earth, and his angels were thrown down with him . . . And they [the saints] conquered him by the blood of the Lamb and by the word of their testimony, for they loved not their lives even unto death* (Rev. 12:9,11).

REFLECTION: In one sentence, how would *you* describe Satan's response to God's worldwide purpose? In practical ways, how should this vision affect what you pray for and look for in your own missions involvement?

You Might Explore: Once More Around Jericho: The Story of the Founding of the U.S. Center for World Mission by Roberta Winter.

11

CATCH THE VISION! SEE A WORLD FULL OF POSSIBILITIES THROUGH CHRIST!

KEY QUESTION: Do I see the Church's potential for closing the Gap in our generation? (The following studies will help you answer the question.)

FACT: There IS a World Full of Possibilities

Almost three billion people have no opportunity to make an intelligent decision for Jesus Christ. But the World Christian doesn't despair. We know that God is not finished yet. The Kingdom still comes! Throughout the earth God's purpose presses on, full and overflowing with possibilities for closing the Gap through His humble, obedient servants among the nations. The possibilities are as infinite as the God who gives them.

We must be careful here. A vision of possibilities—including past victories, present world trends, available personnel, money, and resources—should never overshadow the clear biblical principle that when we are weak then we are really strong because God's power is allowed full expression through our weakness (see 2 Cor. 12:9-10). The task before us should drive the Church daily to the Master in a sense of utter dependence. Our greatest "possibility" lies in our helplessness before Him. But we also need eyes to see all the ways He has prepared to release His power once we rise from our knees to go forth.

Why is it so hard for us to see the possibilities? Often we look at the persecuted church (as in Uganda in the seventies) or at the more resistent peoples of the world (like north African Muslims) and not at data on the tremendous harvestings (as in Brazil or Nigeria or Korea). Sometimes we're simply over-whelmed by the numbers to be reached, unaware of bold new strategies being developed right now to meet this challenge. On the other hand, a pessimistic outlook provides some Christians a smoke screen for noninvolvement: for their unwillingness to seek what God has promised to do, for their lack of compassion, or for their fear of the sacrifices they might need to make.

Marked by its spiritual vitality, global diversity, and available options, the Church has never been better equipped to close the Gap. The time has come to double our efforts. We stand on the threshold of a new era if we but believe and obey. Together we must mobilize to meet the "sunrise of missions" before us.

REFLECTION: How often do you hear other Christians express an enthusiasm about the world missions movement? How full of possibilities do you think world missions is today? In practical ways, how should this vision affect your outlook on daily Christian living?
You Might Explore: On the Crest of the Wave; Becoming a World Christian by C. Peter Wagner.

CHURCH HISTORY Points to the Possibilities

As we look over the world missions landscape we see the potential for closing the Gap only if we look through two-lensed spectacles. The biblical foundation for God's worldwide purpose prescribes the first lens. Church history prescribes the second. The more we know of the Spirit's accomplishments throughout the centuries (beyond Acts 28), through Christians from all parts of the world and in many walks of life and in all kinds of situa-tions, the more we'll be reinforced to believe in great possibili-ties today. No other movement has so dramatically changed the face of the world and the course of history. You can't retain a clear perspective on world missions if you survey its advance with a monocle!

Unfortunately, many of us have succumbed to the *BO-BO theory* of church history (a term coined by Ralph Winter). This theory postulates that the Spirit has "Blinked-On" (BO) and "Blinked-Off" (BO). During the past two thousand years, so the theory goes, He has often "Blinked-Off"—at least that's what our personal facts on the matter would suggest to us. Mistakenly, we look at the familiar high points of Paul and Luther and Moody and John XXIII and assume that in between God has been "off"; He's not been too involved. (After all, they *were* the Dark Ages, weren't they?) If this were the kind of God we served we could be excused for shifting uncomfortably when someone talked about reaching the whole world in our lifetime. Maybe God is about ready to blink off again. Maybe for good.

However, another theory is needed to explain a movement that is eighty-three million times as large as when it began in A.D. 31. Obviously, God's love has been relentless. And we need to know the facts.

We inherit what has gone on before us—and what a rich treasure it is. What will we do with it? How will we build on it? There have been great periods in the advance of Christ's global cause. We must not be willing to settle for anything less now.

REFLECTION: Can you give some illustrations of God's missionary activities in at least ten of the last twenty centuries that would help you catch a vision of mission possibilities today? For example, what do you already know about:

- Paul's missionary team around A.D. 50?
- the fourth century work of Martin of Tours in France; Ulfilas among the Goths; and Patrick in Ireland in the fifth?
- Columba's missionary training center in Iona in the sixth century?
- the work of Boniface (680-754) in Germany?
- Francis of Assisi (1181-1226) and the Franciscan Friars?
- John of Monte Corvino's mission to China in the early 1300s?
- the missionary work of the Society of Jesus in the sixteenth century that spread to Goa, South India, Malay Peninsula and Japan?
- the Danish-Halle Mission launched in 1705 and the Moravian mission work begun by Zinzendorf in 1732?

- the London Missionary Society (1795), the Society of the Brethren (1808), the American Board of Commissioners for Foreign Missions (1810), or the China Inland Mission (1865)?
- the present day missionary efforts of such groups as Greater Europe Mission, Overseas Missionary Fellowship in East Asia, Latin America Mission, Regions Beyond Missionary Union in Irian Jaya, the Presbyterians in Korea or the Southern Baptists among ethnic enclaves in urban America?

In practical ways, how should this vision affect your sense of the possibilities for your own missions involvement?

You Might Explore: From Jerusalem to Irian Jaya: A Biographical History of Christian Missions by Ruth A. Tucker.

SPIRITUAL RENEWAL Points to the Possibilities

The Holy Spirit is a missionary Spirit. Whenever He stirs up His Church He always has one historical end in view: her mission to the ends of the earth. The world waits to see what God's Spirit will do through a global Church that is renewed, surrendered, and empowered together for that mission. Today this dream may become a reality. Many believe Christians are entering a time of unequalled spiritual ferment through which God will finally complete His worldwide purpose. As revival comes to His people on a global scale, He will sweep us past the renewing changes and into the missionary impact for which He has given that renewal.

Such revival has flamed hot in Korea for decades, with thousands joining in 5:00 A.M. prayer meetings every day. In 1980 a World Evangelization Crusade brought together one million Korean Christians for each of six evenings of challenge to worldwide outreach. On the last night thousands stood to offer themselves to go anywhere God would send them.

Bessie Porter Head, caught up in the Great Awakening in 1905, wrote of its direct impact on world evangelization. The words of her hymn are equally true for any generation.

O Breath of Life, come sweeping through us,
Revive Thy Church with life and power;
O Breath of Life, come cleanse, renew us
And fit Thy Church to meet this hour.

Revive us Lord! Is zeal abating
While harvest fields are vast and white?
Revive us Lord, the world is waiting,
Equip Thy Church to spread the Light.

This ferment may be accompanied by intensified persecution. That should be expected, for Satan cannot remain idle and people cannot remain neutral when the Kingdom expands. Yet the attacks we suffer will only intensify the renewal as the Church is driven to a total dependency on Christ for further evangelizing power. Her weakness is always her greatest opportunity to be renewed for missions because she's compelled to pray:

> *"Lord, look upon their threats, and grant to thy servants to speak thy word with all boldness, while thou stretchest out thy hand"* . . . *And when they had prayed, the place in which they were gathered together was shaken; and they were all filled with the Holy Spirit and spoke the word of God with boldness* (Acts 4:29-31).

REFLECTION: Can you give specific illustrations of this spiritual renewal in various parts of the world and among various kinds of Christians? What are your impressions, for example, of the significance of:

• the awakening in the Greek Orthodox, Coptic and Catholic churches?
• the increase in global-wide cooperation for world missions, such as the two meetings in 1980: The Consultation on World Evangelization (Thailand) and the World Consultation on Frontier Missions (Edinburgh).
• the worldwide, trans-denominational charismatic renewal?
• the maturing of the Third World Church and of its missionary efforts?
• the worldwide spread of student movements like Campus Crusade for Christ and Navigators, and the International Fellowship of Evangelical Students (of which Inter-Varsity is a part)?

- the vitality of the persecuted church in communist countries like Poland, Russia, and China?

In practical ways, how should this vision affect your sense of the possibilities for your own missions involvement?

You Might Explore: The Eager Feet; The Fervent Prayer; The Flaming Tongue (Evangelical Awakenings from 1790-1920) by J. Edwin Orr. Also *Key to the Missionary Problem* by Andrew Murray.

WORLD TRENDS Point to the Possibilities

As surely as God's hand is upon His People in their global mission, even so He is at work within the great forces that are making our world what it is today. Nothing escapes His sovereign purpose to prepare the way for fulfilling the Great Commission among all nations. Just as the New Testament world was prepared for the new beginnings in Christ's global cause—Christ came "when the time had fully come" (Gal. 4:4)—so today God is preparing our world to allow the gospel its greatest opportunity for total saturation.

One trend in our modern world is rapid change, a change which produces more change; a trend that leads to more trends. In the upheaval of change, people around the earth are searching for meaning for their past, an identity for their present, and a foundation on which to build their future. At such an hour the gospel comes offering them that meaning, a new self-image, and the only sure foundation. People in the midst of change will listen as never before.

Another example is the growing cry for caring servants to identify with the poor and oppressed, to bring them to their feet with lasting, personal, and social deliverance. In Christ's love we can step forth to offer ourselves and our message of hope for a hurting world as no other human community can. What a day to win a hearing if Christians, particularly in the West, assume the radical life-style shifts that make us available to them and involved with their cries.

At first, some trends may seem defeating to our cause. But God can work through a crisis to fulfill His purpose. For example, when mainland China fell to the Communists in 1949, and thousands of missionaries were expelled, it seemed a victory for

Satan. But as Cliff Westergreen, a Hong Kong based missionary and China watcher, observes: "Although political, physical and psychological barriers have been raised by communism, the more difficult barriers of tradition, ancestor worship, confucianism, superstition, illiteracy and language diversity to a large degree have been broken down. In a real sense, Maoism has conditioned China for Christianity!"[1]

We've never had a greater hour through Christ. We have the best news whether for tribal animists, materialistic capitalists, fervent Muslims or revolutionary Marxists. So often their search is for the right things but in the wrong places. The gospel points them to the living Christ—the right place!

REFLECTION: Can you give specific illustrations of present world trends that could open up possibilities for Christ's global cause? What are your impressions, for example, of the significance of:
- the worldwide migrations of people?
- increased urbanization?
- rise of Muslim missions to the West?
- opening of China?
- political upheavals in Africa or southeast Asia?
- the sweeping impact of modern technology?
- the population explosion?
- the energy crisis?
- world hunger awareness?
- advances in world literacy?

In practical ways, how should this vision affect your sense of the possibilities for your own missions involvement?
You Might Explore: What in the World Is God Doing? by Ted Engstrom.

THE EVANGELISTIC ACCELERATION
Points to the Possibilities

Increasingly Christianity is a force the world must reckon with. In 1790 William Carey estimated that only one-third of the countries had any gospel witness. Today all do with one or two exceptions. More people have become Christians and more churches have been planted in this century than in all the rest of

Church history combined. There are almost twice as many Christians (one billion) as adherents of any other religion, except Islam (750 million). The gospel's impact is accelerating at sixty thousand new people a day claiming the name of Christ and sixteen hundred new churches opening their doors for the first time every Sunday. In 1900 most Christians were found in Europe and North America. By the end of this century projections indicate that 60 percent of all Christians will be found in the Third World.

One example of this is sub-sahara Africa. In the past twenty years Christians there have increased by thirty million. It took a thousand years for the gospel to do that in Europe! There were four million African Christians in 1900 (3 percent of the population). The projection for A.D. 2000 is 351 million (46 percent of the population). The church in Africa is growing four times faster than the population at large—by sixteen thousand every day— making it the largest Christian community on any continent. The story of the Maguzawa people, in northern Nigeria, is typical. There the number of converts are responding so fast that church leaders claim they have lost all count!

True, there are areas where the re-evangelization of former church members is needed. In 1979 about 1,815,100 adult professing Christians in Europe abandoned the church to become agnostics, atheists, or adherents of non-Christian religions. North America also registered a net decline of almost one million. But, according to the Nairobi-based Center for the Study of World Evangelization, over the same twelve months Africa revealed a net gain of 6,052,800 new Christians, or 16,600 new believers each day. And, the Christian movement in South Asia evangelized just over 34,813,000 previously unevangelized persons, a rate that is significantly increasing each year. Without indifference to the apostasies, World Christians are spurred on by the greater vision of God's grace found in a worldwide acceleration in evangelism.

None of this is to the Church's credit. It does not call for a mood of Christian triumphalism. This acceleration is often in spite of follies and faithlessness on our part.

Rather, these responses point more to a spiritually ripened condition throughout the world. In many parts of the earth there is an unprecedented receptivity to the Lord Jesus. More individuals and more segments of population may be open to Him than at any other time in history. In it all we can trace the sovereign hand of our God on the hearts of the nations as well as on the revived remnant who boldly serve Christ's cause at any cost to reach them.

Of course, not every response can be measured as a legitimate new birth into the Kingdom; nor does every newly planted church truly seek to follow Christ. But statistics indicate an acceleration in the evangelistic *penetration* of the ends of the earth. More people are able to render an intelligent verdict for Christ than ever before. The number of churches planted worldwide speaks of new beachheads within which God's Spirit can work to renew and mobilize Christ's witnesses among all nations, to close the Gap as never before.

REFLECTION: Can you give other illustrations of evangelism's acceleration worldwide as it breaks through barriers to reconcile receptive peoples, especially those at wider ends of the Gap? What are your impressions, for example, of the evangelistic acceleration in:

- sub-Saraha Africa, especially Nigeria, Uganda, Kenya, Liberia, and Zaire?
- Asia, especially South Korea, Philippines, Indonesia, and India?
- Latin America, especially Brazil, Bolivia, Columbia, and Ecuador?
- the translation, distribution and study of the printed gospel around the world?

In practical ways, how should this vision affect your sense of the possibilities for your own missions involvement?

You Might Explore: The World Christian Movement: 1950-1975 by Ralph Winter.

AVAILABLE PERSONNEL Point to the Possibilities

Ours is not a post-missionary era. As never before the Spirit is multiplying potential laborers for the harvest. If they would all suddenly decide to become cross-cultural missionaries, for example, there might be enough evangelical Christians in South

Korea alone to close the Gap within the next twenty years!

The 1981 missionary force is no small cluster, however. There are over 80,000 Protestant missionaries: 4,209 from the United Kingdom; 5,500 from Europe; over 15,000 from the Third World church; and 42,300 from North America. (Of course, we mustn't discount the role of the 138,000 Catholic missionaries, 5,870 of whom are from the U.S.)

But more are needed, too. Are they available? Some mission strategists have estimated that over a fifteen-year period one missionary couple can effectively learn the language and culture, share the gosepl and plant a vital, witnessing church among a group of 5,000 people. If this is so, we would need 600,000 more missionaries to complete the task of total world evangelization in this century. It is further estimated that *evangelical* Protestants alone field a worldwide body of over 75 million able, Spirit-filled witnesses committed to sharing Jesus Christ with the unreached. Certainly, out of that Body God's Spirit can raise up the needed 600,000 cross-cultural witnesses for the other 74.4 million evangelicals to send out!

This potential can be seen in the North American church where World Vision International estimates that out of the current evangelical ferment over 200,000 new missionaries could be mobilized within the next two decades, with a little more planning and effort. For example, recently the Christian and Missionary Alliance denomination, with 100,000 members, supported 900 missionaries, or 1 for every 110 members. They work in 43 countries. If the whole evangelical movement here were to keep the same ratio for the confessed 40 million "born again" Christians, we could field 365,000 right now! 1981 brought good news of the first significant increase in career missionaries from North America since 1967—up almost 5,000 over 1975.

It can also be seen in the increase of Third World missionaries. More than four hundred Third World mission societies in forty-four countries have sent out over 15,000. By 1979 India had 2,208, followed by Nigeria's 850, 600 from Brazil, 450 from Third World ethnic groups in the U.S., 300 from the Philippines, 140 from Japan and 100 from Korea. Missionaries have gone from Singaporean churches to the Philippines, Thailand, New

Zealand, and Africa. Japanese missionaries (sent out by eleven societies) are witnessing in South America and Indonesia. Koreans are helping reach India. Africans are sending missionaries within their own continent, from one tribal or language group to another. (For example, the Evangelical Missionary Society of West Africa has 130 couples sent out by fourteen hundred churches at work among fifty distinct language groups). The Aymara Indians of Bolivia (who themselves were reached only recently with the gospel) have formed a missionary association to send their own workers to Navajo Indians in the U.S.!

Asia alone is sending out more missionaries today than the whole European missionary force to Asia in 1810. The All-Asia Mission Consultation in 1976 called for 10,000 Asian missionaries trained and sent by A.D. 2000. In Japan, efforts are underway to send out 1,000 Japanese. From Korea, it is projected, we can expect 2,000 missionaries by 1986. In March 1978 the Chinese Conference on World Evangelization in Hong Kong set a goal to have every Chinese church outside the Peoples Republic send 10 of its own to evangelize the 60 million Chinese in noncommunist lands. If in ten years their goal is reached these four thousand churches will have commissioned 40,000 personnel! No wonder the Asia Region of the International Fellowship of Evangelical Students conducts regular missionary conferences throughout the year to challenge Asian students to all-out involvement in Christ's global cause.

As never before, Christians who learn to serve one another internationally can join together under the Lordship of Christ to reach an unreached world. The human resources within His worldwide Church are immeasurable. World missionary strategy, effort, and personnel should spring from an internationally shouldered enterprise, consisting of hundreds of thousands of local churches that develop an army of mobile missionaries, mission societies, and mission teams, sent from all nations to all nations.

REFLECTION: Can you give other illustrations of the available personnel in Christian movements and strategic locations in various parts of the world? What do you know of personnel possibilities in the Third World church? In practical ways, how should

this vision affect your sense of the possibilities for your own missions involvement?
You Might Explore: The Last Age of Missions by Lawrence Keyes.

MODERN RESOURCES Point to the Possibilities

The Church throbs worldwide with a creative potential that's intrinsic to her very life in the Spirit. This fact alone should spur us on to be creative, responsible stewards of all the modern technical advances within our world community. Twentieth-century tools have extended our voices, our time, our minds, and our bodies. Of course, evangelism is basically a meeting of persons. And, world missions is the meeting of persons across major human barriers. But many contemporary resources, tools, and methodologies provide new ways of creating more opportunities under the Lordship of Christ to make this meeting of persons happen more quickly and more effectively.

Take, for example, the tool of radio. Over sixty-five radio stations are owned and operated by Christian missions in the Third World. The first missionary radio station in Africa, ELWA, was founded twenty-five years ago. Beginning with only four-and-a-half broadcast hours a day, it now carries programming in forty-five languages, with forty-three transmission hours a day covering most of west, north and central Africa. HCJB in Quito, Ecuador, is one of the most listened to short wave stations in the world. Rated by International Shortwave Club of London as one of the top ten, its correspondence in 1978 showed a total of 170,000 letters and reports from 131 different countries. Their Japanese department received the most—63,000 pieces of mail.

Trans World Radio, which also began twenty-five years ago as the Voice of Tangier in Morocco, North Africa, now carries programming in more than eighty languages, employs 350 missionaries and 250 nationals, and has six transmission sites around the world with a combined power of five million watts. Eighty percent of the world's population will soon be able to hear evangelistic broadcasts from these six stations.

And, a recent visitor touring much of the People's Republic of China reported that over 80 percent of its population is able to receive AM broadcasts of the gospel from Far Eastern Broadcasting Company. With increased tolerance in China the impact for these programs can be more easily measured. Whereas for the past twenty years FEBC had not received more than twenty or thirty letters a year, in 1979 the mail increased to more than ten thousand a year. Over 95 percent of the letters were from non-Christians.

But, as amazing as this modern resource is, we must not forget the words of a mission leader with station ELWA: "Beaming the gospel inland has made people very receptive, but it's going to take church-planting teams in face-to-face contact before we see the harvest we know God wants."

Another example of modern resources is the growing international discipline called *missiology,* the science of the strategy of the Christian mission. Knowledge from many other disciplines—anthropology, sociology, geography, linguistics, computer technology, statistical analysis, ethno-history, ethno-theology, ethno-psychology, management theory—has provided immeasurable insights to increase our effectiveness at communications, evangelistic strategy and church planting. Joining these modern resources to the recorded lessons gleaned from tens of thousands of years of composite missionary experience gives us renewed hope, under Christ, for fulfilling the Great Commission.

REFLECTION: Can you give illustrations of modern resources that increase the possibilities for Christ's global cause? What are your impressions, for example, of the possibilities already tapped through:

- mass communications, especially radio, television, films and cassettes?
- use of planes and ships?
- the growth of international organizations that specialize in particular kinds of missionary endeavor?
- Theological Education by Extension?
- the sacred tool of money, especially within the Western church?

In practical ways, how should this vision affect your sense of the possibilities for your own missions involvement?
You Might Explore: Rich Christians in an Age of Hunger by Ron Sider.

"CLOSED DOORS" and a Vision of the Possibilities

Right now there are enough open doors to claim the attention of tens of thousands of new missionaries around the world. We must fight with hard facts the inaccurate picture that missionaries are not wanted or needed. Close to 90 percent of the nations are presently open to some form of cross-cultural evangelism—generally more so than in any previous era of the Christian movement.

For example, of the sixteen most populous nations, note how many (in 1981) are open to missionary and/or evangelistic activity (designated with*):

China—985 million	Nigeria—79.7 million*
India—688.6 million*	Mexico—69.3 million*
Soviet Union—268 million	Federal Republic of
USA—229.8 million*	Germany—61.3 million*
Indonesia—148.8 million*	Italy—57.2 million*
Brazil—121.4 million*	United Kingdom—56 million
Japan—117.8 million*	Vietnam—54.9 million
Bangladesh—92.8 million*	France—53.9 million*
Pakistan—88.9 million*	

Furthermore, Inter-Cristo, a North American computer matching service for Christian ministries, lists the following overseas opportunities as a percentage of their total twenty thousand job openings: Far East—17 percent, Ocean Area—4.8 percent, Australia/New Zealand—2 percent, Europe—8 percent, Middle East—5 percent, Latin America—20 percent, Africa—21 percent.

Open countries are our responsibility. These we must never neglect. There are hundreds of millions of unreached people to whom missionaries can be sent. For example, over 200 million unreached peoples are still accessible throughout East Asia to direct missionary outreach. As the Church moves on these waiting fields, fervently praying for God to open new fields and new channels for outreach, He will not fail to respond.

Actually, what we sometimes interpret as "closed" may be better understood as people and places we have *neglected*. More concentrated effort on a closed area, in faith, could turn the tide. For example, in the U.S. we have one pastor for every six hundred people. In Central America there is one missionary or strong national leader for every fifteen thousand. But in the supposedly closed or resistant Muslim world there is less than one missionary for every 500 thousand! What if the worldwide Church attempted to pour the same intensity of prayer, manpower, research, money and literature into reaching Turkey or the seventy-one million Muslims in India as we put into reaching North or Central America? What doors might God open?

Of course, there are legitimate illustrations of "closed doors." Often that means no more, however, than that a particular nation doesn't grant visas to Western missionaries. Even so, there are many "back doors" which any Christian can use to reach people in such a country, if we have eyes to see those doors. For example, there are alternative approaches through literature and Scripture distribution, radio, and through self-supporting missionary personnel like businessmen, teachers, tourists, and exchange students.

Closed doors have always been temporary. The dramatic and unexpected change in attitude of the People's Republic of China verifies that any door can suddenly open to us. Today, China is permitting Bibles to be brought in by visitors. And, she is asking for 500 thousand teachers of English, German, French and Spanish, the greatest emphasis being on English. The need for native speakers of English to do the teaching is apparent. How many English-speaking Christians are ready to walk through the open door?

With this perspective on the possibilities, South America Mission, faced with the temporary closing of four of their fields in 1978, refused to sink in despair. Instead, they determined to ask God for sixty *new* missionary couples to enter these four countries if and when the doors opened, or to pioneer newly opening fields.

REFLECTION: Can you give illustrations of some *open* doors in the world where we are taking full advantage of the missionary opportunities? Can you name some where we aren't? Can you give some illustrations of seemingly *closed* doors in the world which could be or are being opened to the gospel through other channels besides direct missionary outreach?

In practical ways, how does this vision affect your sense of

the possibilities for your own missions involvement?
You Might Explore: Today's Tent-Makers by J. Christy Wilson.

The AMERICAN CHURCH'S INVOLVEMENT
in the Possibilities

The American missions movement has worked its way out of many jobs but certainly never out of the main job: persuading unreached peoples to become disciples of Christ and responsible members of His church where they live. Even so, present missionary outreach from the U.S. is alive and well and planting churches all around the globe.

Christians in America are often intimidated, however, by the rumor that U.S. involvement in the world arena and in missionary outreach specifically is no longer wanted or needed. But as long as great opportunities for planting churches among earth's massive unreached peoples await new missionary advances, any permanent withdrawal of any Christians from Christ's global cause could be disastrous. Christians in the U.S. should see themselves as Christians first, then Americans. Our citizenship is in the Kingdom of God, and our calling is to the ends of the earth.

Furthermore, the positive contributions of the American missionary movement suggest God's willingness to continue to use us if we are faithful and obedient to Christ alone. As African mission leader, Patrick Johnstone, notes: "Much of the burden for world evangelization rests on believers in the U.S.A.—about 63% of all missionaries, and 90% of all funds." Campus Crusade for Christ estimates that 80 percent of the world's trained Christians and 70 percent of the evangelical church's material resources can be found in our country. The *fact* of this reservoir holds great promise for worldwide evangelization wherever its supply is released through humble, responsible World Christians.

Surveying this reservoir, Gordon-Conwell church historian Richard Lovelace has caught a vision of the possibilities spiritual renewal could give the American church. It demands serious reflection:

> While the broad mass of the laity in American churches continue to be exhaustingly absorbed in the rat race of business life, at least a portion of their finances is being

diverted to furnish a substantial economic foundation for a remarkable missionary program abroad. One cannot help but wonder what the result would be if this mass of lay people could be spiritually released from their servitude in the American success system and reoriented to channel their major energies toward building the kingdom of God. Foreign missions would be enriched with a new flow of personnel and resources . . .

If America were . . . to be "born again" for a generation as England was "born again" during the Second Awakening: if America were to become a showcase of justice as well as liberty; if Christian opinion were visibly to compel the sharing of America's resources to feed and train the whole human community; if the network of multi-national corporations were tanned and brought into service as a rail service for the gospel, as the Clapham leaders tamed the British empire and used it for world mission; then "the Great Century" of missionary expansion, the nineteenth, would in all likelihood yield to an even greater successor.[2]

Of course, America's involvement in the possibilities must not permit a disguised resurgence of the nineteenth century's "manifest destiny." The new reality is *partnership:* missionaries from all nations to all nations; and missionaries within a nation in partnership with the Christians already involved there in the total evangelization for their countrymen.

We need to maintain a right balance in this picture. As one Third-World missionary views this partnership: "World outreach must marry the missions experience of the West and the suffering experience of the East to effectively evangelize the world."

During the seventies many called for a "moratorium" on Western missionaries, but this is often misunderstood. The Third World Church isn't asking so much for fewer Western missionaries as for more missionaries who are spiritually mature, cross-culturally sensitive, and able to demonstrate the reality of the gospel by their lives as well as their message. The church anywhere—America included—has a responsibility to provide *that* kind of missionary every time.

Wherever they come from, there is one kind of missionary everyone wants: one who will identify with the people, love them, and serve them for Christ's sake. This possibility belongs as much to missionaries from the American church as it does to all of God's people.

In light of the possibilities, the openings and the urgency of the unfinished task, the primary question for the American church should not be "Are we wanted?" but rather, "How shall we most effectively get on with the cause?" The fact of almost three billion unreached people assures us that God is ready to work through any of His children if they trust Him and are obedient. Christians in the U.S. must pray, plan, and move forward on the fundamental assumptions that we *will* be needed and *are* essential to Christ's global cause, right out to the ends of the earth.

REFLECTION: Can you give illustrations of positive contributions, past or present, from American missionaries? Can you give illustrations of the potential for future contributions from the American church? How do these illustrations help you catch a vision of mission possibilities today? In practical ways, how should this vision affect your sense of the possibilities for your own missions involvement?

You Might Explore: Winds of Change in the Christian Mission by Herbert Kane.

Notes
1. Cliff Westergreen in *World Vision* magazine, February, 1979.
2. Richard Lovelace, Dynamics of Spiritual Life: An Evangelical Theology of Renewal (Inter-Varsity Press, 1979), pp. 151,425.

12

CATCH THE VISION! SEE A WORLD FULL OF *PEOPLE* WITHOUT CHRIST!

KEY QUESTION: Do I see the great scope of earth's unreached peoples, especially the billions at the widest end of the Gap who have yet to clearly hear the gospel? (The following studies will help you answer the question.)

FACT: There IS a World Full of People

God's vision of the world goes beyond land mass or political boundaries. He sees a mosaic of billions of people and thousands of culture-groups.

This mosaic is not a global curio shop full of curiosity pieces nor a global warehouse full of machinery with various degrees of usefulness. Unfortunately, we humans tend to regard those who are "different" from us as either one or the other. Even our concern for people can be more with hunger than the hungry, or more with poverty than the poor, or more with evangelism than the unevangelized.

Nor may Christians rightly think of people as merely "souls," attaching little value to their bodies or their communities. Rather, we should see a world full of "body-soul-in-community" people (to use John Stott's phrase) with their own unique personal and cultural strengths, qualities, and contributions, as well as their weaknesses, felt needs, and sin.

World Christians, if they have God's vision, will never become "cultural imperialists" believing that the ways of any one group of people make them more valuable than another. We maintain that the Kingdom of God is actually incomplete without those "other" people who seem so different from us, simply because they *are* people—people with tremendous capacity to glorify God with us through Jesus Christ, in their own culturally unique ways. That's the great reason we want them to learn about Him and put their faith in Him.

Whenever you feel your heart beating, remember: by your seventy-third birthday it will beat, not 100 million times or even a billion, but almost three billion beats. That's also how many people remain to be evangelized in today's world. Three billion. That isn't just a statistic. It is a world full of real people who suffer and die without hope and without God. This isn't because they are more evil than you or I, or because they are less deserving of the gospel. They are people just like us, just as needy and just as special in God's sight except, in most cases, they lack the opportunity to hear and believe.

And that's why our hearts go on beating, isn't it? Our physical life in Christ is interwoven with all of earth's unreached—one heartbeat for each person. That's a people-to-people world vision!

REFLECTION: How do you look at a world full of "other" people? Do you see them as objects, curiosities, threats, causes, strangers, or neighbors? Do you have indifference, prejudice, or compassion for them? What could you give to them? What could they give to you?

You Might Explore: A Geography of Mankind by Jan O.M. Broek and John W. Webb.

Problems with VISIBILITY

Many are the reasons we struggle to see and care for people as God does. Among them are: the overwhelming numbers of people for us to see (over four billion); the multitude of complex human boundaries that separate us from one another (geographical, social, cultural, racial, linguistic, religious); and our own lack of information about what comprises the many thousands of culture-groups around the world.

American Christians, particularly, have problems with their vision because we master only one language, English. Many of the world's peoples learn three or four and think nothing of it. To know someone's language is to know their heart. As linguist Dr. Tom Brewster observes: "Americans suffer from mono-lingual myopia—a disease of the tongue that affects the vision."

All of this can foster in us that universal human malady called *ethnocentrism*. When our whole life revolves around people who are ethnically just like us we are *ethno*centric. When we avoid strangers simply because we can't predict how their group works or figure out why they operate the way we do, we're ethnocentric. When we quickly critique and judge others by our own cultural assumptions and values, instead of attempting to understand their behavior within their own world-view, we display ethnocentrism.

Ethnocentrism may evaluate other people by the phrase "So-and-so-people *are better than* so-and-so-people." For example, "Whites are better than mulattoes" or "Europeans are better than Asians" or "Israelis are better than Palestinians" or "the rich are better than the poor" or "the educated are better than illiterates." How foolish to consider someone "better" simply because we feel more at home in their group and less at home in another.

And certainly a phrase like "Christians are better than Muslims" indicates a problem with seeing people as God does. This is the most destructive kind of ethnocentrism for Christ's global cause. Usually what is meant is "Middle-class-Protestant-Americans are better than ignorant camel herders surviving in hot, dusty Egyptian villages." Unfortunately, this sense of superiority gets communicated when we try to share the gospel with a Muslim visitor in the U.S.; and so, he doesn't see Christ at all. The only thing better about Christians is *"Christ* in us, the hope of glory." But then, He is the better way for all kinds of people, not just middle-class Americans.

We have a problem with visibility because we haven't taken time to learn about people. Having a vision for people means learning to actually appreciate their rich potential to glorify Christ. We must cease being armchair tourists of the world. We must become its *students,* even before we become its servants. We must let people very different from us teach us how they see themselves, until we can see through their eyes. Then, and only then, can we build a strategy that loves them for Christ's sake in ways they understand, trust, and to which they can intelligently respond.

There are almost three billion people alive at this moment whose opportunities to hear of Christ, or never to hear, rest largely with those whom God has called to a sacrificial vision. Learning to have a vision for people—to look out of the boxes of our own familiar, comfortable, and predictable relationships—takes hard work. We must love the world with our *minds* as well as our hearts. And the "view" is tremendous! As we learn to value people as people, compassion both for their present and eternal destiny won't be far behind.

REFLECTION: What are some of the problems *you* have with visibility—with seeing "other" people the way God sees them? Where are there different kinds of people that you could start to learn from right now? How would you do this? What would be your first step? What could be the long-range impact of this on your own missions involvement?
You Might Explore: The Church and Cultures by Louis S. Luzbetak.

A Vision of How We're SIMILAR

Human beings, wherever they are found, are similar in so many ways. Cultures differ widely but not wildly. We are similar, for example, in the symbol systems we use for verbal and non-verbal communication (words, graphics, sound, motion, spacing, timing); in our basic survival needs as human beings (food, drink, elimination, sex, security, belonging, love); in the need to adjust to major global forces around us (technological advances, energy shortages, rapid urbanization, nuclear threat); down to the built-in capacity in each of us to hear the gospel, believe in Christ, and follow Him.

People also hold in common a basic center to their lives— what the Bible calls "heart." It is an allegiance to something or someone or some purpose that makes sense out of life. The diversity of the human race can be uncovered by asking: "What do you think the meaning of your existence is?" There are many answers, often contradictory. But our unity is uncovered by the *need* of all humans to answer that question. Every person needs a way to explain, validate, and harmonize everything that goes on in their own thoughts, in their daily living and in their society.

Furthermore, all people have a heart *problem.* We experience evil from within our hearts and in our relationships with others. Separated from our Creator by sin, all of us suffer physical, psychological, social, and eternal consequences of evil. Therefore, we all share the same spiritual need: that our hearts be changed. The world's universal sickness (called by E. Stanley Jones "homesickness") demands the very same remedy: reconciliation to the Father through Christ.

Though we're all sinful, we're also all redeemable. God hasn't declared anyone anywhere impossible of new birth. We all have a common capacity and ability to change and be changed, especially when the gospel comes with clarity.

One example of similarity important for missions is that of religious outlook. So many societies in the world hold to the following basic religious categories: a supreme being or high god, belief in an afterlife which gives meaning to the present life, a sense of moral evil, a struggle between powers of good and evil with man caught in the middle, expectations that a special deliverer will come, prayer as an act of communication and submission, and a reverence for creation with some sense of a divine purpose in it all. The gospel can speak directly to seven key issues on which all people reflect.

Because we are so similar, cross-cultural communications is not nearly so difficult. From the outset we should always have a sense of oneness with any of the earth's unreached peoples. Humanity's solidarity assures us that God's grace can surmount any human barrier as it breaks through any of His people to fulfill His worldwide purpose among any other group of people.

REFLECTION: Think of one people-group you know about from another part of the world or some other U.S. ethnic group, and try to list all the ways you are similar to one another. Specifically, how could knowing these facts make it easier for you to reach them for Christ? In practical ways, how should this vision of similarity affect your own missions involvement?

You Might Explore: Customs and Cultures by Eugene Nida.

A Vision of How We're DIFFERENT

Mankind is also a large assortment of thousands of varied perspectives, experiences, and needs clothed in a great variety of cultural, racial, economic, political, and religious forms. With over nineteen thousand different cultural units worldwide (some with as few as three thousand members, others as large as 30 million), the picture is very complex. Like thousands of finger-prints these cultures differ widely.

For example, there is no typical African or African culture. Africa's 330 million people break down into one thousand languages and dialects, with six major ethnic categories that break down into hundreds of ethnic groups or tribes. When a single country like Nigeria incorporates scores of languages and five hundred tribal groups we begin to see that human differences are far greater than a United Nation's list of 210 political boundaries.

There are many worlds in our one world. By Bishop Stephen Neill's count, we could number seven major blocks: the communist-dominated world; Eastern and Southern Asia; the Muslim world; Africa; Latin America, including the Caribbean; the Pacific world; and the free world of northwestern Europe and North America. But the earth is also diversified into various age categories, climates, class structures, and standards of living. The illiterate, the dispossessed, and the hungry each live in worlds most North Americans know nothing about. Of course, the tongue divides the human race into almost six thousand worlds or languages. And, language differences are directly tied into world-view differences, too. Finally, we might distinguish the various religious worlds: Judaism, Shintoism, Hinduism, Animism, Buddhism, and Islam, to name a few. But even within Islam, for example, there are at least five major (and sometimes internally explosive) sects.

Don't let the differences discourage you. These differences have provided God with thousands of audio-visual aids by which His eternal truths can be illustrated, visualized, comprehended, encoded, and transferred to people everywhere. Furthermore, the diversity of needs and even tragedies within the human community provides multiplied opportunities for the Body of Christ to show the world His love and convince people of their need for a Saviour. As the Church moves out to plant churches and meet those needs among such a diverse humanity, God's grace receives a multitude of new ways to demonstrate how rich and how unlimited it can be. It is within this diversity that the missionary movement and the Kingdom of God can thrive, if we're willing to expand on all fronts!

REFLECTION: Think of one people-group you know about from another part of the world or some other U.S. ethnic group, and try to list all the ways you are different from one another. Specifically, how do these differences present significant challenges to a missionary outreach among them? In practical ways, how should a vision of differences affect your own missions involvement?
You Might Explore: A World of Difference: Following Christ Beyond Your Cultural Walls, by Thom Hopler.

A Vision of the MANY WORLDS IN AMERICA

Since Acts 1:8 focuses our evangelistic activity as much on the cultural as the geographical widths of the Gap, the "ends of the earth" may often be found living right next door to American Christians. The unique U.S. ethno-cultural panorama includes 120 ethnic groupings speaking over a hundred different languages. In the last census 75 million Americans classified themselves as members of ethnic subcultures, including everything from the earliest inhabitants—native American Indians—up to recently resettled Russian immigrants and over 455,700 Indo-Chinese refugees. In this panorama we have Black Americans (26.5 million), those of Spanish descent (14.7 million, our fastest growing minority group with over 600,000 immigrants yearly), the Indian, Eskimo, Aleut (1.4 million located in a hundred distinct tribal groups, speaking over fifty distinct languages), Japanese - Americans (almost one million), Chinese-Americans (almost one half million). Many of these groups can only be reached when lay Christians, not merely professional missionaries, make conscious, planned, missionary-style efforts to cross major barriers to give them the gospel and plant the church among them—here—in America.

In fact, Conservative Baptist urban missionary Mark Marchak suggests that New York City may be America's biggest missionary challenge. More people (eight million) live there than in forty-four of the fifty states, but the evangelical population is no more than 3 percent—probably much less. And there is no strong evangelical base in the suburbs trying to plant churches within the Big Apple. Overall, the world of America's urban underclass, incorporating forty million people in all, is as needy, as difficult to reach, and as dangerous to penetrate as few mission fields anywhere today.

What's more, the culture-groups in our country are growing. At this writing, there are almost eight million legal resident aliens in the U.S., with one and a half million aliens entering each year to become permanent residents. Detroit, for example, receives between ten and twelve thousand new immigrants a year. One third of our immigrant growth is Spanish-speaking; another third is Asian. How many middle-class evangelicals are willing to help take the gospel across the social, linguistic, and economic barriers that these many immigrant worlds present to us?

In Los Angeles County, for example, there are more "minority peoples" than Anglos. Its three million Chicanos are outnumbered only in Mexico City. In response, the Southern Baptist church-planting work in Los Angeles has produced worshiping communities in twenty-three different languages thus far.

World religions, some Eastern in origin and some strongly Muslim, are successfully recruiting followers in America. They present a unique cross-cultural opportunity right next door. Muslims in America, for example, estimated to be three million with eighty-four mosques, grew as much as 400 percent in the past ten years. This makes Islam the third major religion in the U.S., and it is finding converts, often among Black Americans. Further, a University of Chicago study claims that twenty million Americans belong to "fringe religious cults" like Hare Krishna and Rev. Moon's Korean-based mixture of Bible and eastern mysticism.

Similarly, the American campus scene presents many different worlds to be reached. The total of all minority groups rose 25 percent between 1974 and 1979, and now represents 16 percent of college enrollment. Each ethno-cultural unit requires special styles of evangelistic communication. Furthermore, almost three hundred thousand internationals from 150 countries study on our campuses each year, 30 percent from OPEC nations. By 1986, ten thousand of these may be from the People's Republic of China. Our feebleness of outreach to these Internationals may be (in Mark Hanna's words) "the great blind spot in missions today."

Admittedly, the predicament of most people in America is vastly different from the billions outside the U.S. who have yet to hear the gospel once, and who have absolutely no culturally-near neighbors or missionaries to tell them. Only 2 percent of the people in our country live at the widest end of the Gap. In most ways those in the Third World are much farther removed from the Christian witness than anyone here.

Still, we must not lose a vision for those next door that demand special communication efforts from American Christians if they are ever to be reached. Often they have little opportunity to hear of Christ from the tens of millions of evangelicals here, because so few of us are trying to share God's love with them in a way that makes sense within their own unique, separate worlds.

REFLECTION: Who do you know personally, or who do you know about near you, who is culturally, ethnically, or socially different from you and whose differences are presently cutting them off from any vital, ongoing evangelistic effort? What would it take to effectively reach them for Christ? Specifically what could you imagine yourself doing about this during the next year? In practical ways, how should a vision of the many worlds around you affect your own missions involvement?
You Might Explore: Missions in the Mosaic: Ministries to American Ethnic Minorities by W. Wendell Belew.

The Crucial Vision of the HIDDEN PEOPLE
The number of those to be won to Christ in Africa and Asia

has more than doubled since 1900 and will more than triple by the year 2000. Almost three billion people today have little or no knowledge about Christ and His salvation. Never has the challenge been greater for total, global missionary advance.

Most of those to be reached are often called the "Hidden People." Why? Because major cultural, racial, linguistic, social and other barriers "hide" them from the eyes and the concerned efforts of most evangelizing Christians. For example, if every Christian were to win his culturally-near neighbor to Christ two and a half billion non-Christians would still remain totally untouched because they live outside the cultural home base of every active Christian in the world.

To put it another way, 300 million of the world's unreached people can be reached by their Christian neighbors. But 400 million can only be reached by missionaries prepared to bridge medium cultural differences. And more than two billion can only be reached by significant new efforts to cross complex cultural and other human barriers. The latter two groups—the two and a half billion Hidden People—consist of the Hindus of Southeast Asia (656 million); the Muslims, primarily in the Middle East, North Africa and Indonesia (750 million); the Buddhist and Confuscian peoples of south and southeast Asia, including almost one billion mainland Chinese; and the almost 265 million unreached animists or tribal peoples, scattered around the globe, but very evident in Africa.

Where can some of these Hidden People be found? Consider just a few illustrations:

- In *Japan* the total Christian population is only 1 percent, most of whom live in the cities. But in the thousands of towns and fishing villages there is absolutely no Christian witness, and no missionaries to reach them. They are hidden.
- For every Christian in *Thailand* there are 999 Buddhists, most of whom have never once heard of Christ.
- The Baptist church in *Burma* is very strong, but its membership is entirely tribespeople. The 28 million Burmese who are Buddhists are practically untouched after 160 years of Christian witness.
- For every 10,000 villages in *India,* 9,950 have no Christian community whatsoever. Furthermore, less than 10 of its

3,000 castes and tribes have any Christians in them. And who is reaching the 490 thousand Indians living and working in the Arab Gulf states?

- The world's 265 million *animists* are, according to Wycliffe Bible Translators, "sealed off, confined to their own language which is unique in itself. Most of them have never learned their nation's official language; no one has ever cared enough to learn theirs. Without a common language there can be no communication. Without communication there can be no understanding of God's love. Two thousand languages still have no written form." Hidden.

- Despite the strong Christian movement in *Latin America* there are still many Hidden People. In the jungle lowlands there are at least six hundred small primitive tribes with over five million. Many have yet to hear of Christ. Even in Brazil, with one thousand missionaries, many slum dwellers in major urban centers are completely missed by church or missions activity. Right now two million young children are abandoned in the streets of Brazil's cities, most uncared for by any Christian anywhere. Hidden.

- In the *Soviet Union* only 60 percent of the people are Russians. The rest are minority groups, scattered throughout, Bibles in the Russian language are scarce, but they are nonexistent for the fifty million who belong to these ethnic and linguistic minorities.

- Many *Europeans* are "hidden" from evangelistic efforts. Of course, we are more aware of Europe, can more easily identify with its cultures than with many in Asia or Africa, and can build our missionary strategy on a foundation of almost two thousand years of Christian influence there. Still, when faced with one-half million towns and villages with no adequate gospel witness, we know much remains to be done. Although 85 percent claim to be Christian (overwhelming when compared with the Third World) only 4 percent attend church regularly. (Fortunately, the missionary force to Europe has doubled in the past ten years and resident evangelicals are increasing rapidly.)

- In Tanzania and its surrounding territory the *Chinese* are entering at a rate of one thousand each week. Mozambique,

Africa, contains sixty thousand Chinese families of 250 thousand individuals. In France reside over 150 thousand Chinese refugees, speaking at least five dialects and served by only two small Chinese churches in Paris. The Chinese population for Central and South America and the Caribbean totals 260 thousand. But missionaries to Africa or Europe or South America aren't equipped to reach Chinese peoples. Normally they are unaware of these communities. In fact, although more people speak Chinese Mandarin than any other language in the world, including English, very few non-Chinese Christians speak it or are even attempting to. No matter how much we talk about Christ, most Chinese will remain "hidden" to our words until this is changed.

- The 750 million *Muslims* are concentrated in forty-four countries and dispersed throughout forty others. Only 120 million are actually Arabs. And yet in the face of such diversity and with such numbers there are only about five hundred Protestant missionaries reaching them. Hidden.
- There are Hidden People among *students* as well. Representatives of the International Fellowship of Evangelical Students from sixty nations met in mid-1979 to set plans in motion for "pioneering" work among hard-to-reach student populations in our world. There are thousands of campuses without a single Christian student. For hundreds of students their only present contact with the gospel is the IFES staff in their country.

We must not be misled by the statement that in many countries "the church has been planted." The Christian movement in a nation may hold only a token presence. Within many countries we find numerous cultural and linguistic groups in which no church or missionary is at work. Often, as it turns out, the "planted" churches within a country exist within small ethnic pockets, like ethnic islands surrounded by oceans of men and women who, as yet, have heard nothing of God's love—the Hidden People.

"Oceans of Hidden People" expresses both an *extent* of need and a *depth* of need. These billions (the extent) have little sense of their lostness unless the Light of the World Himself penetrates their darkness with the gospel in the hands of cross-cultural messengers. Truly they dwell at the widest end of the gap of opportunity. And unless major new efforts are made immediately to cross the barriers that separate them from the gospel, they will die in their darkness (the depth of their need). Thousands of new missionaries must be called, specifically trained and sent out specifically to plant churches for the first time among each of the 16,700 culture-groupings where no churches exist at this moment. That must be the great goal of Christ's global cause within the next twenty years.

The needs around us should always be seen in this perspective. Although we need evangelistic work on all six continents, not all six are equal either in resources, population or in present opportunities to know of Christ. Asia and Africa—where most of the Hidden People can be found—demand far more of our actual concern and effort. By contrast, in America there is a gospel surplus. According to Don Hillis of the Evangelical Alliance Mission, the 106 million functionally unchurched Americans are not unevangelized. Actually, America is the most evangelized nation—the most gospel saturated—of any nation in history!

A vision of the Hidden People will convince us, for example, of the evangelical church's gross imbalance in sending out only one U.S. missionary for every twenty pastors we place at home. The U.S. isn't twenty times larger than the world—world population is twenty times that of the U.S.

To say that everyone is important and equal before God leads to an inescapable conclusion: those with no Christian witness culturally near to them, as well as geographically near, must have more of our concentrated efforts to reach them. A true world vision cries out against such immense neglect and blindness in the Church and its missionary movement. We must take drastic new measures. Carelessness about those who are presently "hidden" from the gospel is indicative of carelessness toward the One who died for them. For *many* Christians around the world these Hidden People must become our highest priority, or they will never be reached.

REFLECTION: What facts do you know about specific groups of Hidden People around the world? Do you know of any in your own state or city? Specifically, what could you or your church do about helping to plant churches among one group of them right now? What would be your ten-year plan? What would be your first step? In practical ways, how should the crucial vision of the Hidden People affect your own missions involvement?

You Might Explore: Unreached Peoples '79; Unreached Peoples '80; Unreached Peoples '81; Unreached Peoples '82; Unreached Peoples '83 by the MARC Division of World Vision International.

A Vision of STRATEGIES THAT FIT THE MOSAIC

A strategy for total world evangelization must be sensitive to earth's beautiful mosaic of peoples. We must keep the uniqueness of individuals and their culture-groups in clear focus and learn to love them in their own contexts. People are lost within their own socio-cultural context. They are lost as members of a particular group, and this is also how they must be reached. Therefore, every piece of the world's mosaic—every single one of the twenty-five thousand culture groups—requires uniquely designed strategies, methods and emphases that clearly *fit* that piece if the message is to make sense to them. This is especially true of the groups among the two and a half billion Hidden People where no church has yet been planted and where our witness, in many ways, must begin from scratch.

The gospel message itself remains forever the same, but the keys to unlock each piece of the human mosaic to the gospel differ vastly. The challenge before the world missionary movement today is to design keys that fit thousands of different locks, especially within the diversities of Asia.

We need sharp insight into the special ways each culture approaches its own language, art, technology, education, economic system, marriage, and family patterns, definitions of status and roles, laws and taboos, and its religious beliefs and rituals. True, what we learn in designing a key for one culture-group may help us with another. But in many ways, cultures do not duplicate one another. Each lock demands special attention. This is the challenge of cross-cultural communication.

For example, the mosaic in Taiwan consists of nine million Taiwanese-speaking peoples, both urban and rural, three million Mandarian-speaking, one million Hakka-speaking, plus two hundred thousand aboriginal highlanders in six main tribes, speaking six major dialects. Each piece of the Taiwanese mosaic demands a specially-built key or evangelistic strategy to unlock it for Christ.

A denomination in the U.S. has developed a number of keys to unlock unreached peoples in one urban situation. They have formed separate worship centers (number in parentheses) for the pieces of the mosaic they found there: Taiwanese (1), Ceylon (1), Romanian (1), Estonian (1), Arabic (1), Ukranian (2), Portuguese (2), Italian (2), Indonesian (2), Hungarian (2), Filipino (2), Mandarin-speaking (6), Russian-speaking (7), Native American Indian (8), Cantonese-speaking (9), Japanese (10), Spanish (97), for the deaf (25); plus many for Black Americans and for other whites.

Our missionary objective is to make our message understandable and accessible among all peoples. The witness-bearer, therefore, is as important a link in the strategy as the one who receives that witness. If we want our gospel to get through we must look seriously at ourselves as the communicators. Like two mountains, two cultures may never meet, but people who live on those mountains—who belong to separate cultures—can meet. One person can make himself and the good things he has to share fit into the world of the other. As Christians, we are called off our mountains to become bridges which others confidently use to come to Christ. Our effectiveness in this will determine whether or not strategies of communication are built in our generation to span the gulf for cultures at the widest end of the Gap, where over half the human race waits to hear of Christ for the first time.

REFLECTION: What are specific kinds of mission strategy you know of going on somewhere in the world today? Which piece of the mosaic is it aimed at? How effectively is it spanning the gulf in that part of the Gap? How do you know? In practical terms, how should a vision of such strategies affect what you pray for and look for in world missions today?

You Might Explore: That Everyone May Hear by Ed Dayton.

13

CATCH THE VISION! SEE MY OWN WORLD-SIZED *PART* WITH CHRIST!

KEY QUESTION: Do I believe that I, along with other Christians, can have a strategic impact on Christ's global cause right now? (The following studies will help you answer the question.)

FACT: There IS a World-Sized Part

There's nothing superficial about discipleship in the world dimension! As an Inter-Varsity Christian Fellowship publication puts it: "If Christians can once see what God Himself says about their responsibility toward the world, then superficial images will no longer stand in the way of His work."

A frequently quoted "law" claims: "God loves you and has a wonderful plan for your life." It's true that my loving Father wants to be very personal with me as He leads me into His perfect will. But if His "plan-for-me" ever becomes divorced from His "plan-for-the-nations" then I will lose the fundamental basis for a personally significant role in the Kingdom's advance around the world. The familiar adage might better be: "God has a wonderful plan for the nations and He loves you and me enough to give us a strategic place in it!" My part in Christ's global cause can literally touch the ends of the earth!

Notice how Paul puts together our individual purpose in life and God's plan for the world:

> *God has made known to us in all wisdom and insight the secret of His will according to His purpose which He set forth in Christ, His plan for the fullness of times, to unite all things in Christ, things in heaven and things on earth. According to this plan—designed by Him who accomplishes all things according to the counsel of this plan—we who first hoped in Christ have been destined and appointed to live for the praise of His glory* (Eph. 1:10-12, author's paraphrase).

REFLECTION: How would *you* define in one sentence the part you have in Christ's global cause? In practical ways, how should this vision affect your own self-image? Or, your sense of personal significance?

You Might Explore: Don't Just Stand There by Martin Goldsmith.

The Vision: WITH CHRIST—"Follow Me" (Mark 8:34)

There are no legitimate alternatives for those in Christ's global cause. All Christians have been conscripted by Christ to go with Him into the Gap. To all of us who have made peace with the Father by Christ's cross, our Lord's very next words are: "Come. Follow me." The fact that He is Lord implies others are following right behind.

So the vision of our world-sized part depends not so much on who we are, why we're here, or where we're going. Rather it depends on who *Christ* is, why He's here, and where He's going—because we are following Him. World Christians never journey in the Gap alone. Christ and His global cause create the larger dimension to our lives because our part is *with* Him. World missions is His initiative always. He has chosen us to join Him but never to launch out ahead of Him. He alone leads the way.

Jesus is on the move. And He wants us to follow Him out across the borders of our own world—beyond our familiar friends and family and our own social and cultural securities. He wants to lead us out of the limitations our culture puts on our understanding of God's worldwide purpose, on our sense of the tremendous possibilities for fulfilling it, and on the specific people we ultimately choose to care about. He wants to take us across all our personal barriers into His global cause, out where there are no limits on who He will touch through us.

And, because He stays with us we can have the courage to move out. He never takes us anywhere He has not already gone before us. He never asks us to face anything He has not already faced, or to love anyone He does not already love, or to give anything He has not first given.

The Apostle Paul witnessed to how this breakdown of his self-imposed borders began for him:

> *You have heard of my former life in Judaism, how I perse-cuted the church of God violently and tried to destroy it; and I advanced in Judaism beyond many of my own age among my people, so extremely zealous was I for the traditions of my fathers. But when he who had set me apart before I was born, and had called me through his grace, was pleased to reveal his Son to me, in order that I might preach him among the Gentiles, I did not confer with flesh and blood* (Gal. 1:13-16). *And the Lord said, "I am Jesus whom you are persecuting. But rise and stand upon your feet; for I have appeared to you for this purpose, to appoint you to serve and bear witness to the things in which you have seen me and to those things in which I will appear to you [as I con-tinue] delivering you from the people and from Gentiles—to whom I send you to open their eyes, . . . that they may receive forgiveness of sins and a place among those who are sancti-fied by faith in me." Wherefore, O King Agrippa, I was not disobedient to that heavenly vision* (Acts 26:15-19).

REFLECTION: What are some "borders" in *your* life across which Jesus wants you to follow Him? In practical ways, how will following Him enlarge your involvement in His global cause? How might this happen in the next month? The next year?
You Might Explore: The Master Plan of Evangelism by Robert E. Coleman.

The Vision: OUR PART—"Lose Your Life" (Mark 8:34-35)

As faithful stewards of all we've received in Christ, He asks us to actively *invest* our lives for the greatest possible returns in reaching the unreached around the world. Ultimately that investment is in people.

Losing ourselves for Christ's cause—denying ourselves and taking up the cross—is the greatest love we can ever show the world. Our world-sized part isn't fulfilled simply by being involved in mission activities and enterprises, but in love that fully invests our all, no matter who we love or what it costs to do so. No sacrifice which a lover would make for his beloved is too great for us to make in order that the earth's unreached might be wed to our Saviour. We are called into a world-sized part which asks us to be willing to even die if that will help bring them into the reality of God's greater love for them.

And dying may be the part Christ gives some of us. The missionary in the pot was an old joke, but today's "sunrise of missions" springs from many who did die, and the pot is heating up again. "The missionary of tomorrow will be met, not by cringing awe, not by smiles and outstretched hands, not even by spears and leather shields, but by automatic weapons," writes columnist Jenkin Lloyd Jones. "Martyrdom is coming back, and it will be a testing time for Christianity."[1]

On the other hand, the cost for most of us may be in areas such as: physical comforts, reputation, personal plans, family and friendship ties, sleep, and recreation, or, for those who venture cross-culturally, familiar surroundings and one's mother tongue. But whatever its form, there will be a price to pay for everyone who stands in the Gap.

One's greatest fear, however, is usually not fear of suffering; it is fear of suffering for something which makes no ultimate difference. Even in the face of martyrdom, Christians can be sure that our life investment is always in a cause that *will* make the ultimate difference, both for unreached peoples and for the outcome of history.

With Christ we are serving a Kingdom that will remain forever because it is built of people. When you've found out that people are worth dying for, then you've found something and someone worth living for. So, we always live whenever we invest ourselves in Christ's cause and His Good News for the sake of people.

Paul's missionary thrust was marked by weakness, vulnerability, suffering and aggressive sacrifice. But this remained in the context of a strategy for people and a sense of victory:

> *[Don't shift away] from the hope of the gospel which you heard, which has been preached to every creature under heaven, and of which I, Paul, became a minister. Now I rejoice in my sufferings for your sake, and in my flesh I complete what is lacking in Christ's afflictions for the sake of his body, that is, the church . . . to make the word of God fully known, . . . for this I toil, striving with all the energy which he mightily inspires within me* (Col. 1:23-25,29).

REFLECTION: Who are the people in whom you're presently investing your life? How are you doing this? What does it cost you? Are there people at wider ends of the Gap for whom you could be doing the same kinds of things? What would you do? How would you start?

You Might Explore: By Their Blood: Christian Martyrs of the 20th Century by James and Marti Hefley.

The Vision: WORLD-SIZED—"Find Life" (Mark 8:35)

In the context of Christ's global cause, what does it mean to find life? Like our Saviour we should give our flesh for the life of the world—we should stand in the Gap for those for whom He died. But that's not the end of it! As His blood opened the way of reconciliation, so our investment in His cause, no matter how costly, has its returns also. We help harvest those who are reconciled from among the nations. We share with Him in bringing new sons and daughters into God's family. We help fill the Kingdom with people who will praise our Lord forever. And all that adds up to finding real life.

Fufilling a world-sized part points us beyond knowing ourselves, or purifying ourselves, or improving ourselves. Christ calls us to *multiply* ourselves! Miracles big enough to change the world, big enough to penetrate peoples where the gospel has never come before, can happen through any who follow Christ and lose their lives for His sake and the gospel's. God wants to use finite, often fallible Christians to unleash His redeeming work on the very ends of the earth.

It is no coincidence that the same century that has seen more people become Christians and more churches planted than in the previous nineteen hundred years put together, may also have seen more believers martyred for Christ worldwide than in the rest of church history combined. The nations *have* found life because so many were willing to die for Christ's sake and the gospel's.

All of this indicates that we are actually *creators* for Christ's cause rather than just puppets in it. Though we may represent little or nothing in ourselves we have become strategic "some-bodies" who make a life-or-death difference for nations because we serve the King of life. In one sense, the fate of the world rests in the hands of nameless but committed saints through whom eternal life is multiplied to the widest end of the Gap.

Despite his costly ministry among Thessalonian people, Paul found plenty of life there as he multiplied himself through them:

> *For our gospel came to you not only in word, but also in power and in the Holy Spirit with full conviction . . . . And you became imitators of us and of the Lord, for you received the word in much affliction, with joy inspired by the Holy Spirit; so that you became an example to all the believers in Macedonia and Achaia. For not only has the word of the Lord sounded forth from you in Macedonia and Achaia, but your faith in God has gone forth everywhere* (1 Thess. 1:5-8).

REFLECTION: Have you found life in this way? Where across the earth are people coming alive in Christ because you person-ally cared and helped reach out to them with the gospel? In what specific ways could you multiply yourself even more in the Gap? How would you know for sure it was happening?
You Might Explore: Peace Child by Don Richardson.

The Vision of Those Who SET THE PACE
As we follow Christ, who is better qualified to set the pace

than those whose world-sized parts have placed them more directly at the cutting edge of world missions? These pacesetters stand at wider spans of the Gap, having made sacrificial efforts to cross major cultural, geographical, and theological barriers to reach the unreached. I'm talking about the missionary.

Who is better qualified to define for all of us what our "wartime priorities" should be than the "soldiers" who have invaded territory Satan never had to defend before? Why should Christians who aren't professional missionaries not deliberately adopt a missionary life-style and discipline, in the same way the whole U.S. Olympic Track Team adopts the same rigors in training and planning that is required of any who run the main event.

The faith, commitment, readiness, mobility, character, and sacrifice expected of missionaries are equally valid expectations for any Christian serious about fulfilling his world-sized part. To put it another way, when God gave the missionary He did not lay aside the need for a missions-minded Church. Missionaries make an excellent example for *all* of us to follow as they follow Christ into the "sunrise of missions."

In 1910, for example, a group of World Christians out of the Student Volunteer Movement gathered from many parts of the country. They came to share with the whole movement their reasons for going overseas that year as missionaries. Their testimonies reflect the burning vision for every generation of disciples. Listen:

> Because I want my life to tell in a place where Christ is unknown.
> Because I am able to go
> The gift of life is my only answer as a Christian in light of the tremendous need.
> Because I believe profoundly that it is more blessed to give than to receive.
> Because I hear God's voice and the voice of peoples' needs.
> With the desire to be obedient, I want my little light to shine in the greatest darkness.
> Because there is nothing too precious for Christ.
> Because of the present opportunity.

Because God has opened the way, and that was all I was waiting for.

Because the Master has many sheep in that fold.

One of the Church's great missionary statesmen offered himself as a pacesetter for everyone:

So, whether you eat or drink, or whatever you do, do all to the glory of God. Give no offense to Jews or to Greeks or to the church of God, just as I try to please all men in everything I do, not seeking my own advantage, but that of many, that they may be saved. Be imitators of me, as I am of Christ (1 Cor. 10:31–11:1). For it has been granted to you that for the sake of Christ you should not only believe in him but also suffer for his sake, engaged in the same conflict which you saw and now hear to be mine (Phil. 1:29-30).

REFLECTION: Think of some missionaries you know more personally: specifically how are they fulfilling their world-sized parts? What, about their vision or character or ministry, should every World Christian imitate? In practical ways, how should missionaries set the pace for your own missions involvement?
You Might Explore: The Deep-Sea Canoe: The Story of the Third World Missionaries in the South Pacific by Alan Tippett.

A Vision to GO AS FAR AS WE CAN GO

The concern with our world-sized part isn't first of all a question of where we are physically serving the cause. Rather, the question is: *Why* are we where we are and doing what we're doing? Whether or not we ever move to another country, still we must justify our activities by how they help us to fill our world-sized part to the furthest point God wants us to go.

To put it another way, World Christians don't evaluate their part by where in the world they are involved so much as by *who* in the world they are touching: At what *cultural distance* from existing Christians is the person I'm reaching? World Christians desire to be personally involved in reaching beyond people for whom the gospel is readily available to those at wider spans of the Gap. Of the two and a half billion people without any gospel witness, which ones will have an opportunity to hear and become Christians because *I* have pursued my world-sized part as far as I could go with it?

Are we searching for all kinds of ways to be used in reaching the unreached? As God directs, are we seeking to take on any role, at any time, in any place, by any means, with anyone, and at any cost that will help advance Christ's global cause to the ends of the earth? Do we actively fight any personal sense of permanence?

Or do we freeze up over the reasons why "it can't be done" or why "I can't be used"? Do we welcome new ideas and approaches because they might help us go farther? Or are we boxed up in routines and in fears of the unknown? Do we refuse to back away from a mission when our part seems too difficult or too out of the ordinary? Are we willing to move into the Gap even when all our questions aren't answered or our success in outreach fully guaranteed or our friends fully sympathetic?

Paul never lost this vision:

> *For I will not venture to speak of anything except what Christ has wrought through me to win obedience from the [Nations] . . . Thus [I make] it my ambition to preach the gospel, not where Christ has already been named, lest I build on another man's foundation, but as it is written, "They shall see who have never been told of him, and they shall understand who have never heard of him." . . . I hope to see you in passing as I go to Spain, and to be sped on my journey there by you* (Rom. 15:18, 20-21, 24).

REFLECTION: How far have you gone with your world-sized part until now? How do you measure this? What still holds you back? How could you go farther? In practical ways, how should this vision affect your own missions involvement next month? Or, a year from now?
You Might Explore: John R. Mott: 1865-1955 by C. Howard Hopkins.

My Part Needs the HOLY SPIRIT
Our world-sized part with Christ is a theological fact of Scrip-

ture and a daily experience developed through the Holy Spirit. The Spirit has come to make our world-sized part as defined in Mark 8:34-35—following, losing and finding—a permanent, daily event that brings a world-sized blessing.

Our part in world missions is always complemented by His part through us. As the Spirit led and empowered Christ's own earthly mission—in words and miracles, in confrontations with Satan, in sensitivity to the Father's will, all the way to the cross and out of the tomb—He continues to do so for all who follow the Lord. As we open to His forward looking power, as we cast aside our fears of change, the Spirit will be to us all that He was to Him.

Whenever Christians give top priority to fulfilling their world-sized parts, the Spirit has His greatest freedom in our lives. He is free to produce His fruit in us, to transform our characters to make us more like the One whose mission we're on. He is free to build the Body up in love, to unify us into a family with a world mission. He is free to develop in us the skills and abilities He has given us to effectively serve the cause. In summary, the Spirit is free to bring many unreached people into the Kingdom when He has ambassadors of Christ whom He has changed, unified, and equipped for that very calling.

The world-sized impact of Paul's stand in the Gap was directly attributable to the Spirit:

> *When I came to you, brethren, I did not come proclaiming to you the testimony of God in lofty words or wisdom. For I decided to know nothing among you except Jesus Christ and him crucified. And I was with you in weakness and in much fear and trembling; and my speech and my message were not in plausible words of wisdom, but in demonstration of the Spirit and power, that your faith might not rest in the wisdom of men but in the power of God* (1 Cor. 2:1-5).

REFLECTION: What are specific things you want and need God's Spirit to do with you if you're to effectively fulfill a world-sized part? In practical ways, how should the Spirit affect your own missions involvement or that of your group or church? How would you know when He is doing this? When do you expect

Him to do this—before, during, or after you get started on that mission?

You Might Explore: Pentecost and Missions by Harry R. Boer.

My Part Needs the WHOLE BODY

At its deepest level God's family can be defined by its mission. It was Jesus Himself who stated that those who do the will of His Father are His brothers and sisters. Doing the ultimate will of the Father for this generation—reaching those who have yet to even hear of Christ—is what His family's life is ultimately about.

Within this family there are many ministries, but only one mission. Within this family is beautiful diversity, but God intends it to be unity-in-diversity because we are united in the same global cause. Each of our world-sized parts are interdependent and indispensable for our overall mission. The gifts and resources in the Body, both locally and globally, are there to make it strong and life-giving for the world beyond itself that needs to know our Head.

This is not a vision of uniformity, however. Our diversity is our strength. It equips us to deal more effectively with the diversities in human culture. Instead, this is a vision of global *partnership* in missions, as we learn to respect the potential within churches of various nations and cultures; and as we draw on that in forming and implementing our missionary strategy. The Lausanne congresses and consultations organized around the world since 1974 provide many examples of partnership at work.

For each of us, following Christ, losing our lives for His cause, and finding our lives multiplied in others around the earth aren't to be isolated experiences. The principle is this: "The whole of world missions is greater than the sum of our individual, world-sized parts." World Christians were not meant to be lone rangers. We are to believe and act together, not as an organization *of* a self-contained spiritual unit, but *for* a world-sized spiritual movement to close the whole Gap.

Even Paul's missionary triumphs would never have happened if the whole Body of Christ in his day was not given a world-sized part with him:

[I am] thankful for your partnership in the gospel from the first day until now. And I'm sure that he who began a good work in you will bring it to completion at the day of Jesus Christ. . . . I hold you in my heart, for you are all partakers with me of grace, both in my imprisonment and in the defense and confirmation of the gospel . . . . And it is my prayer that your love may abound more and more (Phil. 1:5-9).

REFLECTION: Are you working together with other Christians to play a part in Christ's global cause? Is more accomplished together than if you each would do your part separately? What more could you share with Christian friends that could increase the world-sized impact of each of your lives? In practical ways, how should this need for the whole Body of Christ affect your own missions involvement for the next year?

You Might Explore: You Can So Get There from Here by Edward R. Dayton.

My Part Needs MANY MISSION TEAMS

To make our world-sized parts *manageable,* they need to be expressed in practical strategies carried out by mission teams. The world missionary movement works best in disciplined, organized, mobile communities. This is demonstrated, for example, by the teams during Paul's missionary era, by the sixth century thrust of Celtics out of Columba's training center in Ireland, in the twelfth century movement of Franciscan Friars, as well as in the Protestant Moravian communities, and the Serampore Covenant team of William Carey, down to today's seven hundred North American and three hundred Third-World missionary societies.

Smaller mission teams can help expedite the Church's many mission opportunities around the world. As specialized groups—with sending members and going members—they become direct agents to plant the church among specific groups of unreached peoples.

Think about this: If every one of the world's remaining 16,700 unreached culture-groups were adopted by one substantial mission team, pledged to the long-term goal of reaching them and planting churches among them by direct missionary efforts, the global Body of Christ would experience a monumental advance in its world-sized part for this generation!

In fact, a 1979 recommendation by the Missions Advanced Research and Communications Center (MARC) calls for this very thing. They suggest as a starting point that four thousand existing missionaries be reassigned in teams of four to reach one thousand specific unreached groups. New missionary recruits would undergo special training to add to the number of teams. The ultimate goal MARC recommends is twenty-five thousand teams working to reach twenty-five thousand groups by 1990. Furthermore, this could fulfill the world-sized parts of twenty-five thousand local churches who were equally committed to the teams and their mission goals, as the sending-members of the teams, one church for each team.

The New Testament church "turned the world upside-down" through its mission teams. Consider some of the people involved on Paul's team:

Paul, Silvanus, and Timothy, to the church of the Thessalonians . . . we were ready to share with you not only the gospel of God but also our own selves (1 Thess. 1:1; 2:8) *I have sent [Tychicus] to you for this very purpose, that you may know how we are . . . and with him Onesimus, the faithful and beloved brother, who is one of yourselves . . . . Aristarchus my fellow prisoner greets you, and Mark the cousin of Barnabas . . . and Jesus who is called Justus . . . . Epaphras, who is one of yourselves, a servant of Christ Jesus, greets you, always remembering you earnestly in his prayers . . . Luke the beloved physician and Demas greet you* (Col. 4:7-14).

REFLECTION: Can you name any North American protestant mission societies or missionary teams working in other parts of the world? Why is it important, in specific ways, that they fulfill their world-sized parts as societies or teams? How can the existence of such groups give your world-sized part a more effective expression? In other words, how would you or your church work through them to fulfill your own part? Have you ever considered

forming a team to make your own missions involvement more
manageable?
You Might Explore: Committed Communities Fresh Streams for
World Missions by Charles Mellis.

Notes
1. Jenkin Lloyd Jones, "Christianity Put to the Test," *Los Angeles Times*, September 16, 1979.

Step One—Catch a World Vision!
—The Vision Every World Christian Should See

Step Two—Keep a World Vision!

The Decision Every World Christian Should Make

14. The World Christian Decision
    Will I choose to be a World Christian?
    Will I choose to *join* with other World Christians?
    Will I choose to *plan* to obey my vision?

14

KEEP THE VISION! THE WORLD CHRISTIAN DECISION

The first step of the journey is over. Have you caught a world vision? If so, this widening perspective leads to the logical question: What will I do with my new vision? You're faced with a three-fold decision:

- Will I choose to *be* a World Christian?
- Will I choose to *join* with other World Christians?
- Will I choose to *plan* to obey my vision?

All three issues are interlinked. One decision implies the other two, because none can ever survive by itself. All three taken together constitute the *second* step in the journey: Your decision to *keep* a world vision at the center of your life in Christ.

One of the great leaders of the Student Volunteer Movement was John R. Mott. As a World Christian he recognized the need for every Christian to face this decision:

Without a doubt there comes to many of us the choice between a life of contraction and one of expansion; a life of small dimensions and one of widening horizons and larger visions and plans; a life of self-satisfaction or self-seeking and one of unselfish or truly Christ-like sharing.

To keep a world vision at the center of your life in Christ is no small step. But you can't really take the step until you've caught a sense of what that vision entails.

Let's see if you've caught it. Determine how many of the facts under Step One you could give a check (✓) that says: "Yes! I see that! I accept that! I know it's important. I want *that* area to enlarge my relationship with Christ and to strengthen my commitment to His cause." Try it with this review of what we've studied:

Fact: There is a world-wide purpose in Christ
_____ Christ: the center
_____ The nations: the target
_____ The gospel: the power
_____ The Church: the agent
_____ Missions: the process
_____ Multiplied congregations: the strategy
_____ Numerical growth: a measure
_____ Compassion: the pulse
_____ Cultural transformation: the impact
_____ Satan: the enemy

Fact: There is a world full of possibilities through Christ
_____ Church history
_____ Spiritual renewal
_____ World trends
_____ The evangelistic acceleration
_____ Available personnel
_____ Modern resources
_____ "Closed doors" and the possibilities
_____ American church involvement in the possibilities

Fact: There is a world full of people without Christ
_____ Facing problems with visibility
_____ A vision of how we're similar
_____ A vision of how we're different
_____ A vision of the many worlds in America
_____ The crucial vision of the Hidden People
_____ A vision of strategies that fit the mosaic

Fact: There is a world-size part with Christ
_____ The vision: with Christ—"Follow me"
_____ The vision: our part—"Lose your life"

_____ The vision: world-sized—"Find life"
_____ A vision of those who set the pace
_____ A vision to go as far as we can go
_____ My part needs the Holy Spirit
_____ My part needs the whole Body
_____ My part needs many mission teams

In other words, do you see the following areas well enough to prepare you to *act* on them:

- the big picture of Christ's global cause?
- the Church's potential for fulfilling that cause?
- the great scope of earth's unreached peoples?
- the strategic impact you can have?

If your answer is YES! then you're ready for *Step Two:*

YOU'RE READY TO BE A WORLD CHRISTIAN

What does this entail? You choose to be a World Christian when you catch the vision enough to say:

My whole relationship with Christ will be unified around His global cause. Among every people-group where there is no vital, evangelizing Christian community there should be one, there must be one and, God willing, there shall be one! I want to help make this happen. I want to get involved in the cause where I'm needed most, to close the Gap at some point so that precious lives can be won to Christ and brought home to the Father, so that God's Kingdom can break through.

That's one way of saying: I choose to be a World Christian! Can you think of other ways? How would *you* say it?

YOU'RE READY TO JOIN WITH OTHER WORLD CHRISTIANS

What does this entail? You choose to join other World Christians when you catch the vision enough to seek out others who have also caught it. One team of World Christians on the West Coast called "The Haggai Community" drew up a community covenant that expressed what this meant to them:

> We commit our lives together to pray and work for the cause of Jesus Christ to the ends of the earth. We realize something of the dimensions of the yet unfinished task of world evangelization and are willing to give ourselves, risking our careers and reputations, to live a life-style that enables God's worldwide purpose to be fulfilled through us. Realizing this community alone is not adequate for the completion of this task, we shall pray for others to clasp hands with us in this expanding endeavor.

Each of the World Christians in that group made a momentous, life-changing choice to join other World Christians to stand in the Gap. Can you think of other ways to say it? How would *you* say it? How would you go about doing it? Who would you seek out?

Remember: World Christians are stretching their hearts and nerves and strength and resources to care about wider parts of the Gap. So it is essential that they have people around them who share a world vision, to love and to be loved by on a day-to-day basis. This is the only way obedience to that vision can last the strain of such deep involvement. That's why a decision to become a World Christian must include your decision to be part of a team.

YOU'RE READY TO PLAN TO OBEY YOUR VISION
What does this entail? You choose to plan to obey your vision when you catch it enough to *organize* your efforts for Christ's global cause. Most World Christians do this around these essential components:
- Regularly *build* your vision
- *Reach out* in love
- *Give* your vision to other Christians

This plan forms the highway you'll travel for the rest of your journey, the rest of your life. It is described in more detail in the following pages.

But it is at this crossroad that you must choose to plan for obedience in the Gap. You must believe that God has specific ways He wants to involve you, and that His Spirit will help you develop specific plans to fulfill that calling. Can you say: "I choose to plan to obey my vision"? What does that mean to you? What plan of action would *you* follow? (Appendix II suggests one way to think about planning.)

That's the essence of **Step Two**. That's what it means to *keep* a world vision. What do you think? Are you ready to become a World Christian? Are you willing to join with other World Christians as you stand together in the Gap in obedience to your world vision?

If so, the sample World Christian Decision Card (figure 1) will be a helpful tool for registering your intentions (as it has been for hundreds of others). Take a moment right now to read it. Would you like to sign it? Go ahead. But remember: the decision is something between you and the Lord with whom you stand in the Gap.

Now that you've considered the World Christian Decision Card, spend a moment in prayer about the response you've made to the Lord Jesus.

Next, write down some of the implications becoming a World Christian may have for your life this next month. For example, will a desire to wrap your life in Christ around His global cause change your quiet times? your sharing in a Bible study group? your prayers? your use of extra cash? the way you relate to people on campus or in your church? any decisions you face this month? (Record your thoughts in figure 2 at the end of this chapter.)

Now, make a list of people you might approach to join you to grow as World Christians. (Record three or four names in figure 2 at the end of this chapter.) How will you approach them? Could you share with them the World Christian Decision Card and what it means for you?

Finally, looking over the Personal Strategy Guide in Appendix II, begin to dream about plans for obeying a world vision. As the following pages move you ahead in the adventure of World-Christian discipleship, be on the lookout for specific ideas God gives you to incorporate into your plans *to build* a world vision, *to reach out directly* in love, and to give your vision to others.

WORLD CHRISTIAN DECISION CARD

I have caught a vision of Christ's global cause. This means I acknowledge that:

1. God has a worldwide *PURPOSE* in Christ that encompasses all history, all creation and all peoples everywhere, especially those yet to be reached by the gospel.
2. There is a world full of *POSSIBILITIES* through Christ to significantly advance that purpose in our generation among all earth's peoples.
3. There is a world full of *PEOPLE* without Christ, most of whom must be reached by major new missionary efforts by all Christians everywhere.
4. God has given all Christians a world-sized *PART* with Christ that can make a strategic impact on reaching unreached peoples to the ends of the earth.

Therefore, I choose to keep this world vision. I choose:
- To *BE* a World Christian, unifying my whole relationship with Christ around His global cause.
- To *JOIN* with other World Christians, as we team up to serve the cause together.
- To *PLAN* to obey my vision in three areas:
  —To regularly *BUILD* my vision by taking time to study the cause
  —To *REACH OUT* directly to the world in love to fulfill the cause.
  —To *GIVE* my vision to other Christians, leading them into the cause of World Christian discipleship.

_____

Signature

_____

Date

Figure 1

Step Two is a major turning point in the journey to World-Christian discipleship. Now that you've made it, it's time to head on down the road with *Step Three,* which really consists of steps you take the rest of your life.

In the following pages, you'll study an overview of what it means to *obey* a vision. Don't try to imagine yourself and your fellow World Christians doing everything suggested there. Instead, try for an understanding of the tremendous opportunities for involvement with Christ in the Gap. (Actually, this overview is necessarily brief. For more details and ideas see Appendix III.)

The three major components for obeying a world vision—build, reach out, and give—interact with each other. That means the time commitment and the personal effort required to follow through on these areas isn't nearly as great as it may first appear. For example, a Bible study you have on Psalm 96 (build the vision) may give you new courage to pray for an unreached people-group in the world (reach out) as well as provide something to share on Christ's global cause at your next group or church meeting (give the vision). Or, as you minister to Muslim students on campus (reach out) you'll be reading and learning about Islam and about the countries your new friends come from (build the vision). What you learn can be presented during a training session for next year's small group leaders in your group or church, as you encourage each small group to adopt one international student for God to love through them (give the vision).

Obeying the vision should never be a burden. The challenge of it can be linked very naturally to your day-to-day life and schedule. For example, you can build your vision by considering the world dimension of the Scripture you read at daily devotions; or by reading one chapter a day from a recently published book on world missions. Or, you can reach out by adjusting your lifestyle and spending habits on a gradual basis in order to free up two dollars a week to give to a hospital mission work in Bangladesh; or by praying for one new country each day as you drive to work. You can give your vision to fellow Christians just by the subjects you introduce in conversation during mealtimes; or by bringing an international friend to church on Sunday; or by posting a world map at all chapter meetings.

Under Appendix II you'll find "A Personal Strategy Guide" to help you organize your efforts quickly and easily.

The point is this: you can have a practical, manageable strategy for involvement in the Gap that allows you to say each night, as you lay your head on the pillow: "I know *this* day my life has counted strategically for the global cause of Jesus Christ, especially for those currently beyond the reach of the gospel."

Wouldn't you like to be able to say that every day for the rest of your life? What disciple wouldn't?

I have a growing world vision and I want to keep it. I want to wrap my life in Christ around His Global Cause.

As I do this, I expect to see important changes in my day-to-day life in the following areas (describe one change in each area):

My daily Bible study

My daily prayer life

My involvement in my small group

Use of financial resources

Ministry on campus or in my neighborhood

Involvement in my local church

My plans for the future

Other

Who could I approach to grow with me as a World Christian (list their names below)?

Figure 2

Step One—Catch a World Vision!
     The Vision Every World Christian Should See

Step Two—Keep a World Vision!
     The Decision Every World Christian Should Make

Step Three—Obey a World Vision!

A Plan Every World Christian Should Follow

15

A PLAN: OBEY AS YOU REGULARLY *BUILD* YOUR VISION

KEY QUESTION: Do I take time to study the cause? Am I letting my world vision grow?

To keep a world vision warm we need to band together like coals gathered in a hearth. But World Christian groups can only burn *hot* when they are regularly fired-up with combustible world-sized facts! We need to *study* Christ's global cause. An informed world vision will ignite us to make significant strides as we reach out in the Gap and as we share our world vision with other believers. In all of our other studies and reading the building of a world vision must remain central. One of the most important subjects we can ever tackle concerns what God is doing throughout the earth, and how to be co-workers in it with Him.

What percentage of your efforts at Christian discipleship in the next year will be spent just educating yourself for more effective involvement in the Gap? How will you move beyond just accumulating missions facts and start building them into a *framework* for strategic action?

Let me illustrate why this is so vital. We've all tried a connect-the-dots picture puzzle. Scattered around the page the numbered dots make little sense until they're drawn together by individual lines. Then a picture emerges. Even so, you can't clearly see the big picture of world missions until you connect together, in manageable and meaningful ways, the grand themes that comprise a genuine world vision.

The "Catch a World Vision!" chapters (10-13) provide the "dots" that help form this big picture. You'll discover that what you read these days on world missions will either sharpen your understanding of one or more of those dots or draw lines for you that connect some of the dots together. (In fact, you may want to keep the outline in mind summarized on page 190 whenever you're studying the cause. It provides an excellent set of categories into which you can place the facts you uncover. It can become your framework for action.) Only those disciples actively doing this—who regularly *build* the world vision they've already caught—will be able to move out creatively and intelligently to fulfill that vision and give it to others.

There is another supreme benefit from these efforts, however. J.B. Phillips once cautioned: "Your God is too small!" But an equally important warning is: "Your world is too small!" The world you care about will be no bigger than the "tribal deity" you've made out of God. But if your world is too small then you'll never fully appreciate how big your God is nor desire to glorify Him the way He deserves to be glorified: worldwide. All efforts to build your vision are really efforts at getting to know *God* better, as well as make Him better known throughout the Gap.

Resources and ways to develop a plan to regularly build your vision are abundant. Certainly the place to begin is through Bible study with a world dimension. It's important that you learn all you can about the key biblical passages on Christ's global cause. And there are hundreds of them!

How to Create a World Christian Bible Study

Focus your Bible study on *four basic questions:*

1. What does it *say*? Investigate the passage with what? where? when? how? why? And then ask, How do my various discoveries relate to one another?

2. What does it *mean?* What is God trying to say through this passage? What are its implications for other biblical truths? What

warnings does He give? What promises? What principles for daily living? What should be the impact of the passage on God's people anywhere?

3. What does it mean to *me?* Apply the passage in a very personal way: What does it mean to my walk with Christ? To my dreams? My needs? My life-style? My daily responsibilities? My priorities? My relationships to other people? To my church? My family?

4. What does it mean to me as a *World Christian?* What aspects of my world vision does it help me build? Purpose? Possibilities? People? Part? How could it help equip me, train me, direct me, and challenge me in the specific ways I'm seeking to reach out in love right now? How could it help me give a world vision to someone else? What have I found here that I could share with another Christian to help them grow as a World Christian?

For a *group* Bible study you may want to wrap up with a fifth question: What does it mean to us as a team of World Christians? How do the discoveries we've made in the study apply to our ongoing plans to follow Christ together into the Gap? How does it stimulate, reinforce, or reshape all we're trying to do together with Him?

Finally, here's a *bonus project* in World Christian Bible study. Purchase an inexpensive edition of the Scriptures. Then use a colored marker to highlight every verse that refers to God's concern for, evaluations of, intentions toward, actions toward, or involvement with the nations. You might go book by book from Genesis to Revelation. Look for references to specific nations outside of Israel (small and large) as well as references to "the nations" in general. For example, a passage on Edom, or the sojourner, or worshiping Baal or other gods and idols, or foreign kings or "the peoples," or the ends of the earth, or Creation (the heavens, the earth)—all would be eligible for your pen. Determine what all this means to your understanding of the passages that remain uncolored. After completing one book, go back and read the colored passages only. What do you learn in them about God's worldwide purpose in Christ? Or about the possibilities today for closing the Gap? Or about reaching unreached people? Or about your own world-sized part in it all? How should the discoveries change your life? See Appendix IV for passages to get you started. Or read *The University of the Word* by Dick Eastman. Or write to Inter-Varsity Christian Fellowship for the booklet *How to Create World Christian Bible Studies.*

Besides Bible study, here are . . .

Other Ways to Build a World Vision

1. Keep a *map of the world* handy (one without the U.S.A. at the center!). At most map stores you can secure a large world map containing insets of smaller maps coded to show where major religious, linguistic, economic and other realms are located. Or, write to Operation Mobilization for a special "prayer map" (for $2.00): P.O. Box 148, Midland Park, NJ 07432. Use your map to locate missionary reports, news events, places you read about, places your friends go. Let the world become your friend!

2. Study key *books on world missions.* Write to Inter-Varsity Christian Fellowship for their listing of the best: *The World Christian Book Shelf.* The list indicates which books help to build the four aspects of a world vision. Or you might want to join the Global Church Growth Book Club, from William Carey Library, which qualifies you to order, at a discount, books covering the whole spectrum of world missions. (You might begin with one of the book suggestions found in chapters 10-13.)

3. Subscribe to key *missions periodicals* from the leading evangelical mission societies. Of the *Magazines for World Christians* listed in Appendix III, I highly recommend *World Christian* as the best overall magazine on missions. Many of these are free. Or take the Evangelical Missions Information Service, offering up-to-date news of world missions events and monthly study papers on key issues in missions today. (Write: Box 794, Wheaton, Illinois 60187.) (See Appendix III for more ideas.)

4. Subscribe to key *secular periodicals* with international perspectives. They can keep you informed of world events, personalities, and needs that might relate directly to missions strategies and activities you learn about from Christian literature. Some of the best include: *Atlas: World Press Review, New York Times, Wall Street Journal, U.S. News and World Report, Christian Science Monitor, National Geographic, Time, The Economist, South: The Third-World Magazine,* plus many of the publi-

cations from the U.S. Printing Office in Washington, D.C., especially their *"Area Handbooks"* series for many world nations. (Write for their complete listing.) Consult your local library on these and other helpful publications.

5. As a part of a weekly World Christian small-group meeting you might have one team member give a "World Missions Update" each session. Present a particular mission work, a current world event and how it relates to missions, or report on some unreached people-group. Another approach to the Update would have each member assigned to a certain continent or a specific missions issue about which they bring brief updates at every meeting.

6. Take *world-related and missions-related courses* as part of an ongoing education project. Linguistics, world history, cultural anthropology, and international politics are a few possibilities. You may want to study the correspondence course called "Perspectives on the World Christian Movement" available through the U.S. Center for World Missions. It can be taken for credit or non-credit, and at any speed you desire. Another option is to spend a summer or a semester studying the big picture of God's global purpose at the Institute of International Studies at the U.S. Center for World Missions in Pasadena, California. With other like-minded students and mission professors from around the country, I.I.S. students walk through God's unfolding purpose in the Bible and history, gaining a panoramic perspective of current possibilities in world evangelization. Credit can usually be transferred back to your campus if you are a student. The Theology and Education Group of the Lausanne Committee for World Evangelization has produced a multimedia learning package that helps small groups get a handle on the contemporary scene in missions, particularly cross-cultural sensitivity and evangelism. Called "Hearing And Doing" it is available from Partnership in Mission, 1564 Edge Hill Rd., Abington, PA 19001.

7. Attend *missions conferences* in local churches. In the fall, contact key churches near you and discuss with them their plans for such conferences that year, such as who will be there, what countries will be presented, and what the schedule is. Then put the most helpful ones into your calendar and plan to get a small

group of World Christians to attend. Consider attending IVCF's Urbana Student Missions Convention (with seventeen thousand students it is the largest of its kind). Or, bring a World Christian Conference to your church via video through the World Christian Video Training Curriculum (see Appendix V).

8. Sit at the feet of *missionaries* who have been involved at the front lines of world missions. Learn to see the world through *their* eyes. Read their prayer letters. Spend time with them during their furlough. For help in developing profitable discussions with a missionary visitor, write for Inter-Varsity's "How to Interview a Real Live Missionary!"

9. Also, learn from *Christian international students,* asking them the same questions you would ask a missionary. Contact Campus Crusade for Christ to get their book *Bridges of Love* by Frank Obien. International Students, Inc. offers literature and staff to get you started in this unique learning opportunity.

10. Take *field trips* that put you into another culture for a day or a weekend. Go to *learn* first, rather than to evangelize. Visit an ethnic enclave in a nearby urban center. Attend an ethnic church even if they don't worship in your language. Get a world vision from how they express praise to God. Catch a glimpse of John's vision in Revelation 7. Another field trip might include a Friday evening when you attend the weekly meeting of the International Club on a college campus.

11. If you haven't done so yet, you might begin your vision-building by working through the *Small Group Study Guide* for *In the Gap* found in Appendix I. Or pick one selection from the "You Might Explore" suggestions in chapters 10 to 13 to read in the next month. Many of these books are available at discount through the World Christian Bookshelf listing of the Global Church Growth Club (see Appendix III).

16

A PLAN: OBEY AS YOU *REACH OUT* DIRECTLY IN LOVE

KEY QUESTION: Am I directly involved in the cause? Am I helping to reach the unreached, especially at the widest end of the Gap?

Dreamers: Awake!

It's OK to dream about all the ways you might reach out in love. World Christians make the best kind of dreamers. Their growing world vision drives them to dream of new ways to let their lives count for Christ's cause. Together they gather the big, world-sized dreams God gives to set them free in love to the ends of the earth!

There are two sides to a World Christian's dreams about reaching out. If we build our world vision on a regular basis we will easily dream about effective personal ways to reach out. But the second side is vital. We must *act* on our visions or eventually we will slumber off with a head full of interesting facts but not a world-sized dream to our names. Direct involvement is essential for the journey into World Christian discipleship.

If you were to boil down the popular suggestions for how World Christians can reach out in love, you would most likely

end up with these six areas:
- Reach out through *prayer*
- Reach out to a *Hidden People*
- Reach out *nearby*
- Reach out through a *missions project*
- Reach out through a *Team-Extension Mission*
- Prepare for *future outreach*.

Most active groups of World Christians will eventually move out on all six fronts. But that may take time. Where should you begin?

In the first place, preparing for future outreach (the sixth area) runs concurrent with the other five involvements. World Christians are always preparing to do more and do it more effectively. So this area should be in our plans from the beginning.

Next, you may find it helpful to consider the other five areas as a logical progession—both in priority and in how they fit together in your overall plan. In that case, you would develop your plan for reaching out by establishing, first of all, an effective prayer life for the world. From that base you would add the next area, the adoption of a particular group of Hidden People to learn about, pray for and in which to take an active interest in bringing them the gospel.

After your efforts focus on the world in general (through prayer) and a specific people group at the widest end of the Gap (your adopted Hidden People) turn then to those nearby. Now you're ready to start looking for those where you live who are most neglected in the Church's outreach and who, because of major cultural and social differences, may be far removed from any Christian witness.

As you bring Christ's love to people nearby, you will gain a credibility and a right to increase your outreach around the world. You will gain a *credibility* because what you do elsewhere will be based on your faithfulness and experiences in the Gap around you. You will gain a *right* because you will have taken responsibility for wider parts of the Gap nearby before putting all your energy into a missions challenge in other lands.

Finally, through your material resources (by supporting a missions project) and through sending out some of your own number as your representatives (in a Team-Extension Mission,

Chap. 17) you can help bring the gospel to the neglected and needy peoples in nations and cultures geographically far from you.

Vision International offers a guide called *Planning Strategies for Evangelism* that may help you organize your overall outreach strategy. For churches, *The Missions Policy Handbook* is required reading from the Association of Church Missions Committee.

Reach Out Through Prayer

Prayer is the one mission to the world that all Christians can share. Through prayer any of us can directly love the unreached, even to the ends of the earth. As far as God can go, prayer can go. Prayer can break through any part of the Gap and begin to close it so that lost sinners will find Christ and come home. Such a mission can be ours right now, right where we are sitting.

Prayer is action. By it we step out in advance of all other results. World Christian praying is an activity upon which all others depend. By prayer we establish a beachhead for the Kingdom among peoples where it has never been before. Prayer strikes the winning blow. All other missionary efforts simply gather up the fruits of our praying.

By prayer we do for people, especially those at the widest end of the Gap, what they cannot do for themselves. We stand in the Gap interceding that they might understand who Jesus is; while in prayer we also combat the forces of darkness pitted against their ever hearing the gospel.

The greatest impact any of us can have on Christ's global cause is to be involved in consistent prayer for the whole world and to teach other Christians how to pray this way. No wonder Paul calls it "the highest priority" (1 Tim. 2:1)!

In the process, however, prayer changes *us* too. It stretches us to love in a world-sized way. It intensifies our own longings to bless the families of earth through Christ's salvation. It makes us more willing and ready to receive all that God wants to give us to fulfill every world mission He calls us into. The scope of our praying will determine the scope of our concern and of all our other activities in the Gap.

Most praying for the world centers around the *fulfillment* of

Christ's global cause (so that all things may be summed up in Him) and the *fullness* of the Body worldwide (so that we can effectively carry out our mission to the ends of the earth). Attempt to build your World Christian prayer life around these two major concerns. (The Lord's Prayer, interestingly, divides this way.)

As this book goes to press the Lausanne Committee on World Evangelization is sponsoring an International Prayer Assembly in Korea to help galvanize the efforts of four thousand prayer mobilizers from across the globe into a visible, united movement of prayer for the world. Never in history has such a meeting occurred. And the two main stresses for this prayer movement will be on fullness and fulfillment.

One step to insure consistent outreach in prayer where you live is to establish a weekly "World Christian Prayer Meeting." It might follow this pattern, with different people responsible for different parts:

- Discuss what you want to pray about (15 minutes)
- Praise and prayer for the world in general (10 minutes)
- Praise and prayer for one area of the world (5 minutes)
- Praise and prayer for one missionary enterprise or person (5 minutes)
- Prayer for one unreached people-group (5 minutes)
- Specific personal praise and prayer needs, expressed in the light of Christ's global cause (15 minutes)

Along similar lines there is currently a strong prayer mobilization effort, spearheaded by the National Prayer Committee (NPC) in consultation with leaders in church, student, and mission organizations to assist the formation of "Concerts of Prayer" in 250 major cities in the U.S. These monthly gatherings have a two-fold stress for united prayer: spiritual awakening and world evangelization. You may want to contact the NPC for information on a Concert of Prayer near you.

A word on *personal requests:* Seek to put them in the world dimension. To pray in "Jesus' name" is to pray for something as it relates to His concerns, His cause, and His redemptive work as Mediator in the Gap. Even your most personal concerns should be related to the full scope of God's great plan for all nations. This may change what you ask for, why you ask for it and what kinds of answers you expect, and what you will do when the answers come. Begin your prayer by interceding for the ends of the earth and then work back to your own needs. It will provide a new perspective on the concerns you most frequently pray for.

Resources to Help us Pray More Intelligently

1. The daily news. Have you ever prayed over the front page? Be more than fascinated by the events. Pray for the people and things that cause these events and are affected by them.

2. Key secular news magazines, particularly sections on world events.

3. *Operation World:* A Handbook for World Intercession contains facts on every nation in the world and what to pray for in each. Available from Send the Light, Inc., Box 148, Midland Park, NJ 07432. Indispensible!

4. *World Christianity Profiles* does for you what *Operation World* does, only the profiles do it in more depth for about fifty-five countries. Available from World Vision International, 919 W. Huntington Dr., Monrovia, CA 91016.

5. The *Operation Prayer Diary* produced jointly by leading Christian campus movements to foster unified prayer by thousands of students for the same country and its needs each day of the year.

6. Missions magazine from evangelical societies are full of suggestions. See Appendix III for a listing of *Magazines for World Christians.* I strongly urge you to begin with a subscription to *World Christian* magazine—a "National Geographic" in missions publications, Box 40010, Pasadena, CA 91104.

7. Letters from missionaries you have met. Be faithful to pray for them if you ask to be on their mailing list.

8. Letters from unknown missionaries who are working among a group of people for whom you have a specific concern. Mission societies will be glad to help you get in touch. Consult the *Missions Handbook* (13th ed.) available from World Vision International.

9. Christian international students on a nearby campus, or Christian internationals working temporarily with U.S. firms (such as oil or computer), can help you pray more intelligently for their own peoples and their country. Talk with them.

10. Returning travelers from abroad, for whatever reasons they went, can help make praying more personal for the places and the people they saw.

11. Concentrate prayer on the major blocks of unreached people groups. Organizations that provide substantial help in this include: Fellowship of Faith for Muslims, 205 Yonge Street, Toronto, Ontario, Canada, MSB IN2; Pray for China Fellowship, c/o David Adeney, 1423 Grant St., Berkeley, CA 94705; and the monthly *Global Prayer Digest* on Muslims, Hindus, Chinese, and tribal peoples published by the U.S. Center for World Mission in Pasadena, CA.

12. When praying, remember to locate your prayer targets on a map. This will make your prayer-mission to the world come alive. Try placing a large world map on the floor, kneeling around it, and praying together from continent to continent, nation to nation—right across the earth. To do this, assign continents to individuals and have them come to each prayer meeting prepared to lead the whole group in intelligent praise and prayer for what God is doing in that area.

13. The National Prayer Committee has prepared a ten-lesson, ten-cassette training packet (with leader's guide and student outlines) that could prove invaluable. Called *Concerts of Prayer,* it's available from P.O. Box 6826, San Bernardino, CA 92412.

For more help on prayer read *The Hour that Changes the World* by Dick Eastman, and *A Call for Concerts of Prayer:* Wake Up for a New Missions Thrust by David Bryant.

Reach Out to a Hidden People

As we learned earlier, "Hidden People" describes the two and a half billion among whom there is no vital witnessing community of Christians, and with whom there are little or no evangelizing efforts from the outside by any existing churches or missionary societies. Of all earth's non-Christians these people are most "hidden" from the direct concern and action of God's people. Cultural, linguistic, social, political, prejudicial, or geographical barriers may create a tremendous gap between them and most of the Church's missions activity.

Our continued silence and neglect toward their plight is a gross injustice. Once we are aware these people exist and that few are trying to reach them, we are under a biblical mandate to respond somehow. Someone, somewhere must take personal responsibility for them—without delay.

Teams of World Christians *can* make a difference, at least for the specific group to which God leads them. Think of it this way: These two and a half billion people are locked away from the gospel in 16,700 culture groups (some three thousand in size, like an African tribal group; some thirty million in size, like a caste in India). If only 5 percent of the churches in America (to say nothing of the churches around the globe) were to adopt and reach out to just one Hidden People per church, making themselves fully available to the Lord, then each people-group would have one community of Christians specifically concerned with planting the Church among them for the very first time. Your team could become the vanguard of such an outreach for your church or chapter, helping them discover the same mission with you.

Here's how it could work. For a period of time (one to three years?) adopt one of the thousands of Hidden People groups as your team's ongoing concern. Make the group you adopt as specific as possible, so that your efforts on their behalf will be as manageable as possible. For example:

- Adopt Turkish people who are immigrant guest workers in the German Federal Republic (there are one million of them) and who reside in a particular city.
- Adopt the Akha people of China who have migrated by way of Burma into Thailand (about ten thousand) and who live in the ridge-top villages in the mountainous regions.
- Adopt Urdu-speaking people who are also Muslims and farmers and residents of the Punjab in India.
- Adopt the Japanese who live and work in Little Tokyo in Los Angeles.
- Adopt the one-hundred thousand Cantonese-speaking Chinese refugees from Vietnam who have resettled in France.
- Adopt the Turkana people who live and work in the fishing vil-

lages stretched around the 160 miles of Lake Turkana in Kenya.

- Adopt Welsh people, but more specifically adopt those of the working class who are also miners.

Stand in the Gap for your group—that's what it means to adopt them. Consider them "adopted" the way you would care for a Korean orphan through a child-sponsorship program, who would probably be otherwise abandoned and forgotten. As you do, follow this . . .

Hidden People Adoption Procedure

- Select one of the 16,700 groups (after some preliminary investigation) for whom your ultimate objective will be to plant the Church among them.
- Research and learn all you can about them, and about what is presently being done to reach them, and what it will yet take to plant a vital, evangelizing congregation.
- Pray regularly for them and for God to use your team, group, and church to help reach them.
- Inform others of your adopted group—who they are and how they can be reached. Ask God to raise up interest from others outside your team so that from this expanding base He can actually draw forth some who eventually go.
- Write to existing mission societies, both North American and Third World, which are reaching out near where your adopted Hidden People reside. Ask them what your team can do to help begin this new missions thrust. Offer yourselves to help in any way the society might recommend. Let that society know there are Christians that really care about what happens with this specific group of unreached people.
- Then, get ready to back up whatever God begins. God will take you seriously! Praise Him as you see Him at work.

How can you locate a Hidden People to adopt? Among the excellent resources: The Missions Advanced Research and Communications Center of World Vision International, with hundreds of these groups on file. The U.S. Center for World Mission, with its research institutes on the Hidden People among Chinese, Hindus, Moslems, and Animists. The books

Unreached Peoples (updated yearly) edited by Ed Dayton and Peter Wagner, published by David C. Cook Publishers and available through World Vision. Or, write to IVCF for its handbook, *How to Adopt a Hidden People.*

Reach Out Nearby

Some of the unreached who are culturally, socially and linguistically far from you may actually live *physically* near. They may be American, but still live at a wide end of the Gap. Any barriers that dull the gospel's impact on people around you must be penetrated by Christians with a missionary-style concern and strategy—by World Christians.

World Christians won't allow a growing concern to reach other parts of the world camouflage a lack of personal interest in those around them. Unless we are reaching out in love today to those around us, we may not be faithful or qualified to do so tomorrow in some other situation.

Remember: it is never an either/or proposition.

The more aware and sensitive we become toward the Hidden People in Asia, for example, the more we'll discover and care about people right around us who are "hidden" from the gospel, like many Asian-Americans with no Christian witness in their native language or in their neighborhood. On the other hand, we may actually reach into other nations by reaching those nearby who will travel "over there" for employment, in the armed services, to vacation or study, to visit relatives, or in the case of international students or employees, to return to their native land.

One thing does distinguish the local evangelism of a World Christian: his eyes will be on those who are most often missed or neglected in the evangelistic programs of other (usually white, middle-class) evangelicals. A World Christian actively looks for unpenetrated barriers and does something, despite all the difficulties, to cross those barriers in love.

For example, many in the U.S. are cut off from Christian outreach because of language barriers. Either they can't read or else English is not their native tongue. Unfortunately, most evangelism here is printed and spoken in English! Aware of this, some World Christians are taking college courses on teaching

English as a second language. Others are enrolling in Laubach literacy workshops (usually four days) to gain skills for helping people with language problems. With such skills they can provide a service that builds bridges of friendship. And they can open to those so often missed by normal evangelism new avenues of exposure to God's message of love. Urban teenagers with a fourth grade reading level or international students who have come with little exposure to English or newly resettled refugees from southeast Asia—all would qualify for such an important ministry. (For information on the Laubach program contact your local literacy council or Literacy International, Box 131, Syracuse, New York 13210.)

Opportunities to Reach Out Nearby

Reach out on campus. In some sense the American university contains the world in microcosm. Significant human barriers keep many students from clearly understanding or intelligently responding to Christ. In many cases, no Christians anywhere are actively reaching them because of these barriers. Unless someone, somewhere, gives them high priority they will study and graduate, tragically underexposed to the gospel.

Some of these groups and subcultures include minority ethnic groups (Chinese-American, Black-American and others); the lonely, depressed or disillusioned; the handicapped and chronically ill; those with alternative life-styles like drugs or homosexuality; and international students (see below). We must learn to fit our campus witness to each kind of person or group if we are to communicate God's love to them. The very same principles that missionaries follow in cross-cultural evangelism will be valuable in campus outreach. World evangelism insights can unlock local evangelism barriers.

As a former pastor of a university-related church, and currently active within a similar congregation next door (literally) to the University of Wisconsin, I can vouch for this: If you are in such a church the campus dimension of outreach is just as strategic in the evangelistic planning of your church members as it is for the students. And when we win students to Christ and send them out, our church actually touches the whole world through them. Over the years we can influence *hundreds* who scatter from our midst to the corners of the earth!

Inter-Varsity Press editor, Andy Le Peau, encourages all of us in *HIS Guide to Evangelism,* to discover a missionary-style vision for our campuses:

> Pray that God will instill in you a desire for penetrating the major areas of your campus—geographically, academically, and socially. Do you believe this is God's will for your [fellowship or church]? Do you then believe God is able to accomplish this through you? . . . each campus is different. So your discussion should begin by finding out what your campus is like. Ask, How many students are there and in what categories (grads, undergrads, majors)? Where are they located (dorms, frats, apartments)? What significant minorities are there? How many students have jobs?[1]

> Assume for the moment, that you have all the resources of time, people and money that you need. The key is to mold [your group] to the campus and so create the ideal "fellowship of evangelism" unit for your campus. Do not fool yourself into thinking you can make the campus fit your fellowship.[2]

A Christian group at Brooklyn College faced violence, prejudice, jealousy, and a great diversity of cultures in the early 1970s. In *The Impossible Community,* their faculty sponsor, Barbara Benjamin, tells how these students and laypeople brought the gospel to bear on campus politics, the struggles of minorities and the deterioration of the city. As the only integrated group on campus—the group members included people of Oriental, Irish, Turkish and German descent—they assumed a challenge of missionary proportions right on campus and saw God use them to reach far beyond their school.

Reach out in your neighborhood. Outside the university world live many types of unreached peoples who need our concerned witness. The 120 ethnic groupings in America provide many examples. So do the struggling families locked away in our often dehumanizing ghetto jungles. To these could be added the forgotten in our prisons, the isolated worlds of the deaf and blind, and the refugees from southeast Asia, Cuba, Mexico, El Salvador, and Russia arriving monthly. (Did you know, for example, that in 1983 we caught and sent back one million illegal aliens from Mexico alone? But hundreds of thousands made it. Who will care for them?)

Eventually, most outreach to the neighborhoods nearby will require a strategy for *urban* evangelism. To Roger Greenway, missionary to urban centers in Latin America, there could be no more important challenge for any of us:

As the cities go, our world goes, intellectually, politically, economically, morally, religiously, and ecclesiastically. For this reason, cities must be regarded as the modern frontiers of Christian missions and they must be given high priority in terms of strategy and the assignment of resources. If we fail to win the cities, we shall have failed indeed.[3]

In *The Golden Cow,* however, John White cautions that such a vision could be costly to those sealed up in "middle-class religious ghettos" as much as to a missionary who travels into forbidden jungle interior. He believes our dress, our hair styles, our customs, our church buildings—all raise impenetrable psychological and cultural barriers that effectively keep us from seeing the unreached around us and at the same time, keep them from ever seeking us out. To change this will take sacrifice on our part.

His words are so pertinent we need to hear him out:

There are quite a few churches like yours in lower-middle class and middle-class sectors in your city. What is going on among the poor? Among the recent immigrants? Among the motley international groups of newcomers struggling to gain a foothold on the lower end of the economic ladder? Do we relegate them all to the ministries of the nineteenth-century downtown missions? Or do we take some responsibility ourselves? . . .

So what should we do? I can think of two suggestions. The first would be for the leadership of the church to meet and prayerfully consider the church's responsibilities to neglected areas such as those I have mentioned. Surely God could place a burden on someone's heart for them. Could there not be a prayerful laying on of hands of some who are called to minister elsewhere? To research specific areas and talk to those who know about them? To raise autonomous home fellowships? The Church of the Redeemer in Houston is only one of many possible models.

My second suggestion . . . Churches should rethink priorities. Can downtown facilities be rented for public meetings? Can home study groups become heavenly leaven changing the nature of the core area? Can imaginative schemes be thought up to attract the youth of the area? If so, let your congregation divide. Let those who feel comfortable in your present facility stay there. Let the rest move out to reach the down-trodden . . .

As for our private wealth and our lovely homes, there are many things we can do. We can see that the "guest room" has a higher occupancy rate. We can set up a church organization through which a distress-alert system brings us the abandoned wives and other temporarily distressed person so that they can find their feet and start life anew themselves. We can invite such needy souls not as guests to whom we show gracious hospitality but as full members of the family who share its joys, its sorrows, its prayers, its celebrations and its day-to-day tasks. Our carpets will get worn faster. Our chesterfields will begin to sag sooner. Our favorite records will get scratched. But since when were we called to live for carpets, chesterfields and stereos?[4]

One resource to help you in urban ministry is World Impact, Inc. A resource for ministry to refugeees is the World Relief Commission of the National Association of Evangelicals. A disciplining work begun by former White House advisor Chuck Colson can help you reach out to prison inmates: Prison Fellowship, Box 40562, Washington, D.C. 20016.

Reach out to international visitors. One way to fulfill Christ's global cause with results that reach around the earth awaits those who enter into friendship evangelism with international visitors, of which there are five million total. Almost three hundred thousand are foreign students. Many will occupy top positions of government and industry in their homelands, making major decisions that will affect both world affairs and missionary activity within their country.

International Students, Inc., reminds us:

> Never in the history of the Christian church has a generation of Christians had a greater opportunity to reach the nations of the world than we in America have today. Can we consistently claim that we are concerned about world evangelism when we are largely ignoring the transplanted foreign mission field which God has brought to us?

Often the International represents a people-group for whom the Gap is still very wide or where missionaries are presently not allowed to enter. To love that International for Christ's sake is to also love the families and villages to which he will return. Since the friendship could last a lifetime, you can continue to span the Gap for your new friend, long after he or she returns home, through letters and even by personal visits.

For more information on principles and resources in this ministry write to the Association of Christian Ministries to Internationals, 233 Langdon, Madison, WI 53703, or contact International Students, Inc. for a list of their staff and training materials.

Think of it this way: if one tenth of the five million international visitors in the United States were won to Christ and established as His disciples, we would see a mighty, witnessing army of five hundred thousand going to the unreached peoples of the world every year. And, what if just one of those were like an Apostle Paul for their culture-group? World evangelization could be fulfilled in our generation!

Reach out to the nations through evangelism and discipleship among your own kind of people. Every time we share Christ with those most like ourselves, who may very well be familiar with the gospel, we again open the opportunity for God's Spirit to call out more laborers for the harvest at the ends of the earth. When people come to Christ within a climate of concern for Christ's global cause, they will be more willing to move out immediately as World Christians.

A World Christian will *evangelize* those like himself in such a way that the global thrust of God's saving purpose is clearly in view for them. For example, in a four-week evangelistic Bible study you might use facts from the past and present world missionary movement to illustrate key Bible truths you're asking inquirers to believe. What God is presently doing in Korea or Uganda or Russia is simply more "evidence that demands a verdict."

Furthermore, when those who know us best observe how willing we are to love people quite different from us and more difficult to approach, our friends may take a second look at the message they have treated so lightly. World evangelism can unlock new understandings of the gospel locally.

The same perspective must be present in our *discipling* of a new Christian. Help that person to see the end of all you're teaching him, which is to stand more effectively in the Gap, especially at its widest part. Right now teach him how to study Scriptures and pray with a world dimension. Right now begin to sensitize her to the Hidden People around her and those in other nations. As you teach them how to discover God's will for their lives, disciple them into a vision of their own world-sized part in Christ and help them to weigh all other decisions in that light. By doing such things, you will provide God's Spirit receptive hearts to hear His call to stand in the Gap. You will be reaching out in love to the unreached *through* those you win to Christ and disciple into World Christians.

At your earliest convenience, make a list of ten non-Christians and ten Christians around you with whom you have a meaningful friendship. For each one, ask yourself:

1. How could the world vision I've caught and kept move them more toward Christ or toward understanding the fuller implications of following Him?
2. What specific dreams can I dream about how God might reach out to the ends of the earth through each one, if I win

them to Christ and disciple them with a World Christian perspective?

3. Do any of their interests, experiences or backgrounds indicate the kind of people-group God might choose to love through them?—that, in fact, *I* could love through them?

Reach Out Through a Project for Missions

There is no end to opportunities to financially support specific missions projects. Some projects might originate with a particular missions organization. For example, Africa Inland Mission might need a land rover for a ministry in Kenya. Other projects may result from the individual efforts of Christians who take the initiative. For example, a church may decide to send relief supplies to a disaster area in India and contact a sister church in Andrha Pradesh to distribute the goods.

Whatever your project, ask some tough-minded questions:

• Will the organization use your funds *responsibly* and *efficiently?* Have you taken a good look, for example, at their yearly financial report to see how much of each dollar goes into overhead? (Be sure you understand their definition of overhead.)

• Will your funds be used in an *effective* way? For example, will it really help people to develop on their own or just make them more dependent on Western Christians? Again, will the project have an impact for Christ's sake on some of the world's unreached peoples or only serve existing Christians and churches? Would you classify the project "effective" if it doesn't ultimately help plant the church among the people it ministers to?

• What is the *real (total)* cost of reaching these people, beyond the cost of this one project? What else will need to be funded to make sure *this* project counts strategically toward this goal?

• How will you and your team *raise the funds* you give to this project? How will you look to God to supply your funds? What sacrifices will you be willing to make?

• What are the *long-term* financial commitments this project may require of you? Can you stick with it over a longer period? Can others be recruited to help share in the financial demands?

Samples of Possible Projects

1. Help fund the missionary work of a Third-World church organization or missionary society (although some want to avoid outside funds). Write directly to those listed in World Vision International's *World Christianity Profiles* or in their book *Asian Missionary Societies*. Also, contact Christian Nationals Evangelism Commission.

2. Get involved in hunger relief programs, especially those that combine Christ's saving love for the body and the soul. Among those that do this: Bread for the World, Food for the Hungry, World Relief Commission of the National Association of Evangelicals, World Concern, Inc., MAP International, and World Vision, International.

3. Work with a local church to fund the resettlement of a refugee family in your city. These programs usually last a full year demanding a large financial commitment from an entire congregation. But every dollar helps. And, with the program come opportunities to help the families on many other levels.

4. Support a homeless or destitute child in another part of the world through an evangelical child-sponsorship program such as those of World Vision or Compassion, Inc., and provide them food, clothing, shelter, education. You can also exchange letters and send gifts for special occasions.

5. Help support Christians living under oppression or deprivation, and thus strengthen their witness where they live. One example of this would be support of Ugandan Christians through African Enterprise, 200 North Lake Avenue, Pasadena, CA 91101.

6. Look for projects suggested in the periodicals of mission societies. Or write them asking for particular concerns or needs of the people-groups which interest you.

7. Discuss the possibility of supporting a project with a missionary who visits with you. Find out how you can support some effort he is making in evangelism right now. Ask the same questions by letter to a missionary you know on the field.

8. Give your support to groups or congressional representatives who actively promote human rights, especially where

such support could affect the welfare of unreached people for whom you are praying or when pressure on dehumanizing regimes might stimulate a new degree of religious freedom in an unevangelized country. (Pressure brought on the Indian government in 1979, for example, by Christians inside and outside the country, helped defeat an "anti-conversion" bill in the Parliament.)

9. Contribute to training centers, seminaries, and centers of missionary research to help prepare a future generation of missionaries and develop more effective missionary strategy. Examples: the U.S. Center for World Mission in Pasadena, California; Missionary Internship in Farmington, Michigan; Columbia Graduate School of Bible and Mission in Columbia, South Carolina; and Trinity School of World Missions, Deerfield, Illinois. There are others.

10. Join the effort to place a Bible in their own language into the hands of each person listed in every phone directory in the world. Contact Bibles for the World, P.O. Box 805, Wheaton, Illinois.

Reach Out Through a Team-Extension Mission

A team of World Christians can relocate their witness by sending out one or more of their members across geographical, cultural, and national barriers. By such a mission your team will become more accountable for the real needs of people, as well as find opportunities to get meaningfully involved at the heart of missionary outreach.

Normally the whole team won't be able to "go over there" together, although this has happened before and is always a possibility. But in another sense, whenever some of your members go out the whole team goes with them. You share together in your faith, dreams, plans, preparations, sacrifices and prayers. For a time your team becomes a *"here-there community."* Although you are still one team, certain members are "there" while the base of sending members are "here." In some ways a Team-Extension Mission concept parallels the dynamics of a family. Even when the children leave home they are still a vital part of the family unit and an extension of what that family is all about.

Team-Extension Mission differs in some significant ways from the missionary-sending process of most local churches:

- The whole group is equally called into a particular mission, not just those who physically go as "missionaries."
- Much of what the "sent ones" are able to give in another culture comes directly out of the shared life and love that the team has found together in Christ.
- The "senders" have a vested interest in the entire mission that goes far beyond financial support. Sending holds equal importance to going, and requires equal amounts of commitment, faithfulness, and personal sacrifice.

How Might a Team-Extension Mission Develop?

It may start when one of your team relocates in some other part of the Gap through a Junior Year Abroad study program, a summer job or temporary employment overseas; a short-term missionary experience; a long-term missionary assignment; the purchase of a house within an ethnic or urban center in the U.S. Or you could invite a new member onto your team, such as a career missionary home on furlough or a Christian international visitor. In both cases the mission work or country to which they return as Christ's witness can become the concern of the whole team.

To move out on any of these possibilities, consider some of the resources:

- *You Can So Get There from Here,* a workbook and catalog of many Christian and secular organizations to help you get among the unreached. Available through World Vision International.
- Arthur Fromer's *Whole World Handbook* on summer employment overseas, published by Simon and Schuster.
- *The Overseas List:* Opportunities for Living and Working in Developing Countries, by Beckmann and Donnelly. Augsburg Publishers, 1979.
- Overseas Counselling Service, a computer service on longer-term secular employment overseas, 1605 Elizabeth St., Pasadena, CA 91104.
- Inter-Cristo Inter-Match, with thirty thousand full-time Christian job openings, thirteen thousand of them in other coun-

tries. Call toll-free 1-800-426-0507.

- Inter-Varsity's short-term missionary opportunities such as Overseas Training Camp and Student Training in Missions. Also Campus Crusade for Christ's Agape Movement and International Summer Projects.
- The short-term training and sending ministries of Operation Mobilization (Box 148, Midland Park, NJ 07432) and Youth with a Mission (YWAM), P.O. Box 4600, Tyler, TX 75712.
- *Summer Missions Opportunities,* a catalog updated yearly by the Student Missionary Union at Biola College, 13800 Biola Avenue, La Mirada, CA 90639.
- *Short Term Missionary Manual* available through the Association of Church Missions Committees, P.O. Box ACMC, Wheaton, IL 60187
- Voice of Calvary Ministries in Mississippi and Trinity Christian Community in New Orleans with summer opportunities for work among American Blacks in either rural or urban settings.
- The Southern Baptists' effective church-planting work among U.S. ethnic minorities. Write about their Language Evangelism Projects, 1350 Spring Street, Atlanta, GA. Or, contact your own denomination for information on similar programs.
- Write for information on career missionary opportunities with any of the Protestant missionary societies listed in World Vision's *Mission Handbook.*

How Might a Team Extension Mission Be Put Together?

1. God has captured the team's heart for a specific unreached people-group.
2. So, you pray together about how to follow through on this concern.
3. As you pray you begin to do some research about the people and about what it would take to send a Christian witness to them.
4. With facts in hand your team begins to dream about what might actually happen. You develop a tentative strategy.
5. Eventually certain members of your team feel called by God to be the "team extension." The whole team evaluates and confirms this call.
6. Your whole team participates in the preparations for going.

They share with the extension members in all they must do.

7. You initiate your mission through prayer for your target people-group long before anyone has been sent to them. You enlist other Christians to pray with you.

8. During all this you are developing a deeper life together as a team. One special concern is for those who will go out. Since they will face unique stresses and complex barriers, they must be as spiritually strong as possible.

9. Throughout, the entire team assumes active responsibility for raising the necessary funds to send their extension members.

10. Finally the time comes to send out the extension members. You might hold a "commission service" with others from outside your team attending.

11. Sending-members commit themselves to faithful, daily prayer.

12. Sending-members couple their prayers with regular correspondence with those who go.

13. Extension-members carry out the mission God has given your team.

14. Your extension-members keep the team informed as the mission unfolds.

15. When the mission has progressed sufficiently, extension-members may return to report all that God has done through the team's mission.

16. The team shares these results with other Christians to give God praise and to inspire others to try the same kind of approach.

17. The team evaluates its next steps: "What shall we do next in the Gap together, Lord?"

For more help on this scenario write for Inter-Varsity's *Setting Dreams Free:* How to Have a Team Extension Mission. Also, one of three different training packages in the *World Christian Video Training Curriculum* concentrates specifically on team-extension missions. Write Gospel Light Publications for information on *Coverage: Becoming Teams of World Christians.*

Prepare for Future Outreach As an Act of Love
Right now we should be preparing ourselves for a lifetime in

the Gap. Such preparation should be going on during all our other attempts to reach out. Preparation for the future is as much an act of love now as anything else we do. Here are some examples.

All we do now to *grow as disciples* can prepare us to count more significantly as parts of a sending/going team in the coming decades of missionary outreach. Fortunately the evangelical church in America is abundantly blessed with opportunities for such preparation through local churches, campus movements, literature, large numbers of training events. The question is not, Should we take advantage of these? Rather, it is, Can we justify all our group and church activities by their influence on our growth and preparation as Christ's disciples for future involvement in the cause? For example, if you are in a Sunday School class, or Bible study, ask yourself: "How do our weekly training programs help me catch, keep, or obey a world vision? How could I modify my approach to the training so that it helps me grow as a World Christian and prepares me for future outreach in wider parts of the Gap?"

Life-style is also involved in preparing for the future. We must learn how to simplify our patterns of consumption and spending so that we release more and more of our material resources into the cause. At the same time this will strengthen the credibility of our love before a watching world. God is calling us to begin to love Him and the nations enough to put people above possessions. We need a life-style conducive to His worldwide intentions. This will prepare us for significant involvement in the Gap for years to come.

To improve your outreach in the future you might consider how you answer these life-style questions right now:
- What most determines my sense of "needs?"—TV? career? status? peers? or Christ's global cause and the needs of unreached people?
- Is my life-style shaped by a desire for more—more possessions, more happiness, more power? Or is it shaped by a desire for increased personal freedom and availability of resources in order to serve the world's unreached?
- What are the excesses in my life? What do I have too much of right now? Where do I presently squander, waste, or overin-

dulge? How will this affect further outreach to the ends of the earth?

- Should my involvement in the cause right now be from surplus or from sacrifice? How might future involvement in the cause be affected by my approach on this?

- Out of my 168 hours a week, can I justify the overall allotment of my time in light of Christ's global cause? What specific time commitments need to be cut back in order to prepare me for increased future outreach? Are there places my investments of time should be rechanneled right now?

- Of the decisions I am making right now which ones will have a lasting impact on how involved I am in worldwide outreach in the future? Which decisions might increase my effectiveness over what it is now? How should love for the unreached guide my choices, such as where to live, whom to marry, what profession to pursue, new friendships to seek, purchases, prayer and Bible reading habits, service on a church committee, family size, magazine subscriptions, or Christian conferences I attend?

One group developing a life-style for the future is the Order for World Evangelization, 1605 E. Elizabeth St., Pasadena, CA 91104. They offer a course that helps you build your world vision while guiding your efforts to scale down spending patterns. Another group, the Bethany Fellowship, is a missionary community of families and students-in-training. They have supported missionaries from their own midst by their simplified life-style, community sharing, and by community-run industries since 1947. Over the years they have been directly responsible for reaching thousands of unreached people around the globe. To learn about their story and how it can help you, write them at 6820 Auto Club Road, Minneapolis, MN 55438.

In addition, *Recovery* and *Breakthrough* of the World Christian Video Training Curriculum (Gospel Light Publications) lay a major stress on various aspects of life-style development. Explore these with other budding World Christians, and then help each other remain faithful to the changes you decide to make.

Finally, prepare for future outreach as you *explore the possibility of a longer-term cross-cultural involvement for yourself.*

Ruth Siemens of the Overseas Counselling Service has discovered there's not a career or a college major that can't, with some adjustments, be used in another culture. And, as already noted, thousands of openings for career missionary work wait to be filled around the world right now, with new openings every day. If you are serious about loving the "ends of the earth" you must love them enough to investigate whether you should live and minister among them. How do you do this?

Remain an active member of a team of World Christians. Depend on people like them, who are closest to you and share your vision, to give you counsel and to stand with you in your praying and searching. Continue to survey the world's needs and to work in the Gap with an eye to how you might fit in by serving the cause in another culture.

Furthermore, every World Christian should touch base with missionary societies, reading their literature, talking with their representatives and even visiting their headquarters. World Christians should explore the openings personalized for them through the Inter-Cristo Computer Matching Service and the matching helps of Overseas Counseling Service (addresses for both in Appendix III). Try to imagine yourself serving Christ through some of these careers. Along with this, take inventory of your own strengths and weaknesses in ministry, evaluating what hearing this might have on future career options in missions.

At Fuller Theological Seminary, Pasadena, CA 91101, Drs. Tom and Betty Sue Brewster have packaged their years of effective training in language learning into a ten-part series of one-hour video cassettes with student workbooks. Their intention is to help convince the timid missionary-to-be that he or she *can* learn a language, any language. The Brewsters believe that the fear of languages is one of the major hurdles any of us face as we seek additional preparation for reaching out. Now you can conquer this fear in your own home. Write to the Fuller School of World Mission for information on the Language Acquisition Video Training Series.

Would you like another map through the maze of getting "from here to there"? Sometimes a clearly marked pathway is all it takes to get us moving. Well, World Vision International has done the hard work for you! Highlighting for you, blow by blow, every phase of missions preparation from exploring options to fruitful ministry in another culture, *You Can So Get There from Here* is a one-of-a-kind self-counseling tool. Write them for it.

Of course, at some point you should "test-drive" your present cross-cultural skills through a short-term experience, either nearby or in another country. Twenty-five percent of all short-term missionaries actually become career missionaries. View this experience both for what you can give through it and for what it can teach you about God's future intention for your life.

Notes
1. Andy Le Peau, *HIS Guide to Evangelism*, p. 126.
2. Ibid., p. 128.
3. Roger Greenway, Guidelines for Urban Church Planning (Grand Rapids: Baker Book House, 1976), p. 6.
4. John White, *The Golden Cow* (Downers Grove, IL: Inter-Varsity Press, 1979), pp. 84-86.

17

A PLAN: OBEY AS YOU *GIVE* YOUR VISION TO OTHER CHRISTIANS

KEY QUESTION: Am I transferring my vision to other Christians? Am I seeking more World Christians to stand in the Gap and serve the cause?

External barriers aren't the only ones hindering the fulfillment of the Great Commission. Barriers within the Church may be just as critical. Along with cultural, linguistic, and political barriers, we face internal barriers of provincialism and self-centeredness that afflict so many. When *any* Christian's perspective and life-directions revolve around pea-sized concerns, less will happen for Christ's global cause than might have otherwise. Christians must be alerted to the thousands of mission opportunities awaiting their personal involvement right now. Only then can we hope to close the Gap in our generation.

Your team can awaken others who are sleeping through the greatest missionary advance of all times and help get the whole Body of Christ behind His cause. As you pass along discoveries from your own journey into World Christian discipleship, you can close the gap of unbelief and increase the total force involved in God's worldwide harvest.

Your team or church doesn't exist by accident, nor has God

brought you together primarily for fellowship and survival. You can be certain that His Spirit intends for you to grow around one overriding cause: to stand in the Gap. Based on that key premise, your team should actively seek to help fellow Christians discover, develop and fulfill your potential in Christ for a strategic impact on the nations. You should seek this for each person and for each small group within your church.

This means helping each individual person to:
- Catch a world vision of Christ's global cause
- Keep that vision at the center of their lives, and
- Obey that vision faithfully.

Your efforts with ongoing small groups should lead them to become another team of World Christians working on the basic plan for obeying the vision:
- Building the vision regularly
- Reaching out directly in love
- Giving the vision to other Christians.

A Model; A Catalyst; A Resource

Any attempt to give your vision to others involves your team in three major roles: You are a *model*—making the vision understandable and believable. You are a *catalyst*—making the vision inescapable and desirable. You are a *resource*—making the vision workable and manageable.

Give the vision as a model. Make a world vision understandable and believable. Set a quiet example before your group or church of what a World Christian is really up to. Without fanfare, carry through on your team's plan to obey your vision day by day. Slowly others will begin to realize that being a World Christian really "fits" today's Christian and his concerns, that it produces significant results and that it fulfills all we are meant to be.

Think of your team as a model of what every Christian and every small group should desire to be. You are not a specialized "missions fringe" within your group or church. Avoid this image at all costs. Instead, help others recognize you as a vanguard, setting an exciting pace in Christian living that everyone should want to follow.

Give the vision as a catalyst. Catalysts are motivators. Almost anyone can be motivated for World Christian concerns.

Once you are providing a good model you will have the right to take a more direct role in motivating fellow Christians to get into the mainstream of the cause. As catalysts, you create an environment in which others can also catch a world vision as you make it inescapable and desirable for them.

In this second role your team resembles a time-release capsule. Slowly you release into the bloodstream of your group or church facts and challenges concerning world missions. Along with the information, you also seek to persuade them to act in practical ways, to get a "feel" of what a World Christian is all about.

Give the vision as a resource. The more a group becomes pro-missions, the more it needs "mission-pros"! So in time, your team assumes a third role: resource. You make the World Christian experience workable and manageable for others.

A good resource needs to stay a few steps ahead of the pack. Your faithfulness to build your vision and to reach out in love will naturally equip you to serve in this capacity. As a resource your team should help others see the ways God is already touching the ends of the earth through them, so they can move out from there. Then help them develop new directions and plans for even further impact in the Gap. Train them to obey the vision through building it, reaching out, and giving it to others.

You may be a resource for a number of people: the leadership of your group or church, new World Christians and "almost" World Christians, small groups who want more of a World Christian dimension, and people investigating cross-cultural possibilities.

Key Questions to keep in mind. As you give a world vision to others by being a model, a catalyst, and a resource, refer to some of these key questions to develop an effective plan of action:

- When does a group or church become truly World Christian? How do we get from here to there?

- Which people in our group would be most open to the vision we want to give them? How could we best approach them right now: In personal conversations? Through special meetings or conferences? With literature? By inviting them to join in on our team and its activities?
- Are there enough budding World Christians in our group or church to form a new team?
- How many ongoing small groups would be open to a World Christian approach? Where would we have them begin?
- Who might surface as a potential cross-cultural worker? Who already has? How can we encourage them to follow through on this? Pray for and with them? Point them toward helpful literature? Make the group or church more aware of them and their dreams? Help them get related to a local church and a mission board? Help them find a short-term missions experience next summer? Get them involved with their own team of World Christians for support and growth?

Specific Ways to Be a Catalyst

Let's assume your team has become an active model of World Christian discipleship. You have consistently obeyed your vision, and you have sufficient rapport with your group or church so that they are free to watch you. Also, let's assume you're prepared to be a good resource to any who might respond. In fact, you're just waiting to teach others all you've learned.

The question remains: How can you be a catalyst? How can you alert fellow Christians to the Gap and to Christ's cause, and help them catch and keep the same vision that has changed your life?

1. Sponsor a World Christian Focus

A World Christian Focus is a "spot" (perhaps ten minutes long) included in every large group meeting. In my own church we do this on an average of twenty minutes a Sunday. During this spot, members are informed, stimulated, challenged, or trained on issues relating to the World Christian theme. The Focus keeps the world "out there" alive and real when people are buried under office deadlines and Visa bills, or personal struggles, or plain middle-class provincialism. A regular, creative, consciousness-raising approach like this will provide facts and attitudes by which God can lead them into deeper involvement in the Gap.

Consider the following suggestions for a *Focus* and then create new ideas of your own:

a. *Present a series on a particular unreached culture-group,* focusing one week on the country where they reside, the culture group itself the next, a typical family the third. Follow this on the fourth week with information on present opportunities for reaching them, the fifth week with information on outreach ministries available to your group or church, and the sixth week with a time of prayer for their evangelization.

b. *Evaluate the theme of a popular hymn or song.* Discuss how the verses might read if the theme were given more of a *world* dimension. Before the meeting, or together at the meeting, write new verses or change certain lines in the old verses so that the song illustrates this added dimension. Then, have your group sing the revised edition.

c. *Prepare and distribute a fact sheet* on a specific kind of outreach opportunity that anyone can get involved in. (Select from the ideas mentioned under chapter 16.) Explain how your listeners might begin to reach out, and offer them assistance. Lead in prayer for the people who might be reached in these ways.

d. *Maintain one missionary's visibility* before the group or church by presenting their prayer letter every time it comes. Ask the missionary to add some details for your group beyond what they might relate in a general letter. Prepare a fact sheet with separate columns on the missionary family, the culture group they are serving, the strategy they are now attempting, and their future plans. Then in each column list previous prayer requests, how they were answered, and the new requests for next month.

e. *Prepare a profile on a specific nation.* Have the larger group break into small groups to pray for the nation. Or have them brainstorm about strategies for reaching that nation for Christ.

f. *Prepare discussion sheets* with some of the questions most often raised about missions or on some of the misconceptions people hold about missions. Introduce these issues through creative skits or with a panel; then open for discussion.

g. *Ask a missionary to send a five-minute taped message* to your group along with ten to fifteen color slides. After the presentation, pray for the missionary and his work. After the meeting, ask group members to say a few words of encouragement on the tape, and return the cassette and slides to the missionary.

h. *Have an international student share* about his own culture group, his home life, and his needs as a visitor to the U.S. If possible, have him return the next week to share about his religion or philosophy of life and what it means to him.

i. *Show how to give a World Christian perspective to the news.* Challenge the group to look for hints of God's work around the world in their daily newspaper during the next week and return to share what they discover.

j. *Break the meeting into buzz groups* of five persons. Have each group do an inductive Bible study on a short passage that teaches the biblical basis of missions, such as those quoted in chapters 10 and 13. You might use the outline from chapter 15.

k. *Give your group a geography lesson.* Many Christians don't know where countries are located. As you teach them the "playing field" for the world missionary movement, they'll be more interested in the "game."

l. If someone from your group or church has been involved in another culture, *solicit a report on where they went,* whom they lived among, what spiritual needs they observed there, and what the experience meant to them personally. Perhaps someone is planning to travel to another culture. Ask them to share along the same lines, and to mention specific needs they have as they get ready to go.

m. *Add some new missions-related books* to your group or

church library. During the Focus, review one of the newest selections, urging members to borrow and read it. Make your book review creative, using pictures or skits or provocative statements.

n. *Many churches have found* Twenty-One Hundred's four fifteen-minute movies entitled *To Every People* to be uniquely powerful in a worship service. Each film vividly highlights one of the four major unreached-people blocks (Muslims, Hindus, Chinese, Tribals). Discussion questions are provided for interaction following each film. Or, you can simply conclude with five minutes of small-group prayer. More information is available: 233 Langdon, Madison, WI 53703.

Besides a World Christian Focus you can be a catalyst on a number of other fronts:

2. Infiltrate the Prayer Life of Your Bible Study Group or Church

This can happen either in large-group settings or in regularly scheduled prayer meetings. Your suggestions to pray for an unfamiliar part of the world may surprise some at first. Others will find world-sized praying awkward. But as you lead the way with information and personal example, you will change attitudes toward praying for the world beyond your group and may even change their attitudes toward personally reaching that world. Prayer with a world dimension could happen during family devotions, in a table grace, or at the end of a one-to-one discipling session with a new Christian. (Review the section on prayer in chapter 16 for more ideas and resources.)

3. Sponsor Special World-Related Events

It might be a World Awareness Breakfast every other Saturday morning. Or you might teach a Sunday School elective on the World Christian theme using a book like *In The Gap* as a guide. You could sponsor a weekend seminar or retreat (using one of Gospel Light's World Christian Video Training packages). You might set up regular prayer cells for specific parts of the world. Try taking some friends along with you for an urban experience, visiting people in a specific cultural enclave. You might sponsor an International Dinner once a month where you gather friends from your group and church to eat with you and some of your international student friends, letting the Internationals cook the meal while you provide the supplies. Of course, every three years you can help students get to Inter-Varsity's Urbana student missions convention, as well as the Urbana Onward conferences that follow in February. Or you can take church people to the annual National Conference of the Association of Church Missions Committees, where you will share and learn about missions and mission mobilization in an inter-denominational setting.

4. Invite Missionaries on Board

Make missionaries available to church meetings, to lead small-group Bible studies, to visit with families over dinner, or to give counsel in a one-to-one setting. Have them relate to your friends their own insights into spiritual growth and victory learned in active missionary involvement. Have them share as well about issues that pertain to world missions in general and to their field of work specifically. Be sure your team takes active responsibility to set up the schedule and appointments before your missionary guest arrives.

5. Work Directly with Existing Small Group Structures

Prepare inductive Bible studies on key world mission passages that the small groups can use during a special month of emphasis. (Write for Inter-Varsity's *How To Create World Christian Bible Studies*.) Or give a taste of involvement in world missions by having each small group suggest one kind of missions project for six months. If someone from your church or group is going into a cross-cultural ministry, ask a small group to take interest in that person through prayer and encouragement. Also, you might suggest that a small group take charge of a World Christian Focus once they've learned how to do it by watching you. Finally, most of the ideas for motivating and informing listed above under "World Christian Focus" can be applied at the small group level with positive results.

6. Operate a World Christian Book Table

Once a month set up a table where your group or Sunday

School class meets. Make it attractive. Creatively spotlight some of the best books during announcements. Order books directly from publishers, a local Christian bookstore or from the Global Church Growth Book Club (see Appendix III). Along the same line, when you prepare World Christian fact sheets for distribution during a large-group meeting, mention one good book on your booktable that will help them follow up the information on the sheet (as we've done here in chapters 10-13).

7. Coordinate with Other Teams of World Christians

As you discover other groups involved in the same issues you are, trade ideas around or actually share with each other's group or church. This will help other Christians learn there are many concerned with being World Christians, and it will provide you new approaches to giving the vision. Send a team from one group to lead the weekly large-group meeting in a nearby church, for example.

As mentioned already, one such coordinating effort for local churches is the Association of Church Missions Committees, whose motto is "Churches Helping Churches in Missions." In this unique movement World Christians from various denominations in churches large and small share information and experiences that can help motivate the local church. They do this through area seminars like "The Local Church Can Change the World" to which pastors, missions committees, and laypeople alike are invited. ACMC has also developed a *Missions Policy Handbook* and a *Missions Education Handbook* based on tried and proven insights from local church missions committees.

8. Use the "World Christian Decision Card"

A sample is found in chapter 14. It will help those who have caught the vision to take the next step toward World Christian discipleship. Periodically (maybe once a year) you may want to distribute the card to those for whom you have been a catalyst. You can do this in a one-to-one setting over coffee or in a meeting with a small group or as part of a large-group program.

Before you challenge them with the card, however, be sure they have had sufficient opportunity to understand the life-changing implications of World Christian discipleship. Do they have a sense of God's purpose, of the possibilities, the people, and of their own part? Do they understand what's involved in the decision to keep a world vision? Have they considered the scope of the plan they will pursue once they have made the decision to become a World Christian? You may need to review these matters with them before they pray about signing the card.

One appropriate tool for doing this is the *World Christian Checkup*, available from Inter-Varsity. It is fun to fill out in a group and will help everyone get a new perspective on the World Christian approach, and how far they've developed in it. Based on feedback from this thirty-minute "game" you will know how and when to lead your friends toward a more solid World Christian decision. In fact, they will be able to tell you!

World Christian Checkup

The card and *Checkup* provide excellent ways to help you identify those who are willing to move ahead. Once you find them you can better serve as a resource to them.

Where have we come now in the third step of our journey? Here's an overview:

1. *Obey as you regularly build your vision*
   Through Bible study with a world dimension
   Through other vision builders:
      a world map
      key books on missions
      key missions periodicals
      secular periodicals with international perspective
      world missions updates
      world-related and missions-related courses
      missions conferences
      missionaries
      Christian international visitors
      field trips
      group study guide for *In the Gap*
2. *Obey as you reach out directly in love*
   Through prayer
   To a Hidden People
   To the unreached nearby
   Through a project for missions

Through a Team-Extension Mission
Through preparation for future outreach
3. *Obey as you give your vision to other Christians*
   As a model
   As a catalyst
   As a resource
   Through:
   > a World Christian Focus
   > the prayer life of your group or church
   > special world-related events
   > missionaries or international visitors
   > direct work with existing small groups
   > a World Christian booktable
   > coordinated efforts with other teams of World Christians
   > the "World Christian Decision Card"

See how easy it can be to say at the end of each day, "I know *this* day my life has counted strategically for Christ's global cause, especially for those currently beyond the reach of the gospel"? Where would you like to begin?

18

A CLOSING PARABLE: SMOG

That's the plan: Build the vision regularly, reach out directly in love and give the vision to other Christians.

We come now to the end of this introductory volume on World Christian discipleship. Let's wrap up by summarizing all that a World Christian is and does with one more story:

Once upon a time there stood a startling geographical wonder. The San Gabriel Mountains, they called it. As much as the football game itself, these mountains impressed millions of sports fans everywhere during the January First televising of the Rose Bowl from Pasadena, California. How gorgeous they were! So royal!

The San Gabriel Mountains ruled over the San Gabriel Valley. Here thousands of local natives went about their daily tasks—watering lawns, driving trucks, writing term papers, eating Big Macs, selling shoes . . . and planning future Rose Bowl games.

Every once in a while, however, the natives just *had* to look up and draw in a glimpse of those towering rulers. How it made their spirits soar! In a moment, living itself seemed more grand, more majestic, even during their everyday routines.

But a mysterious spell hung over the Valley. Periodically, a brownish mist (evidently some witches' brew) shrouded it unmercifully. This mist had the power to actually make the mountains disappear! In September, for example, they might vanish for a week at a time. Down in the Valley, everyone's horizon rose no higher than the tallest office building. And the mountain climbers in the foothills simply got lost. Nothing seemed to go right without that refreshing, exhilarating vision of the peerless peaks. Truly a sad state of affairs.

But lo! The spell worked another ghastly ill. The trucker, the student, the shoeman, the climber—everyone, in fact, was forced to cough and wheeze as they trudged through their routines. Many people cowered indoors, barely daring to breathe.

The Valley natives cursed the potion, calling it "Smog." It blinded. It suffocated. There seemed to be no relief, except to cry out, "Curses on that wicked witch!"

And so it is that in every generation the *world mission* of Christ's disciples faces the threat of a similarly blinding, suffocating haze. Whenever Christians turn away from the world, things soon end up like the air trapped in the Los Angeles basin. We become small-minded . . . self-centered . . . picky . . . schismatic . . . obese . . . lost. History bears us witness: boxed up spirituality turns stale fast. No outlet means no uplift!

Under this spell Christians eventually go *blind*: blind to God's worldwide purpose in Christ; blind to the world full of possibilities for serving it right now; blind to the world full of people without any knowledge of Christ; blind to the Church's world-sized part in reaching the world for Christ.

What's more, under this spell Christians eventually *suffocate:* unable to build a clear vision of all that Christ's global cause should mean to them; unable to become rescue teams sent out into the canyons of the world with a life-giving mission to those trapped and dying there, especially those whom most other Christians have forgotten; unable to resuscitate asphyxiated disciples, giving them a fresh vision of where Christ is going and of how they can go forth with Him.

One day the ancient Santa Ana winds rose up. Boundless! Breaking the spell, flushing the smog from the Valley, restoring sparkle to the mountains and oxygen to the natives.

Again the stars studded the night sky. Again the robins returned to sing. The natives rejoiced. And throughout the mountain ravines the trapped and dying were rescued. What a glad, glad ending!

Similarly, Christians can escape the sorcery of self-centeredness. Like a mighty wind the Spirit of God can reverse the introverted patterns in our discipleship. He can uncover for us a crystal view of God's majestic horizons—Christ's global cause. He can inject the grandeur of the Eternal Mountains into all our efforts down in the Valley, wherever God places us and whatever He assigns us to do. He can fill the lungs of our souls with His Breath, so that we'll have the strength and vitality to rescue the perishing everywhere.

God's Holy Wind can free us to move out, breathing deeply and seeing clearly. No blindness. No gasping. Released to be all we were meant to be. Free to be World Christians.

Appendix I

A SMALL-GROUP STUDY GUIDE

When John transferred from the state university to a smaller liberal arts college, he came with one intention: "Someday, across this campus I hope to see a movement of World Christians." How quickly his dream stalled . . . in midair!

True, most of the student body made outward claims to faith in Christ. But John also encountered a baffling resistance to anything cloaked in "world missions." In a few weeks, his own enthusiasm for the subject practically relegated his name to the "lunatic fringe." John was in shock. He was ready to transfer again when he finally unearthed a few others who shared similar concerns: Bob, Dave, Mary, Steve, Patty, and Frank. To these friends he proposed: "For one month, let's meet to pray and discuss the uphill challenge of giving a world vision to our classmates." They agreed.

It was during one of these sessions John hit upon an idea so radical and yet so manageable it tingled with possibilities. It was based on an experience with his discipleship group back at the university. Intent on evangelizing their dorm, the men had devised a strategy which began with what they called "Jericho walks." Each day members of the study group would circulate down the hallways of the dorm. As they walked, they prayed silently for the students there, asking God to raise up an evangelistic Bible study on each floor by second semester. Later, they increased their efforts, extending invitations to students to attend a study offered in each hall. And, by the end of the year they thrilled at seeing many come to Christ.

"Why not do the same thing here?" John asked. "Why not infiltrate every floor of every dorm with a world vision until each student is able to make an intelligent response to the global cause of Christ?"

Quietly, they looked around the circle that afternoon. Every eye voted the same decision: this was precisely what they were to do. "Let's jot down suggestions," they said. During the next two hours a plan of action came together so clearly they were sure God was in it.

Here's what these visionaries designed. They too would begin daily "Jericho walks" around the outside of each dorm, no matter what the weather, to pray that students within would catch a larger vision. Next they would invite one key person on every dorm floor to be trained as World Christians and go back to start weekly prayer meetings for world evangelization. Using the ten week study guide for *In the Gap*, they would direct these prayer leaders into the glory, the urgency, and the practicality of Christ's global cause. From established prayer cells, others would be invited into additional "Gap Group" studies, multiplying World Christians on each floor.

Then, in late spring a special three-day, all campus emphasis on World Christian discipleship would bring a speaker to articulate to the larger campus community the World Christian concept. He would be joined by missionaries to interact with students on a personal level. Finally, their strategy would climax the year with a three-week, campus-wide movement of prayer for awakening. Using prepared agendas, everyone would pray for awakening on campus and in the church worldwide for the fulfillment of the Great Commission in this generation.

That was the plan. Did it work? You bet it did! God *was* in it. Eventually, prayer meetings sprung up on over sixty floors.

There were so many *In the Gap* studies going the Chaplain remarked: "It's the most read book on campus!" And, in the second semester the student body participated for three weeks in ten minutes of world-sized praying during regularly scheduled small groups and organizational meetings.

This same story can be replayed for your local church. Simply change "campus" to church, "dorms" to Sunday School classes or home Bible studies, and make the five students be members of your missions committee. Other churches have seen God work in similar ways to raise up World Christians in their congregations. He'll do it in your church too.

Here *In the Gap* is broken down into a manageable ten-week study for small groups interested in what it means to be a World Christian.

Each session lasts two hours to allow for adequate overview and discussion. Preceding the first session one person should be appointed as group facilitator. Hints to the facilitator are listed at the end of this Appendix.

Each session, except the first, follows the same format. This requires about one and a half hours of preparation before the study. A brief assignment is given each week to apply what the study uncovers.

Remember: This isn't intended to be exhaustive. *This is an overview,* designed to help you think more clearly about being a World Christian, and to prepare you for the "Personal Strategy Guide" in Appendix II.

Attention, group facilitator: Be sure to read over the hints listed on page 274 as you prepare to lead.

Ten Session Weekly Outline

1. World news update (10 minutes)

Group members share what they've learned the past week about world situations and events that affect Christ's global cause. Information might come from missionary prayer letters or mission agency magazines, or from newspapers, or television specials, or topics discussed with friends in church. Be sure to have a world map handy to locate where the updates take place.

2. The world in the word (15 minutes)

After the Scripture is read out loud, it is discussed along two lines: (1) What can we learn from this passage about the scope and concerns of Christ's global cause (5 min.)? (2) What can we learn from this passage about how *we* are involved in Christ's global cause (5 min.)?

Note: This is not the time for in-depth inductive Bible study. That can be tackled after the ten weeks (see Appendix IV).

The recommended passages are:

Week 1—See Appendix IV
Week 2—Colossians 1:15-29
Week 3—Psalms 96 and 98
Week 4—Revelation 4 and 5
Week 5—Isaiah 49:1-13
Week 6—Micah 4
Week 7—Haggai 1:1—2:9
Week 8—Romans 15:7-24
Week 9—Zechariah 9:1-13
Week 10—John 12:12-33

3. Praise and prayer (10 minutes)

Based on what you discover through the update and the Scripture, praise God for specific ways His glory is revealed through Christ's global cause. Then, intercede for (1) world mission needs right now, (2) your own personal involvement in the cause, and (3) the Gap study session you are now in.

4. In the gap: review and discussion (70 minutes)

Follow the week-by-week outline below.

5. In the gap: application for this week (10 minutes)

Follow the week-by-week outline below.

6. Closing prayer (5 minutes)

Pray about issues raised in your discussions and ask for God's help to apply what you have learned.

Outline for Discussion and Application

Week one—Based on *From One Egg to Another* **(to be read beforehand)**

I. World Christian warm-up (40 minutes [replaces World News Update])

Most of session one is designed to help your small group get to know one another. Open in prayer. Then, for the first 40 minutes discuss the following questions (keeping your comments *as brief as possible*):

- What are you asking God to do for you during these ten weeks together?
- When did you first become aware that God's concern was global in scope? Under what circumstances?
- When and how did you first meet a missionary?
- When and how did you first meet someone from another culture or another country?
- Prior to these studies, what has been your biggest hang-up about the world missionary movement?
- Prior to these studies, did you have any dreams or plans for the future that carried worldwide implications?
- Prior to these studies, did your small group or church have any dreams or plans for the future that carried world-wide implications?

II. The world in the word (30 minutes)

Discussion
1. How extensive a list can you develop of biblical passages that teach about God's world? For the next 10 minutes brainstorm together and record key passages you can think of.
2. What does your list tell you about your grasp of Scripture? What does it tell you about Scripture's grasp of God's world-wide purpose? What next steps might this brainstorming experience lead you to take? Take 5 minutes to talk this over.
3. Turn to Appendix IV. Divide your group into two parts and

read responsively to each other the 66 passages under "The Global Thread Through Scripture."

III. Gap preview (10 minutes [replaces Prayer and Praise])

For the next 10 minutes the facilitator will guide you in an overview of the table of contents, and then highlight the procedure for the remaining nine sessions of the small group study. Conclude the preview with this question: "Do we agree together to participate in this study enthusiastically and responsibly, including the between session readings and application projects?"

IV. Introduction discussion (30 minutes [replaces Review and Discussion])

In the opening pages, *From One Egg to Another,* Bryant hits at questions and issues that often arise early on in a small-group study of *In the Gap.* Hearing his readers, he presents initial answers to the questions they ask:

- Is Bryant's World Christian concept biblical?
- Where does Christ fit into all of this for him?
- Does he simply equate Christ's global cause with the modern missionary movement?
- How will his book be practical for solid Christian growth?
- Where did the ideas in the book come from anyway?
- What promise is there that it might be helpful for me to study his book?

For the next 30 minutes, discuss Bryant's answers to each of these questions, and share your reactions to what he says.

V. Closing prayer (10 minutes)

Conclude by reading in unison the prayer at the end of *From One Egg to Another,* "Overheard in the Gap." Then have one or two lead in prayer for the remaining nine sessions.

Application for this week

1. Read chapters 1-3.
2. See how many more passages you can find on God's worldwide purpose in addition to those you listed in the first session. Bring the list with you to Session Two.

Week two—Based on chapters 1-3 (to be read beforehand)

Review
1. Share with the group the total of additional passages each of you found this past week.
2. Give the *reference* of the one passage that meant the most to you. And in *one sentence* tell why.

Discussion
1. How does Bryant define the term *Gap* (chapter 1)?
2. What illustrations does he give of this Gap? What illustrations have you seen of it?
3. Why does Bryant maintain hope in the face of the Gap?
4. What is the greatest gap of all and how does Bryant see it often expressed (chapter 2)?
5. Why does Bryant believe it exists? Can you think of other reasons?
6. What evidence do you see of "pea-sized Christianity" in yourself or in other Christians around you?
7. In the face of the gap of opportunity, what response does Bryant call for from the church at large (chapter 3)?

Application for this week
1. Look around you for three other illustrations of the Gap. Also, look for three other illustrations of the Gap in other nations. Record this to share next time.
2. Identify and pray about one box of pea-sized Christianity in your life. Write down one specific step you might take during the next eight weeks to break out of that box. Bring your idea to share.
3. Read *In the Gap*, chapters 4, 5, and 6.

Week three—Based on chapters 4-6 (to be read beforehand)

Review
1. Share some of your illustrations of the Gap.
2. What was your box of pea-sized Christianity and what one specific step would you take to break out of it? What difference could this make in your life?

Discussion
1. What is Bill's real need and what solutions does Bryant provide (chapter 4)?
2. How does Bryant define Christ's global cause? Would you modify his definition?
3. How does Bryant answer Bill's four main objections? Are his answers adequate, in your opinion?
4. According to chapter 5, how can Christ's global cause create renewed health in
   prayer?
   Bible study?
   godliness?
   small groups?
   larger groups?
   outreach?
5. In one sentence, how would *you* define a World Christian (chapter 6)?
6. How would you answer some of the questions Bryant outlines to help you evaluate your progress in World Christian discipleship?

Application for this week
1. Select one of the areas of Christian discipleship in chapter 5 and work at giving it more of a *world* dimension—at making it healthier for you by relating it more to Christ's global cause. Observe what happens and record the results to share next time.
2. Read *In the Gap*, chapters 7, 8, and 9.

Week four—Based on chapters 7-9 (to be read beforehand)

Review
Share the results of putting more of a world dimension into some area of discipleship. How successful were you? Do you feel "healthier"? Why or why not? What more needs to happen?

Discussion
1. What are some examples of World Christians from the past as discussed in chapter 7?

2. What are some examples Bryant gives from the present? What other examples can you give?
3. How do you respond to either Graham's or Bryant's personal journeys into World Christian discipleship? Do you see any similar trends in your own life?
4. How does Bryant define a "Great Awakening" (chapter 8)?
5. Based on the analysis of Dr. Orr, and of Paul in Ephesians 1, how does Bryant expect to see a Great Awakening develop in our generation?
6. Why does he believe it might surface first in the student world?
7. How valid do you think his arguments are that the current mood of the student world is conducive to a new kind of Student Volunteer Movement?
8. Does the parable of the theater describe anything of your own experience with Christ (chapter 9)? How?
9. Does your group feel it is ready for the second section of *In the Gap*, a journey into World Christian discipleship? Why or why not?

Application for this week
1. Be on the lookout for one good example of a World Christian to describe briefly next time. How did he/she become a World Christian, and how is their World Christian commitment being expressed day by day?
2. Read *In the Gap*, chapters 10 and 11. Survey the "Reflection" questions at the end of each essay and mark two or three you would like to have the whole group discuss next time.

Week five—Based on chapters 10 and 11 (to be read beforehand)

Review
Describe for the group the one example of a World Christian you uncovered this past week. Was this example hard to find? Why or why not?

Discussion

This week's reading involves 20 brief essays with accompanying "Reflection" questions. Since you can't cover all this material in the allotted 70 minutes, there are two approaches you can take:

1. See if group members have come with specific reflection questions they want you to tackle with them.
2. If not, read through each "Reflection" section and pause to discuss those the group finds most applicable to their interests and concerns right now.

In either approach, be sure to allow time for discussion on both chapters.

Application for this week

1. In your daily devotions look for other biblical support on any of the areas outlined in chapter 10. Come next time prepared to share what you discover.
2. Look for three other illustrations of the kinds of possibilities outlined in chapter 11. Come prepared to share them.
3. Read *In the Gap*, chapters 12 and 13. Survey the "Reflection" questions at the end of each essay, and mark two or three you would like to have the whole group discuss next time.

Week six—Based on chapters 12 and 13 (to be read beforehand)

Review

Share from the past week discoveries and illustrations you uncovered on God's purpose and on the possibilities.

Discussion

Follow the same approach suggested for *Week Five* above.

Applications for this week

1. Look for three other illustrations of the many worlds in America. Come next time prepared to share them.
2. Look for three other illustrations of the Hidden People to share next time.

3. Complete the sentence: "My world-sized part is _____" and prepare to read it to the whole group.
4. Read *In the Gap,* chapter 15. Bring samples of resources and tools for some of the approaches suggested there. *Note:* We will return to chapter 14 the last week after we have made an overview of what a World Christian *does* in chapters 15, 16 and 17.

Week seven—Based on chapter 15 (to be read beforehand)

Review
1. Briefly describe one illustration you've found on the many worlds in America and on the Hidden People.
2. Have each person read without comment how they completed the sentence about their world-sized part.

Discussion
1. In what ways are you presently studying the cause? How are you letting your vision grow right now?
2. What are some aspects of a world vision that you would like to study? Why do you pick those areas?
3. Discuss the ways Bryant suggests for building a world vision. Have you brought samples of resources and tools for each approach? Share what you have.
4. How would you begin to build your vision if you set this as an important goal for the next six months? How might you do this together as a team? Discuss a plan of action.

Application for this week
1. Begin to build your vision one new way. Observe and record what you learn. Come next time prepared to share this.
2. Read *In the Gap,* chapter 16. Bring samples of resources and tools for some of the approaches suggested there.

Week eight—Based on chapter 16 (to be read beforehand)

Review
How did you try to build your vision last week and what did you learn?

Discussion
1. In what ways are you presently reaching out in love? How are you helping to reach the unreached at the widest end of the Gap right now?
2. How do you react to the six areas Bryant recommends for direct outreach in love? Could you see yourself involved in each of these areas? How? Could you see your team involved in each area? How? What modifications in Bryant's ideas would you anticipate?
3. Have you brought samples of resources and tools for each approach? Share what you have.
4. How would you begin to reach out if you set this as an important goal for the next six months? How might you do this as a team? Discuss a plan of action.

Application this week
1. Try to reach out in *prayer* as well as in one *other* area. Observe and record what you accomplish in both areas in one week. Come next time prepared to share this.
2. Read *In the Gap*, chapter 17. Bring samples of resources and tools for some of the approaches suggested there.

Week nine—Based on chapter 17 (to be read beforehand)

Review
How did you try to reach out in love last week and what did you see accomplished?

Discussion
1. In what ways do you presently help other Christians catch a world vision? In what ways are you seeking more World Christians to stand in the Gap right now?
2. How do you react to the three roles Bryant suggests you should play as you give a world vision to others? Could you see yourself involved in each role? How? Could you see your team involved in each role? How? What modifications in Bryant's ideas would you anticipate?
3. Which of the approaches for giving a world vision would you like to try and why? Have you brought samples of resources

or tools for each approach? Share what you have.

4. How would you begin to give your vision if you set this as an important goal for the next six months? How might you do this as a team? Discuss a plan of action.

Application for this week

1. Try to give a world vision to three other Christians using one or more of the suggested approaches. Observe and record their reactions. Come next time prepared to share this.

2. Read *In the Gap,* chapter 14. What will you do with the World Christian Decision Card?

Week ten—based on chapter 14 (to be read beforehand)

Review

How did you try to give your vision last week and what reactions did you observe?

Discussion

1. There are three questions that Bryant puts at the heart of a World Christian decision. Are these three areas comprehensive enough for such a step?

2. What does it mean to *you* to choose to be a World Christian?

3. What does it mean to *you* to choose to join with other World Christians?

4. What does it mean to *you* to plan to obey your vision?

5. How many in your group are ready to take Step Two outlined in chapter 14? Have each one explain their response to this opportunity.

6. How does each member of your group respond to the specific approach outlined by the World Christian Decision Card? Have each one explain their response.

7. To those who at this time can't make the decision as outlined by the World Christian Decision Card: How will you follow through on all you have explored in these small-group studies? Share with the group.

8. To those who are ready now to make the decision outlined on the card: What will be your next step together after this week? Share with the group.

9. How could the "Personal Strategy Guide" (Appendix II) help any of you, whether or not you can presently make a decision as outlined on the card?

10. Let each member privately complete this sentence:
In response to these nine weeks of study on World Christian discipleship, my next step will be to _____

_____

_____

_____

_____

11. To conclude your ten weeks together, discuss: Over the last nine weeks how has my understanding of Christ Himself been changed? How did I see Him before and how do I see Him differently now?

Hints to the Small Group Facilitator

1. As facilitator, you are responsible to keep your group on schedule and to facilitate discussion so that everyone has an opportunity to share. Ideally, this happens best when the group is no larger than five to eight. Follow the format suggested here. Keep in control so that each component of the weekly schedule receives the amount of time recommended, and no more. *Remember:* These ten weeks provide you an *overview* of World Christian discipleship. Once the framework has been fully explored, *then* you can meet to discuss further all the implications of *In the Gap*. Don't try to do this, however, before completing the ten weeks; there isn't sufficient time to do so.

2. Be sure members read the assigned portions of *In the Gap* before each session, including the introduction, *From One Egg to Another*, which must be read before your first session.

3. If members do not read their assigned chapters or do not work on the weekly applications, encourage them to do so

by pointing out how important it is to the growth of the whole group that each member participate responsibly.

4. Prior to the first session, the facilitator should complete reading the whole book to have some sense of where the ten weeks will take the group in thinking and applications.

5. Prior to the first session you should begin contacting some of the suggested resources in chapters 15, 16, 17. Secure samples that you can share with your group at the appropriate sessions. See Appendix III for a compilation of organizations and addresses.

6. To help you get at these resources, you may want to assign a letter-writing blitz during the week 1 session. Assign each member one of the organizations listed under Appendix III and have them request information this way: "I am part of a missions study group at _____. Would you please send me information on what you do and complimentary samples of your publications that I can share with my group during the next nine weeks. Thank you so much."

7. At the close of the tenth session, be sure no group member leaves with guilt feelings about any decision they have made. If some members wish to continue on as a team, that in no way reflects on the spirituality of the others. Be sure this is clearly understood.

8. For those in the group who want to go on after the tenth week, you may want to begin meeting with the author through one of the series in *World Christian Video Training Curriculum,* described in Appendix VI.

Appendix II

A PERSONAL STRATEGY GUIDE

- I will spend approximately _____ hours total each week in *a personal effort to obey my world vision.* That time will be divided into approximately _____ hours working together with other World Christians and _____ hours working on my own.
- For the next _____ months my strategy will include *three main components:*

I Will Obey My Vision As I Regularly Build It
1. The time I spend each week building my vision will be _____ hours.
2. Of all I could study, I will begin with:
   - _____ Purpose—topic:
   - _____ Possibilities—topic:
   - _____ People—topic:
   - _____ Part—topic:
3. How will I do it? What do I see happening each week? What will be my resources and tools?
4. What will I do alone? What will I do with a team?
5. How will I know there is progress? How will I measure it?
6. How will I know it is time to add something more?

I Will Obey My Vision As I Reach Out Directly in Love

1. The time I spend each week reaching out will be _____ hours.
2. Of the six opportunities to reach out I will begin with these areas:

    _____ Prayer

    _____ Hidden People

    _____ Nearby

    _____ Missions Project

    _____ Team-Extension

    _____ Preparation for Future Outreach

3. How will I work on the areas I select? What do I see happening each week? What will be my resources and tools?
4. What will I do alone? What will I do with a team?
5. How will I know when there is progress? How will I measure it?
6. How will I know it is time to add something more?

I Will Obey My Vision As I Give It to Other Christians

1. The time I spend each week giving my vision will be _____ hours.
2. I will begin by giving my vision to:

    _____ Friends

    _____ Family

    _____ My small group

    _____ My Sunday School class

    _____ My campus fellowship

    _____ My church

    _____ Others:

3. How will I do this? What do I see happening each week? What will be my resources and tools?
4. What will I do alone? What will I do with a team?
5. How will I know when there is progress? How will I measure it?
6. How will I know it is time to add something more?

Personal Strategy in Daily Discipline
Follow the "5-4-3-2-1 Plan"

Build Your World Vision

   5—Spend five minutes some time each day in personal devotions discovering something of what Scripture teaches about Christ's global cause.

   4—Spend an additional four minutes reading current world-related literature such as a magazine article.

Reach Out to the World in Love

   3—Every day take three minutes to carry out a mission to the world through intercessory prayer, using what God gave you in the previous nine minutes of building your vision.

Give Your World Vision to Others

   2—Sometime each day in personal conversation with another Christian (such as your family at evening meal, or in a Bible study group, or in a letter) share for two minutes what God has given you in the previous twelve minutes of building your vision and reaching out in prayer.

That averages out to fourteen minutes a day. Finally, before retiring at night give God one more minute of complete quiet when He can speak to you about who you are becoming as a World Christian, based on the other aspects of your daily discipline.

Fifteen minutes a day. Anyone can do it. Who among us cannot find or release an extra quarter hour out of twenty-four hours to get equipped for the sake of Christ's global cause and the billions currently beyond the reach of His gospel?

Of course, fifteen minutes is a beginning—a minimum—that may eventually grow into much more. But even so, it allows one to come to the close of each day saying with confidence; "I know this day my life has counted strategically for Christ's global cause, especially for those currently beyond the reach of the gospel."

Appendix III

SOURCES AND RESOURCES

Books

Note: Many of these books are available at discount through the Global Church Growth Book Club's World Christian Book Shelf. For their listing write to 1705 Sierra Bonita Ave., Pasadena, CA 91104.

Belew, W. Wendell. *Missions in the Mosaic:* Ministries to American Ethnic Minorities. Nashville: Broadman Press, 1974.

Benjamin, Barbara. *The Impossible Community.* Downers Grove, IL: Inter-Varsity Press, 1978.

Bernbaum, John A., ed. *Perspectives on Peacemaking:* Biblical Options in the Nuclear Age. Ventura, CA: Regal Books, 1984.

Berney, James, ed. *You Can Tell the World:* A Mission Reader. Downers Grove, IL: Inter-Varsity Press, 1979.

Blauw, Johannes. *The Missionary Nature of the Church.* New York: McGraw-Hill, 1962.

Boer, Harry R. *Pentecost and Missions.* Grand Rapids: Wm. B. Eerdmans Publishing Co., n.d.

Broek, Jan O.M. and Webb, John W., *A Geography of Mankind.* New York: McGraw-Hill, 1973.

Bryant, David. *A Call for Concerts of Prayer:* Wake Up for a New Missions Thrust. Madison, WI: Inter-Varsity Christian Fellowship.

Clark, Stephen B. *Building Christian Communities.* Notre Dame, IN: Ave Maria Press, 1972.

Coggins, Wade T. *So That's What Missions Is All About*. Chicago: Moody Press, 1975.

Coleman, Robert E. *The Master Plan of Evangelism*. Old Tappan, NJ: Fleming H. Revell, 1964.

Collins, Marjorie A. *Who Cares About the Missionary?* Suggestions for Those Who Do. Chicago: Moody Press, 1974.

Costas, Orlando E. *The Church and Its Mission:* A Shattering Critique from the Third World. Wheaton, IL: Tyndale House, 1974.

Dayton, Ed, ed. *Mission Handbook:* North American Protestant Ministries Overseas. Monrovia: World Vision International/MARC Division, 1976.

_____ *You Can So Get There From Here*. Monrovia: World Vision International/MARC Division, 1979.

_____ *That Everyone May Hear:* Reaching the Unreached. Monrovia: World Vision International/MARC Division, 1979.

Dayton, Edward and Wagner, C. Peter. *Unreached Peoples '79; '80; '81; '82; '83:* The Challenge of the Church's Unfinished Business. Elgin, IL: David C. Cook Publishing Co.

Douglas J.D., ed. *Let the Earth Hear His Voice:* Lausanne Compendium. Minneapolis: World Wide Publications, 1975.

Eastman, Dick. *The Hour That Changes the World*. Grand Rapids: Baker Book House, 1973.

_____ . *The University of the Word*. Ventura, CA: Regal Books, 1983.

Elliot, Elisabeth. *Shadow of the Almighty*. Grand Rapids: Zondervan Publishing Co., 1958.

Engstrom, Ted W. *What in the World Is God Doing?* The New Face of Missions. Waco, TX: Word Publishers, 1978.

Fromer, Arthur. *Whole World Handbook:* Summer Employment Overseas. New York: Simon and Schuster, Inc., 1978.

Goldsmith, Martin. *Don't Just Stand There*. Downers Grove, IL: Inter-Varsity Press, 1978.

Goener, H. Cornell. *All Nations in God's Purpose*. Nashville: Broadman Press, 1979.

Graham, Bruce. *What Is a Fellowship of World Christians?* Pasadena: William Carey Library, 1976.

Greenway, Roger S. *An Urban Strategy for Latin America*. Grand Rapids: Baker Book House, 1973.

Greenway, Roger, ed. *Guidelines for Urban Church Planting*. Grand Rapids: Baker Book House, 1976.

Giffiths, Michael C. *Give Up Your Small Ambitions*. Chicago: Moody Press, 1970.

_____ . *You and God's Work Overseas.* Downers Grove, IL: Inter-Varsity Press, 1975.

_____ . *Who Really Sends the Missionary?* Chicago: Moody Press, 1972.

Hefley, James and Marti. *By Their Blood:* Christian Martyrs of the 20th Century. Milford, MI: Mott Media Publishers, 1979.

Hoke, Donald, ed. *The Church in Asia.* Chicago: Moody Press, 1975.

Hopkins, Howard. *John R. Mott:* 1865-1955, Grand Rapids: Wm. B. Eerdmans Publishing Co., 1980.

Hopler, Thom. *A World of Difference:* Following Christ Beyond Your Cultural Walls. Downers Grove, IL: Inter-Varsity Press, 1981.

Howard, David M. *The Great Commission for Today.* Downers Grove, IL: Inter-Varsity Press, 1976.

_____ . *Why World Evangelism?* Downers Grove, IL: Inter-Varsity Press, 1974.

_____ . *Student Power in World Missions.* Downers Grove, IL: Inter-Varsity Press, 1979.

Howard, David M. *Declare His Glory Among the Nations:* Urbana 76 Compendium. Downers Grove, IL: Inter-Varsity Press, 1977.

Johnstone, Patrick J. *Operation World:* A Handbook for World Intercession. Midland Park, NJ: Send the Light Publishers, 1978.

Jones, E. Stanley. *The Unshakeable Kingdom and the Unchanging Person.* Nashville: Abingdon Press, 1972.

Kane, Herbert J. *A Global View of Christian Missions.* Grand Rapids: Baker Book House, 1971.

_____ . *Winds of Change in Christian Mission.* Chicago: Moody Press, 1973.

_____ . *Understanding Christian Missions.* Grand Rapids: Baker Book House, 1974.

Keyes, Lawrence. *The Last Age of Missions.* Pasadena, CA: William Carey Library, 1983.

Kyle, John E., Compiler. *The Unfinished Task.*

Latourette, Kenneth Scott. *A History of Christianity.* New York: Harper and Row Publishers, Inc., 1953.

Little, Paul. *Affirming the Will of God.* Downers Grove, IL: Inter-Varsity Press, 1974.

_____ . *How to Give Away Your Faith.* Downers Grove, IL: Inter-Varsity Press, 1970.

Little, Paul, et. al. *HIS Guide to Evangelism.* Downers Grove, IL: Inter-Varsity Press, 1977.

Lovelace, Richard F. *Dynamics of Spiritual Life:* An Evangelical Theology of Renewal. Downers Grove, IL: Inter-Varsity Press, 1979.

Lowman, Pete. *The Day of His Power:* History of the International Fellowship of Evangelical Students. Downers Grove, IL: Inter-Varsity Press, 1983.

Lutzbetak, Louis J. *The Church and Cultures.* Divine Word Publications, 1970.

McGavran, Donald. *The Clash Between Christianity and Cultures.* Grand Rapids: Baker Book House, 1974.

―――. *Understanding Church Growth.* Grand Rapids: Wm. B. Eerdmans Publishing House, 1980.

―――. *Ethnic Realities and the Church:* Lessons from India. William Carey Library, 1979.

McGavran, Donald, ed. *Crucial Issues in Missions Tomorrow.* Chicago: Moody Press, 1972.

McQuilkin, J. Robertson. *Measuring the Church Growth Movement.* Chicago: Moody Press, 1974.

Murray, Andrew. *Key to Missionary Problem.* Fort Washington, PA: Christian Literature Crusade, 1979.

Naisbitt, John. *Megatrends:* Ten New Directions Transforming Our Lives. New York: Warner Books, 1982.

Mellis, Charles J. *Committed Communities:* Fresh Streams for World Missions. Pasadena, CA: William Carey Library, 1976.

Neill, Stephen. *A History of Christian Missions.* Middlesex, England: Penguin Books, 1964.

Nelson, Marlin L. *The How and Why of Third World Missions:* An Asian Case Study. Pasadena, CA: William Carey Library, 1976.

Nida, Eugene. *Customs and Cultures.* Pasadena, CA: William Carey Library, 1974.

Obien, Frank. *Building Bridges of Love:* A Handbook for Work with International Students. San Bernardino: Campus Crusade for Christ, 1974.

Orr, J. Edwin. *The Eager Feet:* Evangelical Awakenings 1790-1830. Chicago: Moody Press, 1975.

―――. *The Fervent Prayer:* The Worldwide Impact of the Great Awakening of 1858. Chicago: Moody Press, 1974.

―――. *The Flaming Tongue:* The Impact of 20th Century Revivals. Chicago: Moody Press, 1973.

―――. *Campus Aflame:* Dynamics of Student Religious Revolution. Regal Books. Out of Print.

Paulson, Hank, with Richardson, Don. *Beyond the Wall:* The People Communism Can't Conquer. Ventura, CA: Regal Books, 1982.

Perkins, John. *Let Justice Roll Down:* Perkins Tells His Own Story. Ventura, CA: Regal Books, 1976.

_____. *With Justice for All.* Ventura, CA: Regal Books, 1982.

Peters, George. *A Biblical Theology of Missions.* Chicago: Moody Press, 1973.

Pippert, Rebecca Manley. *Out of the Salt Shaker and Into the World.* Downers Grove, IL: Inter-Varsity Press, 1979.

Richardson, Don. *Eternity in Their Hearts.* Ventura, CA: Regal Books, 1981.

_____. *Lords of the Earth.* Ventura, CA: Regal Books, 1977.

_____. *Peace Child.* Ventura, CA: Regal Books, 1974.

Richardson, William J. *Social Actions Vs. Evangelism:* An Essay on the Contemporary Crisis. Pasadena, CA: William Carey Library, 1978.

Scott, Waldron. *Bring Forth Justice.* Grand Rapids: Wm. B. Eerdmans, 1981.

Sider, Ronald. *Rich Christians in an Age of Hunger.* Downers Grove, IL: Inter-Varsity Press, 1978.

Sine, Tom. *The Mustard Seed Conspiracy.* Waco, TX: Word Books, 1981.

Smalley, William A. *Readings in Missionary Anthropology II.* Pasadena, CA: William Carey Library, 1978.

Snyder, Howard A. *The Problem of Wineskins:* Church Structure in a Technological Age. Downers Grove, IL: Inter-Varsity Press, 1976.

_____. *The Community of the King.* Downers Grove, IL: Inter-Varsity Press, 1977.

Stott, John R.W. *Christian Mission in the Modern World.* Downers Grove, IL: Inter-Varsity Press, 1975.

Thompson, Bernard. *Good Samaritan Faith:* A Strategy for Meeting Needs in Your Community. Ventura, CA: Regal Books, 1984.

Tippett, Alan R. *Church Growth and the Word of God.* Grand Rapids: Wm. B. Eerdmans Publishing Co., 1970.

_____. *The Deep-Sea Canoe:* The Story of the Third World Missionaries in the South Pacific. Pasadena, CA: William Carey Library, 1977.

Tonna, Benjamin. *Gospel for the Cities:* A Socio-Theology of Urban Ministry. Maryknoll, NY: Orbis Books, 1978.

Trueblood, Elton. *The Validity of the Christian Mission.* New York: Harper and Row Publishers, Inc. 1972.

_____. *The Company of the Committed.* New York: Harper and Row Publishers, Inc., 1961.

Tucker, Ruth A. *From Jerusalem to Irian Jaya:* A Biographical History of Christian Missions. Grand Rapids: Zondervan Publishing House, 1983.

Wagner, C. Peter. *On the Crest of the Wave:* Becoming a World Christian. Ventura, CA: Regal Books, 1983.

_____ . *Leading Your Church to Growth*. Ventura, CA: Regal Books, 1984.

Wallis, Jim. *The Call to Conversion:* Discovering the Gospel for These Times. New York: Harper and Row Publishers, Inc., 1981.

Waren, Max. *I Believe in the Great Commission*. Grand Rapids: Wm. B. Eerdmans Publishing Co., 1976.

Werning, Waldo J. *The Radical Nature of Christianity*. Pasadena, CA: Mandate Press, 1975.

White, John. *The Golden Cow:* Materialism in the Twentieth-Century Church. Downers Grove, IL: Inter-Varsity Press, 1979.

Wilson, J. Christy. *Today's Tent Makers*. Wheaton, IL: Tyndale House Publishers, 1979.

Winter, Ralph. *The World Christian Movement:* 1950-1975. Pasadena, CA: William Carey Library, 1976.

_____ . *The Grounds for a New Thrust in World Mission*. Pasadena, CA: William Carey Library, 1978.

_____ . *Penetrating the Last Frontiers*. Pasadena, CA: William Carey Library, 1978.

_____ , Hawthorne, Stephen, eds. *Perspectives on the World Christian Movement*. Pasadena, CA: William Carey Library, 1981.

_____ . *Six Essential Components of World Evangelization:* Goals for 1984. Pasadena, CA: William Carey Library, 1979.

_____ . *Say Yes to Missions*. Downers Grove, IL: Inter-Varsity Press, 1974.

Winter, Roberta H. *Once More Around Jericho:* The Story of the U.S. Center for World Mission. Pasadena, CA: William Carey Library, 1979.

Woods, C. Stacey. *The Growth of a Work of God:* The Story of the Early Days of Inter-Varsity Christian Fellowship. Downers Grove, IL: Inter-Varsity Press, 1978.

Mission Policy Handbook. Pasadena: Association of Church Missions Committees, 1978.

World Congress Country Profiles. Monrovia: World Vision International/ MARC Division, 1974-1979.

Area Handbooks. Washington, D.C.: U.S. Printing Office.

Yankelovich, Daniel. *New Rules:* Searching for Self-Fulfillment in a World Turned Upside Down. New York: Random House Publishers, 1981.

Magazines Quoted

Glasser, Arthur. "1980—Where Were the Students." *Missiology*.

January 1981.

Howard, David M. "What Happened at Urbana—Its Meaning for Missions." *Evangelical Missions Quarterly.* April 1977, pp. 141-147.

Jones, Jenkin Lloyd. "It's Time We Stop Feeling Guilty." *L.A. Times News Service/Wisconsin State Journal.* March 11, 1979.

————. "Christianity Put to the Test." *Los Angeles Times.* September 16, 1979.

MacDonald, Gordon. "Your Church in God's Global Plan." *Christian Herald.* November 1980.

Morrow, Lance. "After Proposition 13, Volunteers Needed." *Time.* August 7, 1978, pp. 34,37.

Reapsome, James W. "Youth: Wave or Washout?" *Eternity.* April 1979, pp. 57-58.

Sisco, Joseph J. "Caution, Fragmentation Make Our Image." *New York Times News Service/Wisconsin State Journal.* June 12, 1979.

Stott, John R.W. "The Bible in World Evangelization." *Christianity Today.* February 6, 1981.

Trippett, Frank. "The '70s: A Time of Pause." *Time.* December 25, 1978, p. 34.

White, Jane See. "Quiet Generation Seeking Individual Gains." *Associated Press News Service/Wisconsin State Journal.* May 18, 1979.

Winter, Ralph. "Is a Big Student Missions Movement in the Offing?" *Christianity Today.* May 10, 1974.

"Narcissus Redivivus." *Time.* September 20, 1976, p. 63.

"Out of a New England Haystack." *Time.* January 10, 1976, p. 56.

"Trends: Contradictions, Changes Seen After 10-Year Study of College Youth." *Youthletter.* November, 1977, p. 82.

Non-Denominational Mission Society Magazines

ACMC Newsletter
Association of Church Missions Committees
1021 E. Walnut, Suite 202, Pasadena, CA 91106

Action Report
Language Institute for Evangelism
P.O. Box 200, Alhambra, CA 91802

*Africa Now
Sudan Interior Mission, Inc.
P.O. Box C, Cedar Grove, NJ 07009

The Andean Outlook

Andes Evangelical Mission
508 Central Ave., Plainfield, NJ 07060

Asian Report
Asian Outreach
G.P.O. Box 13448, HONG KONG

Bread for the World Newsletter
207 East 16th Street, New York, NY 10003

Broadcaster
Far East Broadcasting Company
P.O. Box 1, Whittier, CA 90608

Brown Gold
New Tribes Mission, Woodworth, WI 53194

China and the Church Today
Chinese Church Research Center
1564 Edge Hill Rd., Abington, PA 19001

Church Growth Bulletin
Overseas Crusades, Inc.
P.O. Box 66, Santa Clara, CA 95050

CMF Record
Carver Foreign Missions, Inc.
Morris Brown Sta., Box 92091, Atlanta, GA 30314

Communique and *Ambassadors*
Ambassadors for Christ, Inc.
P.O. Box AFC, Paradise, PA 17562

Compassion Magazine
Compassion, Inc.
7774 W. Irving Park Rd., Chicago, IL 60634

The Cross and the Crescent
North Africa Mission
239 Fairfield Ave., Upper Darby, PA 19082

Deaf Witness
Christian Mission for Deaf Africans

P.O. Box 1452, Detroit, MI 48231

Doorways (quarterly)
International Students
P.O. Box C, Colorado Springs, CO 80906

East Asia Millions
Overseas Missionary Fellowship
404 S. Church St., Robesonia, PA 19551

Evangelizing Today's Child
Child Evangelism Fellowship, Inc.
P.O. Box 348, Warrenton, MO 63383

Everybody
World Literature Crusade
20232 Sunburst St., Chatsworth, CA 91311

FAX
Food for the Hungry, Inc.
P.O. Box 200, Los Angeles, CA 90041

Floodtide (quarterly)
Christian Literature Crusade, Inc.
P.O. Box C, Fort Washington, PA 19034

Focus
Missionary Internship, Inc.
P.O. Box 457, Farmington, MI 48024

Focus News
International Students, Inc.
P.O. Box C, Colorado Springs, CO 80906

Global Church Growth Bulletin
Overseas Crusades
3033 Scott Blvd., Santa Clara, CA 95050

Global Report
World Evangelical Fellowship

P.O. Box 670, Colorado Springs, CO 80401

GO and LINK
Bible and Medical Missionary Fellowship
P.O. Box 418, Upper Darby, PA 19082

Gospel in Context: A Focus on the Contextualization
of the Gospel in the Six Continents
1564 Edge Hill Road, Abington, PA 19001

Greater Europe Report
Greater Europe Mission
P.O. Box 668, Wheaton, IL 60187

Harvest Today
World Team
Box 343038, Coral Gables, FL 33134

Harvest
Baptist Mid-Missions
4205 Chester Ave., Cleveland, OH 44103

In Other Words
Wycliffe Bible Translators
19891 Beach Blvd., Huntington Beach, CA 92648

In Touch
IFES
10 College Rd., Harrow, Middlesex HA1 1BE, ENGLAND

Inland Africa
Africa Inland Mission
P.O. Box 178, Pearl River, NY 10965

Intercessor (monthly prayer bulletin)
Mission Aviation Fellowship
P.O. Box 2828, Fullerton, CA 92633

International Viewpoint (monthly)
Christian Literature Crusade, Inc.

P.O. Box C, Fort Washington, PA 19034

Inter-Seminary Student Missions Newsletter
P.O. Box 13053, Portland, OR 97213

JEMS
Japan Evangelical Mission
P.O. Box 640, Three Hills, Alberta, CANADA

Latin America Evangelist
Latin America Mission
285 Orchard Terrace, Bogota, NJ 07603

Lifeline
Unevangelized Fields Mission
P.O. Box 306, Bala-Cynwyd, PA 19004

Link
Interlink
Box 832, Wheaton, IL 60187

Map Miniature Magazine (quarterly)
Map Progress (quarterly)
Map International
P.O. Box 50, Wheaton, IL 60187

Message of the Cross
Bethany Fellowship Missions
6820 Auto Club Rd., Minneapolis, MN 55438

Missiology: An International Review
American Society of Missiologists
1605 E. Elizabeth, Pasadena, CA 91104

Mission Aviation (quarterly)
Mission Aviation Fellowship
P.O. Box 2828, Fullerton, CA 92633

Mission Frontiers
U.S. Center for World Mission
1605 E. Elizabeth St., Pasadena, CA 91106

Missions Advance Research and Communication Newsletter
World Vision/MARC
919 W. Huntington Dr., Monrovia, CA 91109

Newsletter
Daystar Communications, Inc.
P.O. Box 10123, Eugene, OR 97401

Newsletter
TransWorld Radio
560 Main St., Chatham, NJ 07928

Occasional Bulletin
Overseas Ministries Study Center
P.O. Box 443, Fort Lee, NJ 07024

O.M. News (quarterly)
Operation Mobilization
P.O. Box 148, Midland Park, NJ 07432

OMS Outreach
O.M.S. International, Inc.
P.O. Box A, Greenwood, IN 46142

The Other Side: A Magazine of Christian Discipleship
(Not actually a mission society, but good perspectives on world trends
and needs.)
Box 12236, Philadelphia, PA 19144

Outlook
African Enterprise, Inc.
P.O. Box 988, Pasadena, CA 91102

Pray for China Prayer Bulletin
Pray for China Fellowship
1423 Grant St., Berkeley, CA 94703

Prayer Fellowship Bulletin (monthly)
Regions Beyond Missionary Union
8102 Elberon Ave., Philadelphia, PA 19111

Prayer Letters (weekly)
Operation Mobilization
P.O. Box 148, Midland Park, NJ 07432

Prayer News Bulletin
Fellowship of Faith for the Muslims
205 Yonge St., Rm. 25, Toronto, Ontario, M5B 1N2 CANADA

Regions Beyond (quarterly)
Regions Beyond Missionary Union
8102 Elberon Ave., Philadelphia, PA 19111

Reporter
World Relief Commission, Inc.
P.O. Box 44, Valley Forge, PA 19481

SCAN: A Six Contintent Reading Service for the Renewal of Church
and Mission
1564 Edge Hill Rd., Abington, PA 19001

Slavic Gospel News
Slavic Gospel Association, Inc.
P.O. Box 1122, Wheaton, IL 60187

Student World Report
IFES
233 Langdon St., Madison, WI 53703

Student and World Connection
Inter-Varsity Missions
233 Langdon
Madison, WI 53703

Themelios
Theological Students Fellowship
233 Langdon St., Madison, WI 53703

Today's Christian
Fuller Evangelistic Assoc.
Box 989, Pasadena, CA 91102
20th Century Disciple

Youth With A Mission, Inc.
P.O. Box 1099, Sunland, CA 91040

Update
Presbyterian Center for Missions Studies

1605 E. Elizabeth, Pasadena, CA 91104

Update (World Concern)
Box 33000, Seattle, WA 98133

Wherever
The Evangelical Alliance Mission
P.O. Box 969, Wheaton, IL 60187

World Christian (an independent, evangelical magazine created to challenge, encourage and equip Christians who have a heart for the world)
P.O. Box 40010, Pasadena, CA 91104

World Evangelization
Lausanne Committee on World Evangelization
P.O. Box 1100
Wheaton, IL 60189

World Vision Magazine and *International Intercessor*
World Vision International
919 W. Huntington Dr., Monrovia, CA 91109

World Wide Challenge
Campus Crusade for Christ
Arrowhead Springs, San Bernardino, CA 92401

Worldwide News
Pocket Testament League
117 Main St., Lincoln Park, NJ 07035

Worldwide Thrust
Worldwide Evangelization Crusade
P.O. Box A, Fort Washington, PA 19034

The Zwemer Institute Newsletter (to reach unreached Muslims for Christ)
Zwemer Institute, Box 365, Altadena, CA 91001

NOTE: For $32.50 a year the *Evangelical Missions Information Service* provides the following vision-building materials:

Missions News Service—a bi-monthly update on current activities in the whole world of missions

Pulse—a periodical in-depth study of missions in key regions of the world, such as Asia, Latin America, Africa, Europe, etc.

Evangelical Missions Quarterly—news and hard-hitting articles on mission trends and challenges today.

To subscribe, write to: Evangelical Missions Information Services
Box 794, Wheaton, IL 60187

Magazines from Some Denominations with Large Missionary Forces

Alliance Witness
Christian & Missionary Alliance
Overseas Ministries, P.O. Box C, Nyack, NY 10960

Call to Prayer (monthly)
Assemblies of God
Division of Foreign Missions, 1445 Boonville Avenue, Springfield, MO 65802

Commission
Southern Baptist Convention
Foreign Mission Board, Box 6597, Richmond, VA 23230

Firm Foundations (wk)
Churches of Christ
Firm Foundation Publishing House
Box 610, Austin, TX 78767

Good News Crusades (bi-monthly)
Assemblies of God
Division of Foreign Missions
1445 Boonville Avenue, Springfield, MO 65802

Gospel Advocate (wk)
Churches of Christ
Firm Foundation Publishing House, Box 610, Austin, TX 78767

Impact
Conservative Baptist Foreign Missions Society
Wheaton, IL 60187

Secular Magazines with a World Perspective

Aboriginal Identity
Aboriginal Publications Foundation
Box M931, G.P.O. Perth, W.A. 6000

Africa (An international business, economic and political monthly)
Africa Journal Ltd.
Kerkman House, 54a Tottenham Ct. Rd., London W1P 0BT
ENGLAND

Africa News (a weekly newspaper)
P.O. Box 3851, Durham, NC 27702

African Directions
884 National Press Bldg., Washington, D.C. 20045

Americas (The Inter-American Magazine)
Subscription Service Dept., P.O. Box 973, Farmingdale, NY 11737

Amnesty International Newsletter
10 Southampton St., London WC2E 7HF ENGLAND

Aramco World Magazine (The world of the Middle East)
1345 Avenue of the Americas, New York, NY 10019

Asia World
Chatterjie International Centre
33-A Chowringhee Rd., Calcutta 700 071 INDIA

Asian Outlook
1 Tsingtao East Rd., Taipei, REPUBLIC OF CHINA

Atlas: World Press Review: News and Views from the Foreign Press
Box 915, Farmingdale, NY 11737

China Now (for Anglo-Chinese understanding)
152 Camden High St., London, NW 1 ONE ENGLAND

Christian Science Monitor
One Norway St., Boston, MA 02115

Far Eastern Economic Review
G.P.O. Box 160, HONG KONG

The Futurist (a journal about global forecasts, trends and ideas about the future)
World Future Society, P.O. Box 30369, Bethesda Branch, Washington, D.C. 20014

Latin American Weekly Report
Latin American Newsletter Ltd.
90-93 Cowcross St., London EC1M 6BC ENGLAND

The Link: Americans for Middle East Understanding
Room 771, 475 Riverside Dr., New York, NY 10027

Media Today
Living Media India Ltd.
9 K-Block, Connaught Circus, New Delhi 110 021 INDIA

MEED (Middle East Economic Digest)
MABCO, Inc., 61 Broadway, New York, NY 10006

National Geographic
17th & M Streets NW, Washington, D.C. 20036

New York Times
2229 W. 43rd St., New York, NY 10036

Pacific Islands Monthly
2812 Kahawai St., Honolulu, Hawaii 96822

Pacific Research
Pacific Studies Center
Mountain View, CA 94041

The Rotarian: The International Magazine
1600 Ridge Ave., Evanston, IL 60201

The Southeast Asia Record
Asia-Pacific Affairs Association
580 College Ave., Suite 6, Palo Alto, CA 94306

Soviet Life
Embassy of the USSR
1706-18th St., N.W., Washington, D.C. 20009

Travel: The Magazine That Roams the Globe
Travel Building, Floral Park, NY 11001

U.S. News and World Report
Subscription Dept., P.O. Box 2627, Boulder, CO 80321

Wall Street Journal
Dow Jones Co., Inc.
22 Cortlandt St., New York, NY 10007

Women of the World
Women's International Democratic Federation
Unter den Linden 13, 108 Berlin, GDR

World Development (Inter-disciplinary)
Pergarnon Press, Inc.
Maxwell House, Fairview Park, Elmsford, NY 10524

World Issues
Center for the Study of Democratic Institutions
2056 Eucalyptus Hill Road, Santa Barbara, CA 93108

World Student News
International Union of Students
17th November St., 11001 Prague 01, CZECHOSLOVAKIA

The World Today
Royal Institute of International Affairs
Chatham House, 10 St. James Square, London SW1X 4LE ENGLAND

Worldview (ethical scrutiny of international affairs)
P.O. Box 1308M, Fort Lee, NY 07024

Magazines That Move: Mission Films

The following are just a few of the resources available to you for slide/tape and film presentations on world missions. Contact each organization for full information on what they offer and their rental fees (if any). When you write, be sure to specify your audience and request information on the charges to you.

Africa Inland Mission
Box 178
Pearl River, NY 10965

Conservative Baptist Foreign Missions Society
Box 5
Wheaton, IL 60187

Gospel Films
Box 455
Muskegon, MI 49443

International Films, Inc.
1605 E. Elizabeth
Pasadena, CA 91104

Ken Anderson Films
Box 618
Winona Lake, IN 46590

Overseas Crusade
Box 66
Santa Clara, CA 95050

Overseas Missionary Fellowship
404 S. Church St.
Robesonia, PA 19551

Team Films
Box 969
Wheaton, IL 60187

Twenty-One Hundred Productions
233 Langdon
Madison, WI 53703

Worldwide Evangelization Crusade
Box A
Fort Washington, PA 19034

Organizations

Association of Christian Ministries to Internationals
233 Langdon
Madison, Wisconsin 53703
Note: A cooperative effort of more than 20 groups seeking to reach
international visitors to the U.S.

Association of Church Missions Committees
1620 S. Myrtle Ave.   PO Box ACMC
Monrovia, CA 91016   Wheaton, Illinois 60187
Note: Their motto is "Churches Helping Churches in Missions"
Offers:
Training conferences for churches at the local level
National conferences
Missions Resource Center
Missions Policy Handbook
Missions Education Handbook
  . . . plus other helpful literature and consulting services for the local church

Campus Crusade for Christ
Arrowhead Springs
San Bernardino, California 92404
Offers:
International Resources Office
Agape Movement (vocational witness overseas)
STOP OUT! Program (1 year overseas)
International Summer Projects
World Wide Challenge magazine
Here's Life World! campaign
Specialists on international student ministry
Staff openings in over 100 countries outside USA

Christian Nationals Evangelism Commission
1470 N. Fourth St.
San Jose, California 95112
Note: Opportunities to give support ministry to established indigenous evangelistic work in 35 nations.

Evangelicals for Social Action
PO Box 76560
Washington, D.C. 20013
Offers:
World Peace Projects

Workshops on Discipleship and International Justice
Public Policy Task Forces (such as urban concerns)
Updates on a variety of issues that directly or indirectly impinge on
world evangelization

Evangelical Foreign Missions Association (EFMA)
1430 K Street N.W.
Washington, D.C. 20005
Note: Involving both denominational and non-denominational societies,
it is the mission affiliate of the National Association of Evangelicals.
Offers:
Missionary News Service (semi-monthly)
Evangelical Missions Quarterly

Evangelical Missions Information Service
Box 794
Wheaton, Illinois 60187
Offers:
Evangelical Missions Quarterly
Missionary News Service
Pulses (Africa, Asia, Europe, Latin America, Chinese World, Muslim
World)

Global Church Growth Book Club
1705 Sierra Bonita Ave.
Pasadena, California 91104
Offers: A special selection of books (discounted) suited to those exploring the World Christian theme. Also, the major outlet for hundreds of
titles published by William Carey Library. Many books recommended in
In the Gap are available through them.

Gospel Light Publications
2300 Knoll Dr.
Ventura, California 93003
Offers:
World Christian Video Training Curriculum
Regal Books (ask for their catalog and a listing of their titles on world
missions)

Interdenominational Foreign Missions Association (IFMA)
Box 395
Wheaton, Illinois 60187

Note: An association of evangelical foreign mission societies without denominational affiliation.
Offers:
Missionary News Service (semi-monthly)
Evangelical Missions Quarterly

International Fellowship of Evangelical Students
PO Box 270
Madison, Wisconsin 53701

International Students Incorporated
Box C
Colorado Springs, Colorado 80901
Offers:
Literature both for training and evangelism with foreign students
Training conferences
Staff nationwide

Inter-Varsity Missions
233 Langdon St.
Madison, Wisconsin 53703
Offers:
World Christian Handbooks Series
World Christian Conferences
World Christian Video Training Curriculum
Student Training in Missions
Overseas Training Camps
World Missions Training Camp, USA
URBANA Student Missions Convention
Mission Specialists nationwide
Christmas House Parties for international students
Student Foreign Missions Fellowship

Inter-Varsity Press
Downers Grove, Illinois 60515
Note: Ask for their latest catalog and a listing of their titles on world missions.

Lausanne Committee for World Evangelization
Whitefield House
186 Kennington Park Rd.
London SE11 4 BT

Note: An international network to alert Christians to the needs and opportunities in world evangelization and to foster cooperative efforts to that end among the worldwide evangelical community. Publishes monthly the *World Evangelization Information News Service,* free upon request.

National Council of Churches of Christ in the U.S.A.
Division of Overseas Ministries
475 Riverside Drive
New York, New York 10027

National Prayer Committee
PO Box 6826
San Bernardino, California 92412
Note: An interdenominational effort of recognized prayer leaders to mobilize prayer in the church, nationally and locally, for spiritual awakening and world evangelization.
Offers:
Training materials
Conferences
Consultations
. . . and other services

Navigators
PO Box 1659
Colorado Springs, Colorado 80901
Note: Involved in 34 countries, the Navs offer opportunities to students who have been helped first in their specialized training programs. *Nav Log* highlights their work around the world.

U.S. Center for World Mission
1605 E. Elizabeth St.
Pasadena, California 91104
Includes:
Institute for Chinese Studies
Institute for Muslim Studies
Institute for Hindu Studies
Institute for Tribal Studies
Order for World Evangelization
Fellowship of World Christians
Oversees Counseling Service
Frontier Fellowship

304 In the Gap

United Presbyterian Center for Mission Studies
Episcopal Church Missions Community
Fellowship of Artists in Cultural Evangelism
Institute of International Studies
... plus many other organizations
It also offers a correspondence course for World Christians entitled
Perspectives on the World Christian Movement, a periodical *Mission
Frontiers,* and a daily prayer guide, *Global Prayer Digest.*

World Evangelical Fellowship
Wheaton, Illinois 60187
Note: An association of national evangelical fellowships, committed to
mutual support and exchange in fulfilling the task of world evangelization. Publishes a quarterly bulletin *Global Report,* free on request.

World Relief Commission
P.O. Box WRC
Wheaton, Illinois 60187
Note: One of many fine organizations that provides meaningful ways to
minister to physical needs in Christ's name.

World Vision International/Missions Advanced Research and Com-
munication Center (MARC)
919 West Huntington Dr.
Monrovia, California 91016
Includes:
Ministry to the hungry
Community development projects
Training for national pastors
Child sponsorship programs
... plus many excellent materials developed through their MARC
Division, particularly from their research into the Hidden Peoples.
Write for a listing.
    There are many other fine organizations to which you can turn as
you obey your world vision. Write to Inter-Varsity Missions for a listing
of the many that sponsor displays at the URBANA Student Missions
Convention. Or, you may want to consult the resource tool: *Mission
Handbook:* North American Protestant Ministries Overseas, listing 700
such agencies. It is available through World Vision/MARC Division.

Appendix IV

SCRIPTURE AND CHRIST'S GLOBAL CAUSE

Inter-Varsity Missions offers a helpful guide on *How to Create World Christian Bible Studies.* It can equip you to "mine out" of Scripture its rich treasure of teaching on the world mission of the Church. The following pages are excerpts from that handbook. The tool also includes such sections as "Guidelines for World Christian Bible Studies" and "Books on the Biblical Basis," as well as twelve pages listing every key biblical passage on Christ's global cause, giving the reference and theme title.

The Global Thread Through Scripture
Aspects of Christ's global cause can be found in every book of the Bible. Read straight through the passages listed here in one sitting. Watch how this grand theme weaves its way through Genesis to Revelation. Watch how the theme comes through, however, in a way that is compatible with the focus of each book and with that book's place in the Bible's progressive teaching on the cause.

GENESIS—Through you all the families of the earth shall be blessed (12:3).

EXODUS—For all the earth is mine and you shall be to me a Kingdom of Priests (19:5-6).

LEVITICUS—The stranger who sojourns with you shall be to you as the native among you, and you shall love him as yourself (19:24).

NUMBERS—A star shall come forth out of Jacob, and a scepter shall rise out of Israel. It shall crush the forehead of Moab and shall break down all the sons of Sheth. Edom shall be dispossessed, Seir also, his enemies, shall be dispossessed while Israel does valiantly (24:17-18).

DEUTERONOMY—The Lord will establish you as a people holy to himself, as he has sworn to you, if you keep the commandments . . . and all the peoples of the earth shall see that you are called by the name of the Lord; and they shall be afraid of you (28:9-10).

JOSHUA—For the Lord your God dried up the waters of the Jordan for you until you passed over . . . so that all the peoples of the earth may know that the hand of the Lord is mighty (4:23-24).

JUDGES—I will not drive out before them any of the nations that Joshua left when he died, that by them I may test Israel, whether they will take care to walk in the way of the Lord (2:21-22).

RUTH—Entreat me not to leave you or to return from following you; for where you go I will go, and where you lodge I will lodge; your people will be my people, and your God my God (1:16).

1 SAMUEL—This day the Lord will deliver you into my hand . . . that all the earth may know that there is a God in Israel (17:46).

2 SAMUEL—For this I will extol thee, O Lord, among the nations and sing praises to thy name. Great triumphs he gives to his king (22:50-51).

1 KINGS—Thus King Solomon excelled all the kings of the earth in riches and wisdom. And the whole earth sought the presence of Solomon to hear his wisdom, which God had put into his mind (10:23-24).

2 KINGS—So now, O Lord our God, save us, I beseech thee, from his hand, so that all kingdoms of the earth may know that thou, O Lord, art God alone (19:19).

1 CHRONICLES—Sing to the Lord, all the earth! Tell of his salvation from day to day. Declare his glory among the nations (16:23-24).

2 CHRONICLES—Likewise when a foreigner, who is not of thy people Israel, comes from a far country for the sake of thy great name, and thy mighty hand . . . hear thou from heaven thy dwelling place, and do according to all for which the foreigner calls to thee; in order that all peoples of the earth may know thy name and fear thee (6:32-33).

EZRA—Thus says Cyrus king of Persia: The Lord, the God of heaven, has given me all the kingdoms of the earth, and he has charged me to build him a house at Jerusalem (1:2).

NEHEMIAH—Thou art the Lord, thou alone; thou hast made heaven, the heaven of heavens, with all their host, the earth and all that is on it, the seas and all that is in them . . . Thou art the Lord, the God who didst choose Abram and bring him forth (9:6-7).

ESTHER—And who knows whether you have not come to the kingdom [*of Persia*] for such a time as this? (4:14).

JOB—The Lord said to Satan, "Whence have you come?" Satan answered, "From going to and fro on the earth." And the Lord said to Satan, "Have you considered my servant Job, that there is none like him on the earth?" (1:7-8).

PSALMS—Let everything that breathes praise the Lord! (150:6).

PROVERBS—By me [*Wisdom*] kings reign, and rulers decree what is just; by me princes rule and nobles govern the earth (8:15-16).

ECCLESIASTES—I know that whatever God does endures forever; nothing can be added to it, nor anything taken from it; God has made it so, in order that men should fear before him (3:14).

SONG OF SOLOMON—The maidens saw her and called her happy; the queens and concubines also [*from Solomon's international alliances*], and they praised her (6:9).

ISAIAH—It is too light a thing that you should be my servant to raise up the tribes of Jacob . . . I will give you as a light to the nations, that my salvation may reach to the end of the earth (49:6).

JEREMIAH—And this city shall be to me a name of joy, a praise and a glory before all the nations of the earth who shall hear of all the good that I do for them and shall fear and tremble (33:9).

LAMENTATIONS—Who has commanded and it came to pass, unless the Lord has ordained it? Is it not from the mouth of the Most High that good and evil come? Why should a living man complain, a man, about the punishment of his sins? (3:37-39).

EZEKIEL—And I will vindicate the holiness of my great name, which has been profaned among the nations, and which you have profaned among them; and the nations will know that I am the Lord when through you I vindicate my holiness (36:23).

DANIEL—And he came to the Ancient of Days and was presented before him. And to him was given dominion and glory and kingdom, that all peoples, nations and languages should serve him (7:13-14).

HOSEA—Yet the number of the people of Israel shall be like the sand of the sea, which can neither be measured nor numbered; and in the place where it was said to them, "You are not my people," it shall be said to them, "Sons of the living God" (1:10).

JOEL—Multitudes, multitudes in the valley of decision! For the day of the Lord is near in the valley of decision (3:14).

AMOS—In that day I will raise up the booth of David that is fallen and repair its breaches, and raise up its ruins . . . that they may possess the remnant of Edom and all the nations who are called by my name (9:11-12).

OBADIAH—Thus says the Lord God concerning Edom: We have heard tidings from the Lord and a messenger has been sent among the nations: "Rise up! Let us rise against her for battle!" (v. 1).

JONAH—And should not I pity Nineveh, that great city, in which there are more than a hundred and twenty thousand persons who do not know their right hand from their left, and also much cattle? (4:11).

MICAH—He shall judge between many peoples, and shall decide for strong nations afar off; and they shall beat their swords into plowshares (4:3).

NAHUM—The mountains shall quake before him, the hills melt; the earth is laid waste before him, the world and all that dwell therein (1:5).

HABAKKUK—For the earth shall be filled with the knowledge of the glory of the Lord as the waters cover the sea (2:14).

ZEPHANIAH—For my decision is to gather nations, to assemble kingdoms, to pour out upon them my indignation, all the heat of my anger; for in the fire of my jealous wrath all the earth shall be consumed (3:8).

HAGGAI—And I will shake all nations, so that the treasures of all nations shall come in, and I will fill this house with splendor (2:7).

ZECHARIAH—And the Lord will become king over all the earth; on that day the Lord will be one and His name one (14:9).

MALACHI—For from the rising of the sun to its setting my name shall be great among the nations, and in every place incense shall be offered to my name (1:11).

MATTHEW—Go, and make disciples of all the nations (28:19).

MARK—This gospel must be proclaimed to all the nations (13:10).

LUKE—Repentance and forgiveness of sins must be proclaimed in my name to all nations (24:47).

JOHN—There are other sheep which are not of this fold. I must go and bring them. Then there will be one Shepherd and one fold (10:16).

ACTS—You shall be my witnesses to the ends of the earth (1:8).

ROMANS—We have received grace and apostleship to bring about the obedience of faith for the sake of his name among all the nations (1:5).

1 CORINTHIANS—Then comes the end, when Christ delivers the kingdom to God the Father after destroying every rule and every authority and power (15:24).

2 CORINTHIANS—For God was in Christ reconciling the world back to himself, not counting their trespasses against them (5:19).

GALATIANS—In Christ Jesus the blessing of Abraham has come upon the nations, that we might receive the promise of the Spirit through faith (3:14).

EPHESIANS—His plan for the fulness of times is to sum up all things in Christ, things in heaven and things on earth (1:10).

PHILIPPIANS—That every knee should bow and every tongue confess that Jesus Christ is Lord (2:10).

COLOSSIANS—The gospel has come to you, as indeed in the whole world it is bearing fruit and growing (1:6).

1 THESSALONIANS—Your faith in God has gone forth everywhere (1:8).

2 THESSALONIANS—The Lord will be revealed from heaven with his mighty angels in flaming fire, inflicting vengeance upon those who do not know God and upon those who do not obey the gospel (1:7-8).

1 TIMOTHY—Christ was manifested in the flesh, vindicated in the Spirit, seen by angels, preached among the nations, believed on in the world, taken up in glory (3:16).

2 TIMOTHY—I charge you in the presence of God and of Christ Jesus who is to judge the living and the dead, and by his appearing and his kingdom; preach the Word (4:1).

TITUS—The grace that brings salvation to all men has appeared (2:14).

PHILEMON—I, Paul, an ambassador and now a prisoner also for Christ Jesus, appeal to you for my child, Onesimus, whose father I have become in my imprisonment (vs. 9).

HEBREWS—In these last days God has spoken to us by a Son, whom he appointed the heir of all things, through whom also he created the world. He reflects the glory of God and bears the very stamp of his nature, upholding the universe by his word of power. When he had made purification for sins, he sat down on the right hand of the majesty on high (1:2-3).

JAMES—Of his own will he brought us forth by the word of truth that we should be a kind of first fruits of his creation (1:18).

1 PETER—Resist the devil, firm in your faith; know that the same experience of suffering is required of your brotherhood throughout the world (5:9).

2 PETER—But according to his promise we wait for new heavens and a new earth in which righteousness dwells (3:13).

1 JOHN—And we have seen and testify that the Father has sent his Son as the Savior of the world (4:14).

2 JOHN—For many deceivers have gone out into the world, men who will not acknowledge the coming of Jesus Christ in the flesh (v. 7).

3 JOHN—You will do well to send them [*missionaries*] on their journey as befits God's service. For they have set out for his sake and have accepted nothing from the nations (vs. 6-7).

JUDE—To the only God, our Savior through Jesus Christ our Lord be glory, majesty, dominion, and authority, before all times and now and forever. Amen (v. 25).

REVELATION—"Worthy art thou to take the scroll and to open its seals, for thou wast slain and by thy blood didst ransom men for God from every tribe and tongue and people and nation, and hast made them a kingdom and priests to our God. And they shall reign on the earth (5:9-10).

How God Created One World Christian Bible Study-er

The following testimonial comes from Rob Malone, a campus worker for over fifteen years and a leader in mobilizing Pittsburgh churches for World Christian concerns.

I became a Christian in 1969 during my junior year in college. It wasn't long before my study of Scripture led to the inescapable conviction that what I had found in Christ was for everyone. I couldn't imagine a more important reason to live than to share Christ with others, wherever I found them.

But the full implications of this challenge took time to get through to me. In fact, at Urbana '70 (Inter-Varsity's triennial Student Missions Convention) I was soundly turned-off by the big emphasis on foreign missions. Why worry about all those people overseas, I objected, when so many around me still need to hear of Christ?

But by Urbana '73 regular Bible study had created in me a keen burden for unreached people. In His mysterious way, God used His Word to open me up to the whole world—His world. I attended my second Urbana convinced the scope of God's purpose was much larger. This time the needs in other parts of the world contrasted sharply to most of what I saw in my own community.

My Bible study gained wider dimensions still. The following summer I attended IVCF's Overseas Training Camp, my first experience with other cultures. During that program our group combed the book of Amos, learning about God's concern for justice and righteousness and the plights of the poor. It hit me how the implications of most biblical teaching goes beyond a personal application. God's message is the hope of the whole world. Bible study in a cross-cultural context reinforced how the gospel wasn't just for USA students, but for all peoples of earth. That summer I developed a special concern for students in Mexico caught in the winds of Marxism. After OTC I visited the International Fellowship of Evangelical Students' Mexican movement and toyed with the idea of joining their staff. By the fall, however, I decided to return to my campuses in West Virginia where I was on IVCF staff, to influence students toward a biblical commitment to Christ and His worldwide cause.

There my own World Christian Bible studies gained momentum. The global dimension of God's activity sprang out at me from almost every page. He would not let me forget to take what I learned from His Word and challenge students to hear and obey it with me.

In 1975 I started training young adults for short-term missions experiences. It was a chance to influence my generation in even more direct ways by training collegians in cross-cultural evangelism. Through training others, God showed me how most of us Americans need to break out of a mono-cultural interpretation of the biblical message. Having an appreciation for the diverse beauty and the significant values in world cultures could provide exciting new perspectives on the eternal message of Scripture, and on its application to our lives. This was revolutionary! It made me even more committed to making myself study the Bible like a World Christian.

More recently God has used me to stir up churches to prayer and action for missions, while leading church missions conferences and coordinating mission study courses. Again I've found that without the clear teaching of Scripture, nothing else will ultimately mobilize people to be World Christians.

Over the years I've found many helpful ways to do this kind of Bible study.

Often in my daily quiet times I pray for different needs across the earth before I start to study. This automatically affects the things I find in Scripture and the way I apply it to myself before beginning a new day of service for Christ's global cause.

I have discipled new Christians from other churches. As I study Scripture with them, their perspectives on a verse (as a Nigerian or Venezualan, for example) will often help me see a whole new reflection of God's truth for myself.

I've used study guides such as Ada Lum's *Twelve Studies on World Missions*, some older OTC Bible studies, as well as overviews of the biblical basis of missions found in many Urbana compendiums (published by IV Press). David Howard's *Student Power in World Missions* and George Peters's *A Theology of Missions* provide good direction, too.

Preparing studies for others helps me grow. For a small group near Morgantown, West Virginia, I organized a four-week biblical overview of missions which I titled, "Because God Has a Mission, So Do We." At Carnegie Mellon University in Pittsburgh I taught studies from 1 Thessalonians, challenging them to penetrate their campus the same way God used the Thessalonians to penetrate many places in the world far beyond them. When a small group asked me to lead them in a study of Romans 1–5 I began by showing them from Romans 15 that Paul wrote the letter to encourage Christians in Rome to join his mission to the whole world. Then we explored how the theology and principles in the first chapters laid solid thinking for such a joint mission. In the summers, as I direct Small Group Leaders Camp for Inter-Varsity, I teach from Scripture God's desire to have on every campus a network of mission teams through whom He works, not only to reach other students, but ultimately, the ends of the earth.

We need World Christian Bible studies. I'm convinced most of us bypass the world dimension of Scripture. Normally we see what it says about God or about us, but little of its strong appeal for what this means for Christ's global cause. Because most of us have lived our Christian lives in the shelter of one culture and one place in the world, we must continually make concentrated efforts to see all that God is saying about His great purpose of redemption. We must never study the Bible outside the context in which God brought it into being: the whole world of the nations, which was ever on His heart with every word He breathed into His prophets and apostles.

One Model of How to Do It

Orientation weekends to help prepare Inter-Varsity students for a summer cross-cultural experience concentrates on the biblical basis of missions, using the following approach. It has been just as helpful for churches. Maybe you would like to try it. Here's how it's done.

They are given a selection of passages that trace God's activity in making His name known to the nations. The passages are divided into four sections, each showing God's concern and activity in different situations. Then, they are instructed to study each set of passages, looking for what each passage says about God and His activity, and man and his activity. Using categories suggested by Dr. George Peters, they must then organize their finds. (Often, they find it helpful to do this on large charts taped to a wall, to see how everything finally comes together.) The major categories on the chart are:

The Passage Reference
Scope of the Mission Described
Method Used
Message Given
Characteristics of the Messenger

When they complete their study of the four individual sections, they debrief their findings from all the passages with these questions:

1. What do we learn about the scope of God's mission?
2. What do we notice about the methods of God's universal mission? Does it help to compare references from the Old Testament and the New Testament? Do we notice differ-

ences between how this mission is viewed by the Old Testament and the New? Are there similarities?

3. What is the message that God's mission brings to the world? Do certain passages emphasize one part of the message over another? Are there common elements of that message wherever it is described?

4. What are various characteristics of the messengers involved in God's mission? Which ones can you identify with?

5. Based on our investigation, how would you define "missions" in one brief paragraph? (Write it out.)

You could do the study by yourself or maybe with your Sunday School class. Better still, let your small group invite three other small groups from your church (one group for each of the four sections of passages) to join you at someone's home for the study. What a great way to spend the evening together—creating a World Christian Bible study!

Here are the four sections:

1. God's Universal Concern
   Genesis 1:1; 25-28; 6:5-13; 9:1-7; 11:1-9
   Psalm 33:6-9, 67, 96
   Philippians 2:5-11

2. God's Purpose for Israel
   Genesis 12:1-7; 26:1-6; 28:10-16
   Exodus 9:13-16; 19:1-8
   Joshua 4:19-24
   Judges 2:1-23
   Isaiah 48:17-22

3. God's Personal Interaction with Men
   John 1:14
   Luke 4:16-21
   (Notice who/class in society/how Jesus ministered)
   Matthew 22:41-49; 8:5-13
   Mark 1:32-34, 40-45
   Luke 7:36-50; 5:29-32
   John 4:7-30
   Mark 7:24-30
   (Notice who/when/where/what Jesus said)
   Matthew 28:16-20
   Mark 16:14-18
   Luke 24:33-49

John 20:19-21
Acts 1
Philippians 2:5-11
4. God's Purpose for the Church
John 17:14-26
Acts 1:8; 6:1-7; 8:1-8; 13:1-5
Romans 3:19-30; 10:9-17; 15:7-21
1 Corinthians 9:19-22; 12:19-30
1 Peter 2:9-10
2 Timothy 2:2
Revelation 7:9-17

Appendix V

INTER-VARSITY MISSIONS TOOLS AND RESOURCES

Note: Most of the materials are directly applicable to your local church. Others can be quite useful with creative adaptation. Materials specifically recommended in *In the Gap* are starred. (*).

Brochures
(All brochures are free)

_____ **IFES**

Describes the work of the International Fellowship of Evangelical Students

* _____ **Media Tools on Mission** (from IVCF's Twenty-oneHundred Productions)

Crafted to provide practical insights into the Church's world mission, and stimulus for our participation in it.

* _____ **World Christian Book Shelf**

An annotated catalog of some of the best titles available for growing World Christians . . . all at a sizeable discount.

Overseas Training Camp—Africa

Both Kenya and Nigeria offer camps that give exposure to ministry in African cultures.

Overseas Training Camp—China Experience

Travel throughout the Chinese world, including the People's Republic, itself.

_____ **Overseas Training Camp—Honduras**

One-month cross-cultural learning and serving experience in Central America.

_____ **Overseas Training Camp—Philippines**

Six-week learning, training, and serving experience in the Philippine Islands.

_____ **Overseas Training Camp—Europe**

One-month of learning and ministry in various nations of Europe.

_____ **So You're Interested in Summer Missions**
Questionnaire for students interested in serving in a cross-cultural situation for a summer. Personal recommendations are given according to your interests and skills.

Student Training in Missions (Regional)
_____ (1) Information brochure—can be used for prayer, to increase public awareness of the program and in raising funds.
_____ (2) Application request brochure—gives details on the program and the qualifications, plus a request blank for application (sent on an individual basis only).

* _____ **Urbana Student Missions Convention**
Describes the world's largest missions convention for students, held every two years, and how you can attend the next one.

_____ **What in the World Is God Doing?**
Very brief overview of contemporary missions with accompanying facts and figures.

* _____ **William Carey Library Catalog**
Listing of key mission books at a discount price.

_____ **World Missions Training Camp/USA**
Three-week summer camp revolving around Christ and His Word and Christ and His global cause. Looks at evangelism and service in a worldwide arena as well as helps campers inventory personal discipleship for impact upon world missions.

Papers

15¢ _____ **A Balanced Missions Emphasis**
_____ Describes objectives of missions emphasis and gives many suggestions for chapter involvement and programs.

* 15¢ _____ **Directory of Foreign Mission Agencies**
_____ Contains names of Protestant mission agencies with offices in the U.S. and/or Canada.

10¢ _____ **Outline of the History of Christian Missions**
_____ David Howard provides a brief overview of the highlights of the Church within major periods of world history.

10¢ _____ **Recommended Missionaries/Mission Leaders for a Campus Ministry** (speakers)

10¢ _____ **Suggestions for a Chapter Missions Program**
_____ See how "Missions" is the overall picture within which we should see and evaluate all our activities of the chapter.

5¢ _____ **Study Programs in Missions**
_____ Includes addresses and brief description of short-term mission experiences.

Booklets

25¢ _____ **Why World Evangelism?**
_____ Biblical reason why each Christian should personally consider the

global cause of Christ.

50¢ _____ **The Man God Uses**

_____ Daily devotional guide for personal application of scriptural life principles. Eighteen studies.

50¢ _____ **You and God's Work Overseas**

_____ Answers to common questions concerning your possible role overseas.

50¢ _____ **What If I Don't Go Overseas?**

Valuable guidelines for those God calls to form the "sending base" behind the ones who go.

Tools

* $5.25 _____ *Student Power in World Missions*

David Howard surveys the biblical and historical basis for expecting students to play a key role in advancing the world mission of the church.

$1.00 _____ *You Can Tell the World:* A Missions Reader

This book surveys basic issues in missions/mission involvement. Accompanying study guide makes it a valuable tool for missions study/action groups.

_____ *Ten Next Steps*

_____ Containing specific resources and ideas, this booklet provides the key follow-up tool to taking action.

* 25¢ _____ *A Guide to International Friendship*

__ Gives specific suggestions to those who desire to be cross-cultural ambassadors for Jesus Christ at home.

* $2.50 _____ *Operation World*

Great tool for intercessory prayer for the world. This book gives specific prayer needs for each country of the world.

25¢ _____ *Operation Prayer*

_____ Companion guide to *Operation World.* Produced by IVCF, Campus Crusade, Navigators, and International Students, Inc., this "prayer atlas" links you up with thousands of other Christians to pray the same things for the same country each day of the year.

Free _____ *Student and World Connection*

_____ IV Missions student newspaper, published four times a school year. Gives up-to-date happenings of student interest in world missions.

* $1.50 _____ *You Can So Get There from Here*

_____ Workbook designed to work through the process of getting from this country to overseas. Describes the missionary career path in twelve steps.

Student Foreign Missions Fellowship

Free _____ *Directory of SFMF Groups*

_____ Includes name, address, and phone of SFMF group; also names the president and faculty advisor(s). Listed by state, includes Canada.

$6.00 _____ *Student Mission Leaders Handbook*

_____ A training manual for developing and encouraging mission groups on Christian college campuses.

World Christian Handbooks

(These materials are useful for student groups inside and outside the IVCF movement. Also helpful to laypeople and local churches.)

ʳ 20¢ _____ *World Christian Checkup*

_____ A fun quiz-booklet for individual evaluation for growth as a World Christian. Great for a large group event as well.

15¢ _____ *World Christian Chapter/Church Profile*

_____ Helps to determine a world dimension to your life together. Also helps set new directions for involvement in Christ's global cause. Most valuable if filled out together by group or church leaders.

45¢ _____ *Obey the Vision Through Prayer*

_____ Discusses the why/how of praying as World Christians. Provides excellent ideas and resources to help you and your group develop an exciting, creative and meaningful prayer life for the world.

* $1.00 _____ *How to Create World Christian Bible Studies*

_____ Guidelines for turning ordinary Bible study into valuable discoveries of God's grand purpose for the whole world and how all of us fit into it in Christ.

* 10¢ _____ *How to Interview a Real Live Missionary*

_____ This booklet will prepare you for intelligent interaction with a cross-cultural worker and show how you can benefit from such.

* $1.00 _____ *Set World Christian Dreams Free!* How to Have a Team-Extension Mission

Designed for small groups of World Christians interested in seeing God fulfill Acts 1:8 through them in practical, vital ways. A must for any kind of team-extension mission, especially short-term, cross-cultural ministry.

Appendix VI

VIDEO TRAINING WITH THE AUTHOR

World Christian Video Training Curriculum

Over the past nine years, David Bryant has traveled the U.S. presenting his World Christian Conferences to thousands of Christians on campuses and in churches. Benefit from these years of experience as you interact with the author in a class-room setting or informally in your own home, through *video cassettes*.

These video conferences are useful to student groups, lay-people and local churches. Includes five hours of video cassettes for each conference, plus student workbooks/discussion guides, and leaders' guides. Many of the World Christian Handbooks, beginning with *In the Gap,* can be used to follow up the video training.

Each training experience can be pursued in a variety of ways. For example: in a one-weekend event; during six Satur-day morning study breakfasts; over a series of evening sessions for six nights in ten extended Sunday School sessions, etc. Write for the free brochure.

RECOVERY Series: Getting Set for the Coming Global Awakening

Missions motivation by giving the biblical, theoretical, and practical *overview* of what it means to be a World Christian in this generation. Recommended for those who are ready to build a basic *framework* for personal and corporate involvement in the world mission of the Church.

BREAKTHROUGH Series: Explorations into World Christian Discipleship

Missions motivation by giving biblical and practical experimentation with personal aspects of a World Christian life-style. Recommended for those who want to act upon personal implications of the world mission of the Church for their day-to-day life as Christ's disciples.

CONVERGE Series: Becoming Teams of World Christians

Missions motivation by giving biblical and practical experimentation with the corporate aspects of a World Christian life-style. Recommended for those who want to act upon corporate implications of the world mission of the Church for their day-to-day life together as Christ's disciples.

Available for rent or sale from:
>Gospel Light Media
>2300 Knoll Drive
>Ventura, CA 93003
>1-800-4-GOSPEL